Mary Louise Barroll

Around-The-World Cook Book

The Culinary Gleanings of a Naval Officer's Wife

Mary Louise Barroll

Around-The-World Cook Book

The Culinary Gleanings of a Naval Officer's Wife

ISBN/EAN: 9783944350363

Auflage: 1

Erscheinungsjahr: 2013

Erscheinungsort: Bremen, Deutschland

@ Kochbuch-Verlag in Access Verlag GmbH, Fahrenheitstr. 1, 28359 Bremen. Alle Rechte beim Verlag und bei den jeweiligen Lizenzgebern.

AROUND-THE-WORLD COOK BOOK

THE CULINARY GLEANINGS OF A NAVAL OFFICER'S WIFE

BY
MARY LOUISE BARROLL

"One homely thought prevails, the world around;
'Food well prepared;' We meet on common ground."

NEW YORK
THE CENTURY CO.
1913

CONTENTS

PART I

RECEIPTS

	PAGE
BREADS	3
HORS D'OEUVRES	19
SOUPS	24
FISH	38
ENTRÉES	51
MEATS	71
RICE AND MACARONI	100
VEGETABLES	107
EGGS	133
SAUCES	143
SALADS	158
PICKELS AND RELISHES	184
CHAFING-DISHE RECEIPTS	198
SANDWICHES	209
DESSERTS	211
CAKE	235
CANDY	256
BEVERAGES	276

PART II

USEFUL INFORMATION

CLEANING AND REMOVING STAINS	303
CARE OF FURNITURE	315

CONTENTS

	PAGE
CARE OF THE HAIR	321
CARE OF THE SKIN	325
PERFUMES	330
SIMPLE REMEDIES AND FIRST AIDS	336
ALPHABETICAL INDEX	345
GENERAL INDEX	355

PREFACE

All the receipts embodied in this book have been tested and are therefore reliable. They have been gleaned from many sources in many lands. Some of them have been recorded under the difficulty of translating those foreign idioms which correspond to our " fist of flour," " some butter " or " as much sugar as you think it needs "; many have been given by friends, to whom I here return my thanks; some are heirlooms, handed down by thrifty New England housewives, while others come from the old homes of the South; others still have been cut from newspapers, here and there in the odd corners of the world to which my travels have taken me.

To those who are constantly changing their abode and cannot therefore enjoy the conveniences of a settled home, like the families of army and navy officers, the suggestions and simple remedies of Part II may mean all the difference between comfort and discomfort.

It is the aim of this book to introduce into American households some of the toothsome dishes of other lands; and to suggest to the American housewife that she make use of the best cookery of New England, the South and the West,— for the distinctive dishes of these regions should be known and enjoyed throughout the land.

MARY LOUISE BARROLL.

Washington, September, 1913.

PART I
RECEIPTS

AROUND-THE-WORLD COOK BOOK

BREADS

TIMES FOR COOKING BREAD AND CAKE

The following table gives approximately the time for cooking bread and cake. The time will in some cases vary, owing to the quantity to be cooked, the state of the fire, and for other unforeseen reasons.

BAKED

Bread, brick loaf	40 to 60 minutes
Biscuit	10 to 20 minutes
Graham gems	30 minutes
Pie crust	30 to 40 minutes
Rolls	10 to 15 minutes

FRIED

Fritters	3 to 5 minutes
Muffins	3 to 5 minutes
Doughnuts	3 to 5 minutes

BAKED

Plain cake	20 to 40 minutes
Sponge cake	45 to 60 minutes
Cookies	10 to 15 minutes

Custards.	15 to 20 minutes
Gingerbread.	20 to 30 minutes
Rice pudding.	1 hour
Bread pudding.	1 hour
Tapioca pudding.	1 hour

All steamed puddings require from 2 to 3 hours.

NUT BREAD, NO. 1

Graham flour, 2 cups,
White flour, 1½ cups,
Sweet milk, 2 cups,
Brown sugar, ½ cup,
Molasses, ½ cup,
Salt, 1 teaspoon,
Soda, 1 large teaspoon,
Walnuts, chopped fine, 1 cup.

Beat very light, form in a loaf, and bake for 1 hour.

NUT BREAD, NO. 2

Sugar, 1 cup,
Sweet milk, 2 cups,
Nut-meats, chopped fine, 1½ cups,
Flour, 5 cups,
Baking-powder, 5 teaspoons,
Eggs, beaten light, 2.

Sift the flour, baking-powder, salt and sugar together 3 or 4 times, and then add the chopped nuts. Mix in well, then add the milk to the beaten eggs and stir this into the dry ingredients. Make into 2 loaves, let them stand 20 to 30 minutes before baking.

Bake 1 hour in a slow oven. When baked, butter the top.

PULLED BREAD

TO SERVE WITH SALADS

Take a loaf of fresh bread, rather underdone, and still warm, and pull the inside out of it, in irregular pieces, about the size of an egg. Put it in the oven, and toast to a delicate brown.

So crisp, and full of flavor is this "pulled bread," that it makes a delicious accompaniment for any salad.

GRAHAM LOAF

Graham flour, 1 pint,
White flour, 1 pint,
Sour milk, 1 pint,
Molasses, ½ cup,
Soda, 1 teaspoon.

Bake for 1 hour.

PARKER HOUSE ROLLS

Flour, 2 quarts,
Lard, or butter, 1 large tablespoon,
Cold boiled milk, 1 pint,
Yeast-cake, 1,
Sugar, ¼ cupful,
Salt, ½ teaspoon.

Dissolve the yeast-cake in ½ cupful of lukewarm water. Rub together the flour and butter, in a pan. Make a hole in the center of the flour in the pan, and pour into this the milk and the yeast. Also put in the sugar and half a teaspoon of salt.

Stir together, and let it then stand overnight. Next morning knead it thoroughly, and put aside in a warm place.

Let it rise till light, then work it over again, and roll out to a thickness of about 1 inch. Cut into circles with a biscuit-cutter, and spread the tops with melted butter. Fold over, and place them to rise in the pan in which they are to be baked; being careful not to crowd them.

Bake in a quick oven until light-brown on top.

WASHINGTON ROLLS

Pastry flour, ¾ cup,
Sweet milk, ½ cup,
Sugar, 2 tablespoons,
Yeast-cake, ½,
Salt, ¼ teaspoon,
Butter, 2 tablespoons,
Egg, 1,
Grated lemon-rind.

Scald the milk, and add the sugar and salt, and let it cool. Add the flour and the yeast-cake, which has been dissolved in 2 tablespoons of lukewarm water.

Cover, and let it rise overnight; and then add 2 tablespoons of melted butter, 1 egg well-beaten, the grated rind of 1 lemon, and flour enough to knead.

Let it rise again, and when light, roll out ½ inch thick, and shape it the same as rolls.

Let it rise still another time, and when light, bake in a rather hot oven.

BATH BUNS

Sifted flour, 1 pound,
Milk, 1 cup,
Salt, ½ teaspoon,
Yeast-cake, ½,
Eggs, 4,

Melted butter, 4 ounces,
Sugar,
Currants,
Candied orange-peel.

Dissolve the yeast in warm water. Add the salt and milk, and mix it with the flour to a dough. Knead, and let it stand till light. Work in the beaten eggs, and the butter. Cover, and set aside, till risen a second time.

Mold into balls a little larger than an egg, and press into the top of each one some currants and shreds of candied orange-peel.

Arrange the buns a half an inch apart on greased pans, and let them stand in a warm place until light.

Brush the tops with warm water; sprinkle thickly with granulated sugar, and bake in a moderate oven for about three-quarters of an hour.

GRAHAM GEMS

Eggs, 3,
Milk, lukewarm, 3 cups,
Graham flour, 3 cups,
Sugar, 1 tablespoon,
Melted butter, 1 tablespoon,
Salt, ½ teaspoon,
Baking-powder, 1 heaping teaspoon.

SODA BISCUITS

Flour, 1 quart,
Butter, 2 tablespoons,
Water, 2 cups,
Baking-powder, 2 teaspoons,
Salt, ½ teaspoon.

Mix well, handle as little as possible, and cut into biscuits and bake.

MINUTE BISCUITS

>Graham flour, 2 cups,
>White flour, 2 cups,
>Butter, or lard, 2 tablespoons,
>Brown sugar, 1 tablespoon,
>Milk, 3 cups,
>Baking-powder, 2 teaspoons,
>Salt, 1 teaspoon.

Chop the shortening into the flour, add the sugar, salt, and milk. Roll out with little handling, and pierce each biscuit with a fork. Then bake.

RICHMOND THIN BISCUITS

>Flour, well sifted, 1 pint,
>Butter, 1 heaping teaspoon,
>Eggs, 2,
>Salt, ½ teaspoon,
>Cream, or rich milk.

Rub the butter into the flour. When the flour feels like fine meal add the well-beaten eggs, and enough cream, or rich milk, to make a dough stiff enough to roll. Roll out as thin as paper, and cut into circles with a tin cutter, prick each biscuit with a fork, dust with flour and place them in a pan and bake to a light brown.

WAFFLES

>Flour, 1 cup,
>Eggs, 2,

Baking-powder, 1 teaspoon,
Salt, ½ teaspoon,
Milk,
Sugar.

Beat the eggs separately and add to them a cup of flour and thin down with sweet milk to a batter, adding half a teaspoon of salt and a teaspoon of baking-powder.

Beat all together, and they are ready to cook.

RICE WAFFLES

Cold boiled rice, 1 cup,
Milk, 1½ cups,
Eggs, well-beaten, 2,
Flour, 2 cups,
Salt, ½ teaspoon,
Melted butter, 1 tablespoon,
Baking-powder, 2 heaping teaspoons.

Add the milk to the rice, and stir so that there may be no lumps. Add to this the salt, and the eggs, well-beaten. Then sift in the flour. Add the butter, melted, and the baking-powder.

Bake at once.

RICE GRIDDLE CAKES

Boiled rice, 1 cup,
Flour, 1 cup,
Butter, ½ cup,
Sweet milk, 1 quart,
Salt, 1 teaspoon,
Soda, 1 teaspoon.

Stir the rice in the milk and let it stand for half an hour, and then add the salt, butter, flour and soda, the latter being dissolved in a little cold water.

RICE PANCAKES

Cold, boiled rice, 1 cup,
Sour milk, 1 cup,
Sifted flour, 2 cups,
Eggs, well-beaten, 2,
Soda, 1 teaspoon,
Salt, ¼ teaspoon.

Dissolve the soda in a little cold water. Mix all the ingredients. Bake on a griddle.

SOUR MILK CAKES

Sour milk, 1 quart,
Flour, 4 cups,
Soda, 2 teaspoons (dissolved in boiling water),
Molasses, 3 tablespoons (put into the milk),
Salt, ½ teaspoon.

Put the flour into a deep bowl and mix the salt through it. Make a hole in the middle of the flour, and pour the milk into it, and lastly add the soda which has been dissolved in boiling water.

GERMAN PANCAKES

Flour, 6 large tablespoons,
Eggs, 6,
Milk, ½ cup,
Baking-powder, 1 level teaspoon,
Salt, a pinch.

The milk should be mixed with ½ cup of water. Beat the eggs, and mix in, slowly, the flour, milk and water. Add a little salt, and 1 level teaspoon of baking-powder.

BERLIN PANCAKES

Flour, 2¼ cups,
Milk, 1 quart,
Eggs, 6,
Butter, ½ tablespoon,
Baking-powder, 1 teaspoon,
Salt, 1 teaspoon.

Stir the flour and salt together, beat the egg-yolks, add them to the milk, mix gradually with the flour to a smooth batter.

In a large bowl beat the whites to a stiff dry froth, then gradually add to them the batter, beating till the whole is entirely mixed.

Place a medium-sized frying-pan over the fire, melt in it the butter or lard. When hot, pour in sufficient of the batter to cover the bottom of the pan. Shake till cooked to an even brown on the underside, then turn over, and cook the other side in the same manner.

Transfer the pancake to a hot plate, and spread it with marmalade, butter, or sugar. Bake in the same manner, till all the batter is used.

WHOLE-WHEAT CAKES

Whole-wheat flour, 1 pint,
Salt, ½ teaspoon,
Baking-powder, 1 teaspoon,
Cold water, 1 pint.

Mix the salt and flour, add the cold water gradually, beat quick and hard, till the batter is filled with tiny bubbles.

Have deep gem pans very hot, and well greased; fill them nearly full with the batter, and bake in a hot oven until risen and brown. This will take about half an hour.

OATMEAL WAFERS

Rolled-oats,
Butter, ½ cup,
Sugar, 2 cups,
Egg, 1
Milk, 2 tablespoons,
Salt, ¼ teaspoon,
Baking-soda, 1 level teaspoon.

Dissolve the soda in a tablespoon of warm water. Cream the butter with 1 cup of the sugar, and add the egg, beaten, and then gradually beat in the other cup of sugar, and the salt.

Add the baking-powder with the milk, and work in enough rolled-oats to make a stiff dough and knead it well.

Roll the dough out into as thin a sheet as possible, and cut into desired shapes. Lift them carefully, and place them on greased pans, and bake in a moderate oven until thoroughly done, light-brown and crisp.

SALLY LUNN

Flour, 1½ pints,
Butter, 1 full tablespoon,
Sugar, 2 tablespoons,
Eggs, 5 (yolks only),
Sour milk, 1 cup,
Baking-powder, 1 teaspoon,
Salt, ½ teaspoon.

Mix the baking-powder with the flour. Rub in the butter, add the sugar, the beaten yolks of the eggs, and the milk. Mix all, and bake in a lightly greased pan, in a moderate oven.

VIRGINIA SALLY LUNN

> Flour, 4 cups,
> Milk, 1 pint,
> Sugar, 1 tablespoon,
> Butter, 1 tablespoon,
> Salt, 1 teaspoon,
> Eggs, well-beaten, 2,
> Yeast-cake, ½.

Scald the milk and cool to lukewarm. Add the salt, sugar, melted butter, and the yeast-cake, the latter dissolved in half a cup of tepid water. Next add the well-beaten eggs.

Pour 4 cups of sifted flour into the mixing bowl, add all the liquid ingredients, and beat well until a smooth batter is formed.

Pour all into a large buttered tube-pan, known as a "Turk's head," lay a piece of cheese-cloth over it, and set it in a warm place to rise. It will probably take about 6 hours to rise. When it has risen, then bake.

POP-OVERS

> Flour, 2 cups,
> Milk, 2 cups,
> Eggs, 3,
> Salt, ½ teaspoon.

First beat the eggs separately, then add the other ingredients, beat all together until quite smooth; pour into well-greased pans, and bake in a moderate oven for three-quarters of an hour.

EGG PUFFS

GERMAN

Flour, 2 cups,
Milk, 2 cups,
Eggs, 2 (well-beaten),
Salt.

To the beaten eggs gradually add, beating in, the flour, milk, and salt. Have very hot buttered cups ready, fill half full of the batter, and bake about 25 minutes. These may be also used with a fruit sauce, as a dessert.

SCOTCH SCONES

Flour, 1 pint,
Butter, 2 tablespoons,
Milk, ½ pint,
Egg, 1,
Baking-powder, 1 teaspoon,
Salt, ¼ teaspoon.

Mix together the flour, baking-powder, and salt while dry. Rub in the butter. Beat up the egg in milk, or in water, then mix all thoroughly together, and bake immediately on a griddle, or in a quick oven.

If milk is not to be had, water may be used; but in case water is used, only ½ pint must be taken.

ENGLISH CRUMPETS

Flour, 2½ cups,
Milk, 1½ cups,
Lard, 1 heaping tablespoon,
Eggs, 2,

Baking-powder, 3 teaspoons,
Salt, ½ teaspoon.

Melt the lard, and add to it the eggs, well-beaten, and the milk. Mix the baking-powder with the flour, sifted, and beat it in with the other ingredients.

Crumpet rings are larger than muffin rings. Put the greased rings on a hot griddle, fill them two-thirds full with the batter, and cook. Turn them when half done.

CHEESE STRAWS

Flour, 1 cup,
Melted butter, 1 tablespoon,
Baking-powder, 1 teaspoon,
Grated cheese, ½ cup,
Salt, cayenne, milk.

Sift the flour and baking-powder together, add the salt, a dash; rub in the butter, and roll out thin, using enough milk to make it roll out.

When rolled out, sprinkle thickly with the cheese and the cayenne (a dash, only), and cut into strips.

Bake in the oven until brown.

YORKSHIRE BREAKFAST CAKE

Flour, 3 cups,
Butter, 1 heaping teaspoon,
Salt, ½ teaspoon,
Baking-powder, 3 level teaspoons,
Milk.

Sift the flour, salt and baking-powder together, and rub in the butter. Mix to a soft dough with milk. Place without cutting, on a hot greased griddle and cover. Cook on a moderate fire 10 minutes. Slip off on a board, turn, return to the griddle, and cook 10 minutes longer. Break into pieces, and serve with butter.

YORKSHIRE PUDDING

Eggs, 4,
Flour, 6 tablespoons,
Milk, ½ pint,
Water, ½ pint,
Salt, ½ teaspoon,
Beef-dripping, 2 tablespoons.

Mix the milk and water together. Take part of this, and with the flour make a smooth batter. Add to this the eggs, one at a time, beating well as you add each one.

Now add the rest of the milk, and the salt, and stir well. Make ready a good-sized dripping-pan, hot, and with 2 tablespoons of beef-dripping. Turn in the batter, and bake for 20 minutes, in a good hot oven.

BOILED CONNIFELA
GERMAN

Sweet milk, 1½ pints,
Eggs, 2,
Salt, 1 teaspoon,
Flour,
Bread-crumbs.

Use enough flour to make a very stiff batter; add the milk, and salt, and when the batter is made have a vessel of boiling water ready and tip the vessel that contains the batter, so that it will be over the boiling water.

Then with a sharp knife cut the batter off in small chunks, and let them fall into the boiling water. Let them boil for a few minutes, then drain off the water from the dumplings, and place them in a dish, and over all pour bread-crumbs which have been fried a golden brown.

The connifela is very nice fried crisp for a supper dish.

FRIED CONNIFELA

GERMAN

Sweet milk, 1 pint,
Egg, 1,
Flour,
Salt.

With the above ingredients make a batter of the consistency of pancake batter. Have ready a skillet that has plenty of lard in it. Pour in the batter, all at once, cover, and let it fry a rich brown on the under side; then turn it over with a turner, and brown it on the other side. Keep turning until you are sure that it is done.

This makes a nice breakfast dish served with butter and maple-syrup.

CINNAMON COFFEE-BREAD

GERMAN

Flour, 1 cup,
Sugar, ¾ cup,
Milk, 1 cup,
Egg, 1,
Butter, 1 tablespoon,
Lemon, 1 (grated rind, only),
Baking powder, ½ teaspoon,
Salt.

For the coating for top

Sugar, ¼ cup,
Melted butter, 1 tablespoon,

Ground cinnamon, ½ teaspoon,
Chopped almonds, 1 tablespoon.

Mix together all the ingredients for the bread, and put it into a baking-pan. Cover the top with a dressing made of the ingredients given, and bake until well-browned on top.

HORS D'ŒUVRES

OYSTER COCKTAIL

Small oysters (chilled),
Tomato catsup, 1 tablespoon,
Grated horseradish, 1 tablespoon,
Worcestershire, ½ tablespoon,
Lemon juice, 1 tablespoon,
Tabasco, ¼ teaspoon,
Vinegar, ½ tablespoon,
Salt, 1 salt-spoon.

Mix well together, and set in the ice-box, or in ice for an hour. Into each of very cold little glasses put 5 of the small chilled oysters, and fill the glasses with the cold sauce.

If preferred, the oysters may be served on the half-shell, with the cocktail glass containing the sauce placed in the center of each plate, and the oysters arranged around it.

ALLIGATOR PEAR COCKTAIL
HAWAIIAN

Alligator pear, 1,
Tomato catsup, ½ pint,
Worcestershire sauce, 1 teaspoon,
Tabasco, 6 drops,
Lemon, the juice of 1,
Chutney pickle, 1 tablespoon,
Salt, 1 salt-spoon.

The alligator pear should be cut in dice (with a silver knife, else it will blacken).

Mix all together, and serve in cocktail glasses. This makes enough for 8 cocktails.

FRUIT COCKTAIL

> Currant syrup, 1 pint,
> Oranges, 5,
> Lemons, 5,
> Pineapple (grated), 1 can.

Add the juice of the lemons and oranges to the currant syrup, grate, and add the pineapple, sweeten to taste with sugar, add 1 cup of cold water, and serve in small glasses.

CAVIAR

> Caviar, ¼ pound,
> Lemon, 1,
> Chopped onion, 1 tablespoon,
> Eggs (hard boiled), 2,
> Soft toast.

Cut the toast into squares or rounds. Mix the caviar and lemon juice well together, and spread it on the toast.

In the center of each slice put some of the chopped onion, crush the eggs with a silver fork, and sprinkle over the top.

TOMATO

> Rounds of toast,
> Tomatoes,
> Anchovies,
> Mayonnaise,
> Hard-boiled eggs.

Put a slice of tomato on the toast, and on top, and close around the edge, put anchovies, and in the middle put a teaspoon of thick mayonnaise. Decorate with the eggs — the whites and yolks chopped separately.

ANCHOVY PASTE

Anchovy paste may be used instead of caviar, in which case decorate the toast with points of lemon, and sliced pimentoes.

CANAPE OF CHICKEN LIVERS

Chicken, or duck livers, creamed, may be served on toast, and ornamented with chopped green, and red peppers, and hard-boiled eggs.

CANAPE LORENZO

Crab-meat, 1 pound,
Butter, 2 heaping tablespoons,
Flour, 1 tablespoon,
Cream, 1 pint,
Slices of toasted bread,
Chopped shallot, 1,
Salt and pepper.

For the paste

Butter, 4 heaping tablespoons,
Grated Parmesan cheese, ½ cup,
Salt, red and white pepper.

Chop the shallot and fry it lightly in the butter without coloring; add the flour, and wet with the pint of cream. Next add the crab-meat, seasoning with salt and pepper, and leave it on the fire until it has just begun to bubble.

Cut slices of bread one-quarter of an inch thick, and trim

them into any desired shapes, either round, oval, or square, and toast them on one side, only.

Then prepare the paste as given above, mixing the ingredients all well together, and having put the crab-meat mixture on the toasted side of the slices of bread, then spread, over the top of all, this paste, in a layer about one-eighth of an inch thick.

Then put the canapes, or pieces of toast, on a buttered dish, and color them in the oven.

CROUTES OF HERRING

ENGLISH

Smoked herring, 4 tablespoons,
Butter, 1 tablespoon,
Hard-boiled egg, 1,
Rounds of buttered toast, 6,
Chopped parsley, 1 teaspoon,
Tomato sauce, 1 teaspoon,
Cayenne pepper, a dash.

The herring should be freed from skin and bone, then flaked, and chopped fine, before being measured. The egg should be divided and the white chopped fine and the yolk powdered.

Melt the butter in a small saucepan, and add the fish and the seasoning of tomato sauce and cayenne, and mix well together.

Put a spoonful of this on each round of toast, and decorate each with lines of parsley, chopped white and powdered yolk of egg. Serve hot, with a lace paper under each.

ITALIAN TOAST

Rounds of bread (about ½ inch thick),
Bacon,

Grated cheese, 1 cupful,
Milk, ½ cupful,
Eggs, 2,
Salt and cayenne pepper.

Beat the eggs; then mix cheese, eggs, and milk together, and season with salt and cayenne pepper.

Cover the rounds of bread with this mixture, and place a thin slice of bacon on the top of each round. Put into the oven, and let it remain until the bacon is crisp. Serve hot.

FONDS OF ARTICHOKE

Fonds of artichoke combined with small vegetables, such as peas, beans, and chopped carrots, placed on a leaf of lettuce, and decorated with chopped hard-boiled eggs, and mayonnaise.

This also may be served as a salad.

RINGS OF ONIONS, OR EGGS

Rings of onions, or rings of the whites of hard-boiled eggs, placed on soft toast, may be filled with any appetizing salt, or smoked fish, or fish paste; and decorated with chopped olives, chopped hard-boiled eggs, chopped peppers, or pickles. The toast should always be soft, and cut in small, attractively shaped pieces.

CELERY

Cut the stalks in 4-inch lengths, and fill the grooved sides with cream cheese, seasoned and mixed with finely chopped green peppers.

SOUPS

WHAT TO SERVE WITH SOUPS

Pea-soup—Serve croutons.

Mulligatawny—Serve boiled rice.

Hare soup—Serve red currant jelly, or cranberry jelly.

Clear soup à la Colbert—Serve poached eggs in a hot dish.

Turtle soup—Serve lemon cut in quarters, and passed on a dish.

Artichoke soup—Serve croutons, or thin brown-bread dipped in soup or stock, and then made crisp in the oven.

Bouillabaise—Serve quarters of lemon and either croutons or brown bread.

Clear soup, with Italian paste—Serve grated Parmesan cheese.

Croute au pot—Serve thin rounds of bread dipped in the soup or stock, and then made crisp in the oven.

CREAM OF CELERY

Celery, 1 bunch (1 root),
Water, 1 pint,
Milk, 1 pint,
Onion, 1 slice,
Parsley, 1 sprig,
Flour, 1 tablespoon,
Butter, 1 tablespoon.

Cut the celery in inch pieces, and boil it in 1 pint of water with the onion and the parsley. When tender, pass it through a colander and put into a double boiler with the milk. Add the butter and flour, which have been creamed together, and boil for 10 minutes.

Cream of cauliflower and cream of asparagus may be made in the same way.

CREAM OF MUSHROOMS

Chicken stock, 1 quart,
Chopped mushrooms, 1/4 pound,
Butter, 2 tablespoons,
Flour, 2 tablespoons,
Onion, 1 slice,
Cream, 1 cup,
Salt, baking-powder.

Remove the fat from a quart of chicken stock and stir into it a quarter of a pound of mushrooms chopped, and a slice of onion. Simmer for 20 minutes, and then run it through a colander and return it to the fire. Thicken with the butter and flour, and stir until smooth; then beat in a cup of rich cream, containing a pinch of baking-powder, and season with salt and pepper.

CREAM BEET SOUP

Beets, 4,
Veal stock, 1 pint,
Flour, 2 tablespoons,
Butter, 1 tablespoon,
Milk, 1 pint,
Egg, 1,
Salt and pepper.

Wash the beets well and boil them in salted water for an hour and a quarter. Scrape off the skin, and put the beets through a meat-grinder, saving all the juice that flows from them. Skim a pint of veal-stock and stir the ground beets and their juice into this.

Simmer for 20 minutes; strain, and set the liquor at the side of the range to keep hot. Cook together, 2 tablespoons of flour, and 1 tablespoon of butter, and when they are well blended pour upon them a pint of milk—half cream if possible.

Stir this until smooth and thick, and beat in, by a few spoonsful at a time, the beet-purée. When very hot, season with salt and pepper, and pour it upon a well-beaten egg, stirring all the time. Serve at once.

ALMOND MILK, CREAM SOUP

>Rice, 2 tablespoons,
>Hot milk, 1 pint,
>Almond extract, 2 drops.

Boil the rice until it can be pressed through a sieve, then add the hot milk, and the extract of almond. Sweeten to taste.

Serve in bouillon cups.

CREAM OF ASPARAGUS

>Asparagus, 1 bunch,
>Milk, 1 pint,
>Flour, 1 tablespoon,
>Butter, 1 tablespoon,
>Cream, ¼ cup,
>Salt and pepper.

Cook the stalks of 1 bunch of asparagus in water or in stock, with sufficient water to cover. Cook until tender. Mash the stalks through a sieve, and return to the liquid in which they were boiled. Allow for each bunch of asparagus, a pint of milk, heat to the boiling point; then thicken with a tablespoon of flour, rubbed smooth with a tablespoon of butter.

Cook 10 minutes, then add to it, the water in which the stalks were cooked. Season with salt and pepper, then add a quarter of a cup of cream, and also the tips of the asparagus, which have been cooked by themselves for 12 minutes in salted water. Serve with croutons.

CHESTNUT AND CELERY SOUP

Chestnuts, 1 pound,
Celery, 6 stalks,
Milk, 1 quart,
Onion, 1,
Carrot, 1,
Butter, 2 tablespoons,
Cloves, 4,
Salt.

Chop the celery, onion, and carrot, and fry them in the butter until brown. Put with them a quart of milk and 4 cloves, and stew together for 1 hour.

Season with salt; strain, and divide the stock into 2 portions. Into one-half of it put the chestnuts which have been boiled 10 minutes, and shelled and blanched, and stew this gently for half an hour.

Set aside a few of the chestnuts to be later put into the soup plates, and chop the remainder fine and put them through a colander, together with that portion of the stock in which they have just been cooked.

Then add the other half of the stock, and cook for 10 minutes longer.

Put a few of the other chestnuts that have been reserved into each soup plate, and pour the soup over them.

CHESTNUT CREAM

>Spanish chestnuts, 1 pint,
>Flour, 1 tablespoon,
>Butter, 1 tablespoon,
>Hot milk, or stock, 2 cups,
>Egg, 1,
>Celery-salt,
>Cayenne,
>Cold milk, 2 cups.

Cook together the flour and butter until they bubble, and then pour on the 2 cupsful of hot milk or stock. Stir until smooth. Add to this a pint of Spanish chestnuts which have been shelled and blanched, a dash of celery-salt, and a little cayenne.

Boil for half an hour, and rub all through a colander, and add the cold milk and 1 egg, stirring them in carefully.

Season to taste, boil, and serve at once.

CREAM OF CARROTS

>Grated carrot, 1 pint,
>Salt, ½ teaspoon,
>White pepper, ¼ teaspoon,
>Butter, 1 large tablespoon,
>Flour, 3 scant tablespoons,
>Milk, 2½ cups,
>Peppercorns, 6,
>Bay leaf.

Cover the grated carrots with 1 quart of boiling water; add the salt, white pepper and a piece of bay leaf, and also 6 peppercorns.

Simmer for 1 hour, and then press through a fine sieve. In a saucepan melt the butter and flour; gradually blend with this 2½ cups of hot milk, stirring until it is smoothly thickened. Gradually add the pulped carrot liquid, and more seasoning if necessary.

CREAM OF CAULIFLOWER

>Cauliflower,
>Onion,
>Milk,
>Salt and pepper.

Soak the cauliflower head downward in salted water, and then cook it until tender. Remove some of the best flowers to serve in the soup, and press the rest through a sieve. Add the water if it is not too strong.

Scald a slice of onion in twice the quantity of milk that you have of pulp. Add the pulp to the milk and onion, season with salt and pepper, and lastly add the flowerlets of the cauliflower.

CHESTNUT PUREE, NO. 1

>Blanched chestnuts, 1 pint,
>Milk, or stock, 1 pint,
>Flour, 2 tablespoons,
>Butter, 2 tablespoons,
>Eggs, 2 yolks,
>Cream, 2 tablespoons.

Cook the chestnuts in sufficient water to cover them. When soft, pass through a sieve while still hot, and add to this the stock, and stir until it boils. Blend the butter and flour together and add it to the stock and chestnuts; also add salt and pepper to taste.

Just before serving, add the beaten yolks of the 2 eggs, and the cream.

CHESTNUT PURÉE, NO. 2

>Spanish chestnuts, 1 quart,
>Butter, 2 tablespoons,
>Cream, 2 tablespoons,
>Onion juice, ¼ teaspoon,
>Salt and pepper.

Shell, blanch, and boil the chestnuts until soft, and then rub them through a colander. Add to them the butter, cream, onion-juice, and salt and pepper to taste. Stir over the fire until thoroughly hot.

This is a delicious purée to serve with roast fowls of any sort, or with game.

TARO, OR POI

HAWAIIAN

If the taro root cannot be obtained, taro flour may now be had from many druggists.

Peel and boil the root until mealy. Pound in a mortar until like dough, adding a little water as you are pounding it. Set it away to ferment, but do not let it get very sour. Fermentation from 24 to 30 hours will probably be long enough.

When preparing for use, mix with water, and make a gruel—there are three thicknesses recognized by Hawaiians; respectively, "one-finger," "two-finger," and "three-finger poi."

For invalids, boil as above, and pound in a mortar, but

do not ferment. Mix with milk instead of water, and always use it when fresh. It should be cold when used, chilled if possible.

TOMATO BISQUE

Tomatoes, 1 can,
Butter, ¼ cup,
Onion, finely chopped, 2 tablespoons,
Flour, 3 tablespoons,
Milk, 2 pints,
Salt, 1½ teaspoons,
Parsley, chopped, 1 teaspoon,
Cloves, 4,
Soda, ¼ teaspoon,
Celery-salt, and cayenne.

Melt the butter and add the onion, and cook for 5 minutes; then add the flour, milk, and seasoning.

Heat the tomatoes and rub through a sieve, and add the soda to it, combine this with the butter and milk mixture, and cook all in a double boiler for 20 minutes. Then strain and serve.

BLACK-BEAN SOUP

Black-beans, 1 cup,
Salt-pork, ½ pound,
Lemon, 1,
Sherry, ½ cup,
Eggs, 2,
Salt and pepper.

Let the beans soak for 6 hours, then boil them with 2 quarts of water, and with the salt-pork. When soft, press the beans through a colander and return to the fire; season with the sherry and lemon, and with the eggs, hard-boiled and cut in slices. It may be necessary to add more water.

LOBSTER SOUP

Lobster, 1,
Milk, 1 quart,
Butter, 2 tablespoons,
Flour, 2 tablespoons.

After boiling the lobster take it from the shell, and chop fine. Put the milk with 1 pint of water; boil, and then add the lobster, and the butter and flour, which have been creamed together.

A little sherry will improve this.

CLAM CHOWDER

Hard clams, 1 pint,
Soft clams, 1 pint,
Potatoes, 6,
Onions, minced, 2,
Carrots, 2,
Milk, 1 pint,
Salt-pork,—cut in thin strips, ¼ pound,
Water, 2 quarts.

The onions and pork should be browned in the bottom of the pot; then add, all chopped fine, the clams, potatoes and carrots.

Add the water and cook slowly for several hours. Just before serving add the milk, and stir it well in.

CORN CHOWDER

Corn, 6 large ears, cut from the cob,
Potatoes, 4, chopped,

Salt-pork, chopped, ¼ pound,
Onion, chopped, 1,
Flour, 2 tablespoons,
Butter, 2 tablespoons,
Milk, 1 pint,
Water, 1 quart,
Salt and pepper.

Put the onion and pork into the pot, and brown slightly; add the corn, potatoes, and 1 quart of boiling water. Boil slowly, until the potatoes are soft.

Cream together the butter and flour; add this to the pint of milk, season with salt and pepper, and pour it into the chowder.

Boil the whole together for 10 minutes.

CHICKEN GUMBO

Young chicken, jointed as for fricassee, 1,
Okra, chopped fine, 1 quart,
Tomatoes, sliced, 1 quart,
Onion, finely minced, 1,
Flour, 1 tablespoon,
Butter, 2 tablespoons.

Place the butter, flour, and onion in a pan, and slightly brown. Add slowly the tomatoes and okra, and let these boil for 15 minutes; then add the chicken, which has been previously boiled, and let these cook together till the okra is dissolved.

LOUISIANA GUMBO

Okra, 1 quart,
Tomatoes, 6,
Onion, 1,

Green pepper, 1,
Beef-stock, 3 pints,
File (powdered sassafras), 1 tablespoon,
Salt and pepper.

Chop the onion, okra, tomatoes and pepper. Put in a pot and add to it the stock, and let it simmer until thoroughly cooked. Then add the salt and pepper and a tablespoon of the "file," or sassafras powder.

PUCHERO

ARGENTINE

Beef, 4 pounds,
Carrots, 2,
Onions, 2,
Cabbage, 1, small,
Potatoes, 6,
Ears of corn, 6,
Peas (in the pod), 1 quart,
String-beans, 1 quart,
Turnips, 3.

Prepare the vegetables as for boiling, except the peas, which should be left in the pods. Put the beef in hot water and allow it to boil for half an hour, then add the vegetables. Season with salt and pepper and let the whole simmer for 4 hours. Remove the meat and vegetables, strain the liquid and serve as a soup; the remainder to be served as another course.

This is a standard dish in Spain, Mexico, and in all other Spanish-American countries. In Mexico it is known as "Caldo."

PLAIN SOUPS

SCOTCH BROTH

Water (in which mutton has been boiled), 1 quart,
Barley, 1 cup,
Carrot, 1,
Turnip, 1,
Onions, 1,
Celery, 4 stalks,
Green peas, ½ cupful,
Beans, ½ cupful,
Butter, 1 tablespoon,
Flour, 1 tablespoon,
Parsley, salt, pepper.

Cut the vegetables up fine and parboil them for 10 minutes. Drain and put over the fire and add the stock. Add the barley which has been previously soaked for 3 hours. Simmer slowly for 3 hours. Just before serving add the butter and flour which have been creamed together, and stir well in.

LENTIL SOUP

GERMAN

Dried lentils, ¼ pound,
Bouillon, or stock, 3 pints,
Butter, 2 tablespoons,
Flour, 1 tablespoon,
Carrot, turnip, onion, celery, parsley,
a small piece of each.

Wash the lentils and soak them overnight. In the morning cook them in fresh water until soft—about 2 hours. Then rub them through a sieve.

Cook the butter and flour in a saucepan until brown. Add

the vegetables and cook for 15 minutes; then add the bouillon, and cook for half an hour; then put in the lentils and rub again through a sieve. Let this whole mixture now boil for about 10 minutes.

BEEF-TEA

Lean beef, 1 pound,
Water, enough to cover,
Salt and pepper.

Cut the meat in small pieces, sprinkle generously with salt and pour on just enough cold water to cover. Let it stand aside for from 1 to 3 hours; then place on the fire, and let it come to a boil. Do not let it remain on the fire longer than 5 minutes.

Pour the liquid from the meat, and season it with pepper.

GRIESMEHL SOUP

GERMAN

Griesmehl (farina may be used), ½ cup,
Milk, 1 pint,
Water, 1 pint,
Butter, 1 tablespoon,
Egg, 1 yolk.

Boil the milk and water together, then add the meal and let this simmer for half an hour, stirring frequently. Take from the fire, and then add the butter and the egg.

Griesmehl is a coarse white-wheat meal, found in German stores in America. Farina is a good substitute.

CLARET SOUP

GERMAN

Claret, 1 quart,
Sago, 1 teacup,

Lemons, cut thin, 2,
Water, 1 quart,
Cinnamon, 2 sticks,
White sugar, 1 cup.

The sago should be soaked for several hours, and this, with the claret, sugar, lemon, cinnamon, and water, allowed to boil for about 10 minutes, or longer.

FRUIT SOUPS

Fruit soups are little more than the juice of stewed fruits. They are, however, very delicious during the heated season. In some cases they are served with cracked ice, but ice should undoubtedly be avoided during meals.

LEMON SOUP

Make a strong hot lemonade; thicken it slightly with cornstarch, or arrow-root, and serve cold, with a bit of preserved ginger, or a cherry in each glass.

Pineapple and currant and red raspberry soups are made in the same way.

BLACKBERRY SOUP

This is but the juice of stewed blackberries, strained, slightly thickened and flavored with nutmeg.

PEACH PURÉE

This can be made by adding a little lemon-juice, bitter almond, and thickening, to fresh or canned peaches, and straining through a sieve.

FISH

TIMES FOR COOKING FISH

The following table gives approximately the time for cooking fish. The times will in some cases vary, owing to the quantity to be cooked, the state of the fire, and for other unforeseen reasons.

BAKED

Halibut (per pound),	12 minutes
Shad, "	15 minutes
Bluefish, "	15 minutes

BOILED

Cod (per pound),	15 minutes
Halibut, "	20 minutes
Salmon, "	20 minutes
Turbot, "	20 minutes
Mackerel,	10 minutes
Lobster,	20 to 30 minutes

BROILED

Mackerel,	10 minutes
Bluefish,	12 to 15 minutes
Small thin fish,	5 to 8 minutes

FRIED

Whiting,	5 minutes
Soles,	5 minutes
Flounders,	5 minutes
Smelt,	5 minutes
Fish-balls,	5 minutes
Trout,	5 to 10 minutes
Slices of fish,	4 to 6 minutes

CORRECT SAUCES TO SERVE WITH FISH

Raw oysters—Tomato catsup, horseradish, and cut lemon.

Baked bluefish—Serve Worcestershire sauce or walnut catsup.

Baked halibut—Serve Worcestershire, or walnut catsup.

Baked shad—Serve Worcestershire, or walnut catsup.

Boiled cod—Serve caper sauce, egg sauce, or cream sauce.

Boiled soft crabs—Serve sauce tartare.

Boiled mackerel (salt)—Serve vinegar and melted butter, or, serve parsley sauce.

Boiled salmon (cold)—Serve vinaigrette sauce, or serve sauce tartare.

Boiled salmon (hot)—Serve hollandaise sauce, or caper sauce, or cream sauce.

Boiled sole—Serve maître d'hôtel butter.

Broiled fish (cold)—Serve sauce piquante.

Broiled mackerel (fresh)—Serve lemon butter.

Broiled mackerel (salt)—Serve maître d'hôtel butter.

Broiled salmon—Serve béarnaise sauce, sauce piquante, or tomato butter.

Broiled shad—Serve cucumber salad.

Fried fish-cutlets—Serve sauce tartare.

Fried eels—Serve sauce tartare.

Fried halibut—Serve sauce tartare.

Fried flounders—Serve Dutch sauce, and quarters of lemon.

Fried smelt—Serve sauce tartare.

Fried soles—Serve anchovy sauce and fried parsley.

Lobster cutlets—Serve sauce tartare.

SALMON LOAF, NO. 1

Canned salmon, 1 can,
Bread-crumbs, 1 cup,
Eggs, 2,
Lemon-juice, 1 tablespoon,
Worcestershire, 1 teaspoon,
Salt and pepper.

Free the salmon from bones and skin, and save all the oil, and use it instead of butter. Pick the salmon all up, fine, mix well together in a chopping-bowl. Pack it in a well-greased bowl and steam for half an hour.

Turn it out on a platter, garnish with parsley and slices of lemon, and serve with a white-fish sauce, made with hard-boiled eggs. This is enough for 6 persons.

This mixture may also be used for making salmon croquettes.

SALMON LOAF, NO. 2

Canned salmon, 1 can,
Bread-crumbs, 1 cup,
Eggs, beaten, 2,
Milk, 1 cup,
Melted butter, 1 tablespoon,
Salt and pepper.

Pick the salmon into small pieces, remove all the bones, add the melted butter, beaten eggs, bread-crumbs, milk, salt, and pepper; mix well, and pack in a small buttered pan, and bake for 1 hour.

Turn the loaf out on a platter, and pour over it the following sauce.

Sauce

Milk, 1 pint,
Cornstarch, 2 tablespoons,
Butter, 1 tablespoon,
Egg, 1, well-beaten,
Salt and pepper.

Heat the milk to the boiling point, add the cornstarch, and butter, season with salt and pepper, stir well together, and just before removing from the fire, add the beaten egg, and stir it in thoroughly.

CREAMED SALMON

Salmon, 1 1-pound can,
Butter, 1 tablespoon,
Flour, 2 tablespoons,
Milk, hot, 1 pint,
Eggs, whites only, boiled and chopped, 3,
Peanuts, chopped, 1 cup,
Salt and Cayenne pepper.

Melt the butter and flour together, and season with salt and cayenne; then add the pint of hot milk. Cook until this is smooth and then add the salmon, which has been freed from bones and skin, and next add the chopped nuts and the chopped boiled whites of the eggs.

This may be served on buttered toast, or in ramekins.

DEVILED SALMON

Salmon, 1 1-pound can,
Butter, 1 tablespoon,
Flour, 1 tablespoon,
Cream, 1 cup,

Eggs, hard-boiled (yolks, only), 3,
Chopped parsley, 1 tablespoon,
Nutmeg, salt, cayenne.

Put the butter and flour in a pan, and when melted add the cream. Stir until it is smooth and thick. Add the yolks of the eggs mashed fine. Season with salt and cayenne, and a little nutmeg, and add the fish and parsley.

Turn it out into a greased baking-pan, or into individual dishes, and bake until light brown. Serve with cucumber sauce.

CODFISH BALLS

Salt codfish, 1 pound,
Potatoes, 6,
Milk, 1 pint,
Butter, 2 tablespoons,
Eggs, 2.

Boil the fish, changing the water once, so that it may not be too salty. While still hot, pick it fine, so that it is feathery. This cannot be done with a fork, but must be done with the fingers. At the same time have ready hot potatoes, boiled. Mash them well, and make them creamy with milk and butter. To 3 cups of the mashed potatoes take $1\frac{1}{2}$ cups of fish. The fish should not be packed down. Beat the eggs lightly, and stir them into the other ingredients.

Then beat well together the whole mixture, till light; then mold it into small balls, handling it lightly, and before frying, roll the balls in flour.

Fry in a basket. The pot must be deep enough to allow the fat to cover them well.

MELTING CODFISH CAKES

Codfish, picked up, fine, 1 large cup,
Potatoes, 2 cups, mashed,
Butter, 1 tablespoon,
Eggs, 2,
Cream, 2 tablespoons.

Boil the picked codfish with the potatoes, and when the potatoes are well done, mash all well together, add the butter, eggs, and cream, and beat all together until it is soft and creamy.

Then drop the mixture from a spoon, into a frying pan of very hot lard. They should be cooked quickly, as too long cooking will make them dry.

PLANKED SHAD

Shad, one of 4 to 6 pounds,
Melted butter, ½ cup,
Salt, ½ teaspoon,
Mustard, ½ teaspoon,
Tabasco, 3 or 4 drops,
Walnut catsup, 1 teaspoon,
Worcestershire, ½ teaspoon.

The "plank" used should be of well-seasoned oak, about 2 inches thick. Those sold in the stores usually have wires attached for fastening the fish. Before using a new board brush it well several times with olive oil, and place it before a hot fire so that the oil will strike in. The wood will absorb considerable oil.

Having the board in readiness, clean the fish, and remove the backbone, rinse well quickly in slightly salted water, and dry it on a soft cloth.

Then fasten the fish on the board, skin downward, tacking it well to the board.

Have made the following sauce, from the above ingredients: To the ½ cup of melted butter add the salt, tabasco, mustard catsup, and Worcestershire sauce, and stir all together. Keep this hot at the side of the fire.

The board containing the fish may be either placed in an oven or stood in front of a hot fire. Baste the fish every 10 minutes while it is cooking, and catch in a pan the surplus which runs off while basting the fish.

When the fish is completely cooked, send it to the table on the board, being careful to remove all the tacks or fastenings before serving.

STUFFING FOR BAKED SHAD

Grated stale bread, 3 slices,
Butter, 1 tablespoon,
Capers, 1 teaspoon,
Sweet marjoram, ½ teaspoon,
Salt-pork, a small piece, chopped.

Melt the butter in a saucepan, and pour it over the grated bread and pork, which latter is chopped fine. Add the capers, and marjoram, and a very little warm water.

Stuff the shad through the cuts in both ends, and place it in the oven to bake.

OYSTERS À LA CREOLE

Oysters, 1 pint,
Butter, 2 tablespoons,
Onion, finely chopped, 2 slices,
Flour, 1 tablespoon,
Stewed tomatoes, 1 cup,

Tabasco, 1 or 2 drops,
Salt.

Melt the butter in a chafing-dish, or stewpan, add the sliced onion, and stir till it is delicately browned; then add the flour, and stir until it is smooth and brown, and then add the tomatoes.

As soon as the sauce thickens, add the oysters drained from their liquor, and cook them until the edges curl. Season with the tabasco and one-half a teaspoon of salt. Serve on toast with parsley.

OYSTERS À LA POULETTE

DELMONICO

Large oysters, 2 quarts,
Butter, 6 ounces,
Flour, 2 ounces,
Cream, ½ cup,
Eggs, 4 (yolks only),
Lemon, ½,
Chopped parsley, 1 teaspoon,
Salt, ½ teaspoon,
Cayenne pepper, a dash.

Put the oysters into a stewpan, and set them on the fire until they boil. Drain through a sieve, saving the liquor. Set the oysters aside, and keep them hot.

Put 4 ounces of the butter into a stewpan with 2 ounces of flour, a little Cayenne pepper, and salt. Blend well together, and moisten with the oyster liquor and with the cream. Stir this while on the fire, and keep it boiling for 10 minutes. Then take it off the fire and pass it through a colander.

Now add the remaining 2 ounces of butter, and the yolks of the eggs. The mixture must not be allowed to cook after the eggs are added.

Just before sending to the table, add the oysters, the juice of half a lemon and the chopped parsley.

CREAMED SCALLOPS

Scallops, 1 quart,
Milk, 1 pint,
Butter, 1 tablespoon,
Flour, 2 tablespoons,
Sherry, 2 tablespoons.

Cream together the butter and flour. Boil the scallops and milk together for 15 minutes, then strain and after chopping them, place them again on the fire with the milk and add the butter and flour creamed together.

Cook the mixture for 10 minutes, then put in the sherry, and bake, either in one dish, or in individual ramekins, until light brown.

BAKED SOLE, OR FILLET OF FLOUNDERS

GERMAN

Fish,
Olive oil,
Lemon-juice,
Seasoned bread-crumbs,
Eggs,
Larding pork,
Onions,
Green olives.

Remove the bone from the fish, and cut the meat into strips. Roll these and fasten with wooden toothpicks. Soak the rolls for an hour, in olive oil and lemon-juice; then roll them in seasoned bread-crumbs, next in beaten egg, and then again in bread-crumbs.

Now put into a baking-dish, and on each roll of fish put a slice of larding pork. Sprinkle generously with chopped onion, and green olive, and bake about 45 minutes, or until it is well-browned.

BRAZILIAN SHRIMPS

Shrimps, 1 pound (or 1 can),
Tomato juice, 1 pint,
Green pepper, 1,
Onion, 1,
Butter, 1 tablespoon,
Flour, 2 tablespoons,
Sugar, 1 teaspoon.

Cut the pepper and onion in long thin strips and place them in the stewpan with the tomato juice. Let this boil about 15 minutes, and then add the shrimps.

Cream the butter and the flour together, and add these to the mixture, and allow the whole to boil together until it thickens, and is smooth.

MACKEREL

CHAMBERLIN'S METHOD

Take one or more mackerel, and soak them for about 48 hours, changing the water once. Then put them in a pan, and cover with cream, or rich milk, or the nearest you can get to it, and put them in the oven and cook until the cream is brown.

FISH CUTLETS

Codfish, or salmon, 1 pound,
Flour, 2 tablespoons,
Butter, 1 tablespoon,
Chopped parsley, 1 teaspoon,

Onion juice, 1 teaspoon,
Lemon juice, 1 teaspoon,
Milk, 1 pint,
Eggs, 2 yolks,
Salt and pepper.

Boil the fish in cheese-cloth for 15 minutes, then pick it to pieces. Heat the milk and add to it the butter and flour which have been creamed, the salt, pepper, parsley, onion juice, lemon juice and eggs. Let it stand 3 or 4 hours on the ice, then form into cutlet shape, dip into egg and breadcrumbs, and fry in a wire basket.

FISH PASTE

JAPANESE

Halibut, cod, salmon, or pompano, 1 pound,
Butter, 1 tablespoon,
Flour, 1 tablespoon,
Milk, 1 cup,
Cream, 1 tablespoon,
Lemon juice, 1 teaspoon,
Onion juice, 1 teaspoon,
Egg, 1.

Boil the fish for a few minutes, and then put it through a purée sieve. To this add the beaten white of the egg, and set it away to cool.

Melt the butter and flour together, and while they are boiling, add the milk. Take it away from the fire, and add the yolk of the egg, and the seasoning. Then return it to the fire, and cook it until it is smooth, then take it from the fire, and add the fish, which was set aside to cool.

Place the whole mixture in small cups, or molds to cool.

This should be served on a bed of rice, and garnished with cresses.

STEWED TERRAPIN

CHAMBERLIN'S METHOD

Terrapin, 1,
Eggs (yolks, only), 4,
Butter, ½ cup,
Cream, ½ cup,
Madeira, or sherry, ½ cup.

Put the terrapin in boiling water for 5 minutes, to loosen the skin; then take it out, skin it and replace it in the hot water. When the claws are soft it is sufficiently boiled.

Take it out, and remove the bottom shell first. Cut off the head and claws, and take out the gall and sand-bag; and then cut up the remainder. Cut up entrails and all, about ½-inch lengths. Be careful to preserve all the juice.

Put the terrapin meat into a stewpan, and make a dressing of flour, yolks of 2 hard-boiled eggs, a third of a pound of good butter, salt, red pepper, a small quantity of rich cream and a half cup of madeira or good sherry to each terrapin.

All of the ingredients should be of the best quality. Stew it well, and dish promptly, and serve smoking hot.

The cow terrapin is the best—besides furnishing eggs, which are a great addition. Some persons have been known to season with spices, but this is not to the taste of epicures.

TIMBALE CASES FOR CREAMED FISH

Flour, 1 cup,
Eggs, 2,
Butter, 1 tablespoon,
Salt, ½ teaspoon.

Separate the whites and yolks of the eggs, and beat the yolks smooth. Add a cup of cold water and the sifted flour, and also the butter—olive oil may be used if butter is not at hand.

Add also the salt and stir well, then heat the mixture hard. Next whip the whites of the eggs to a stiff froth, and add them to the batter, and heat it again, and then put it aside, and let it cool overnight.

Immerse the timbale iron in smoking fat until it is very hot, then lift it up, and let it drain for a second, and dip it carefully into the batter until a layer of batter adheres to it; then plunge it into the fat and hold it there till the batter is delicately colored. Hold it over a paper and tap it sharply with a knife, and the cup will fall off. If the cup is too thick then thin the batter.

When the timbale cups are needed for use for fish, stand them on a paper pan and reheat them in the oven. Then fill the cups with any kind of fish, heated with a cream sauce, seasoned with lemon juice, etc. Put a pinch of parsley on each cup when filled.

FISH TIMBALES
SWEDISH

Boiled white fish, ½ pound,
Bread-crumbs, ½ pint,
Milk, ¼ pint,
Cream, 6 tablespoons,
White pepper, ¼ teaspoon,
Salt, 1 level teaspoon,
Eggs (whites, only), 6.

Boil the bread-crumbs and milk to a paste, and let it cool; then add the fish, which has been put through the grinder; and press all through a sieve. Then add the cream, pepper, and salt, and the stiffly beaten whites of the eggs.

Butter the timbales, and fill them with the fish, three-fourths full. Cover them with oiled paper, and bake for 20 minutes.

ENTRÉES

HADDOCK RAMEKINS

ENGLISH

Smoked haddock, 1 cupful,
Butter, 2 tablespoons,
Eggs, 2 (yolks, only),
Whipped cream, 1/4 cupful,
Grated nutmeg,
Salt and pepper.

Scald the haddock, and put it into the oven with 1 tablespoonful of the butter, until cooked. Remove all the skin and bones, and take 1 cupful of finely flaked fish. To this add the other tablespoonful of butter, and rub all through a colander.

Add the seasoning and the beaten yolks of the 2 eggs. After these are well worked together, then stir in the whipped cream.

Bake at once, in ramekin cases, in a quick oven.

GENOA RAMEKINS

Milk, 1 pint,
Eggs, 2,
Stale bread, 6 slices,
Grated cheese, 1 cup.

Cut the stale bread into thick slices and remove all the crust. Arrange them in buttered pans, or in one shallow baking-dish. For 6 slices, make a raw custard with 1 pint of milk, 2 eggs, and ¼ teaspoon of salt. Baste the bread at intervals with this, until it has absorbed as much as possible, and then cover with a thick layer of cheese, and place it in a moderate oven until the custard sets, and the cheese is melted and slightly browned.

CHEESE CUSTARD

Milk, 1 cup,
Grated cheese, 6 tablespoons,
Eggs, 2,
Green pepper, 1, chopped.

Scald the milk in a double boiler, add the cheese and stir until it melts. Then put in the eggs, slightly beaten, season with salt and pepper or paprika.

Butter 6 individual molds and sprinkle them with the green pepper. Fill with custard and bake.

GNOCCHI

Grated cheese, 1 cup,
Butter, ¼ cup,
Flour, ½ cup,
Cornstarch, ½ cup,
Milk, 2 cups,
Eggs, 2 yolks.

Melt the butter in a pan, and when it is bubbling put in the flour and cornstarch; gradually add the milk and the cheese, and lastly the yolks of the eggs which should be well-beaten. Pour into a buttered pan, and allow it to spread so that the mixture shall not be thick. When it is cool turn it onto a cutting-board and cut it into fancy shapes; diamonds, squares, fingers, etc.

Arrange them on a platter and sprinkle with the remaining cheese. Place them in the oven and bake until brown.

CALF'S HEAD CHEESE

>Calf's head, 1,
>Sweet herbs, finely minced, 1 tablespoon,
>Sage, ½ teaspoon,
>Onion, 1, small and finely chopped.

Boil the calf's head in water enough to cover it, until it leaves the bones. With a skimmer put it into a wooden bowl or tray. Pick out every bit of bone and chop it fine. Add all the seasoning, and lay it in a cloth pressed tightly over it. Put it in a colander and cover with a plate on which a weight is placed.

When cold, slice and garnish with parsley and lemons.

ENGLISH BRAWN

>One small pig's head,
>Salt, 2 tablespoons,
>Bay leaf, 1,
>Cloves, 6,
>Peppercorns, 12,
>Cayenne, a dash.

Clean the pig's head thoroughly, removing the eyes and the brain; then soak it for 1 hour in cold water.

Take from the water, and put it in a pan with 2 tablespoons of salt, and sufficient water to cover it (about 2 quarts).

Bring this to a boil, then draw the pan to one side, and allow the contents to simmer for 3 hours.

Take it out, place on a hot dish, and remove all the bone. If it has been properly boiled, the bone will come away easily. Cut and shred the meat, preserving the tongue whole.

Now discard all but about 2 cupsful of the liquor in which it has been boiled, and to this add the bay leaf, cloves, peppercorns, and cayenne, and boil this rapidly together, until it has been reduced to about half its original quantity.

Arrange the tongue in the middle of a mold, and pack the shredded meat around it. Then gradually pour over it the liquor, and set it away to cool.

When cold, turn out, and cut in slices.

PORK CHEESE

ENGLISH

Cold roast pork, 2 pounds,
Pork fat, ½ pound,
Onions (finely minced), 2,
Gravy, 1 cup,
Gelatin, 1 teaspoon,
Sage leaves, 4,
Salt and pepper.

Cut the pork and the fat into dice, then pack into a mold with salt and pepper to taste, also add the sage leaves, crushed, and the onions finely minced.

Dissolve the gelatin in the gravy, and pour it into the mold over all.

Bake for about an hour, and set aside to cool. When cold, turn out of the mold.

ITALIAN VEAL CHEESE

Veal, 3 pounds,
Lemons, 2,
Whole cloves, 12,
Worcestershire sauce, 2 tablespoons,
Gelatin, 1 tablespoon,

Stuffed olives, 12,
Eggs (hard-boiled), 3,
Celery-salt,
Salt and pepper.

This should be made and allowed to stand about 24 hours before using.

Cook the veal until tender, in just enough water to cover it. Take it from the water and pass it through the meat-grinder, or chop fine. Put the gravy back on the stove and add to it the juice of one of the lemons, the cloves, Worcestershire sauce, salt, pepper, celery-salt and the gelatin.

Cut the eggs, and the remaining lemon into thin slices, and cut the stuffed olives in halves. Line a mold with the slices of egg, lemon and olive, making symmetrical figures or patterns.

Put the meat into the mold, and pour the gravy over it through a strainer, and set it aside to cool.

When ready to serve, turn out of the mold, and the symmetrical figures will appear on the outside of the cheese.

PREPARED MARROW-BONES

GERMAN

Beef marrow-bones,
Flour,
Hot toast.

Have the bones cut between 2 and 4 inches in length. Wash and wipe them dry. Make a stiff dough of flour and water, roll it out until about ¼-inch thick. Cut pieces of the dough into 2-inch squares, and with these cover the ends of the bones.

Pin the bones in a piece of cloth, put them in a stewpan, and cover with boiling water. Let them boil for 1 hour. Take them up, and remove the cloth and paste, and place the bone on a piece of hot toast. Use salt, and cayenne, or black pepper to taste.

VEAL TERRAPIN

Cold veal, 1 pint,
Eggs, 6,
Minced lemon-peel, 1 tablespoon,
Cream, or cream-sauce, 1 cup,
Salt, pepper, nutmeg.

Cut the veal in dice. To each pint of cut veal add 6 eggs boiled fifteen minutes and chopped fine. Sprinkle with pepper and salt. Add the lemon-peel, a little grated nutmeg, or sweet marjoram, or summer-savory, according to the flavor desired, also add the cream or cream-sauce, 1 cup to each pint of cut veal. Let it come to a boil, heat all together, and serve hot.

Garnish with toast-points, and olives.

VEAL SOUFFLÉ WITH MUSHROOM-SAUCE

Butter, 2 tablespoons,
Cornstarch, 3 level tablespoons,
Flour, 1 tablespoon,
Salt, ½ teaspoon,
Chopped veal, 1 cup,
Soft bread-crumbs, ¼ cup,
Eggs, 3,
Hot milk, or stock, 1 cup.

Make a sauce of the butter, cornstarch, milk, and seasoning, salt and pepper to taste, and when cooked and smooth, beat well and add the chopped veal and bread-crumbs. Remove from the fire, add the yolks of the eggs, well-beaten, and stir in the whites beaten stiffly.

Place it in a buttered dish, standing in a pan of hot water, bake in a moderate oven 30 minutes, and serve with mushroom-sauce made as follows:

> Butter, 4 level tablespoons,
> Carrot, 1 slice,
> Onion, 1 slice,
> Cornstarch, 3 level tablespoons,
> Flour, 1 tablespoon,
> Veal-stock, 2 cups,
> Salt, pepper, bay leaf,
> Mushrooms, chopped, 1 cup,
> Kitchen bouquet.

Melt the butter, to which add the carrot, onion, and half a bay leaf, and 1 sprig of parsley, and cook for 5 minutes, then add the cornstarch and flour, season with salt and pepper to taste, and gradually add 2 cups of the stock in which the veal was cooked, and cook again for 5 minutes. Strain the sauce, reheat, and add ½ teaspoon of kitchen bouquet, and the cup of chopped mushrooms.

Serve the veal soufflé with this sauce from a gravy boat.

SWEETBREAD CROQUETTES

> Sweetbreads, 1 pair,
> Fat pork,
> Tongue, ½ pound (cold, boiled),
> Onion, ½,
> Eggs, 3,
> Parsley, bread-crumbs,
> Butter,
> Salt and pepper.

Parboil the sweetbreads for 5 minutes, then trim off the string and pipe. Lard them well with strips of fat pork, about the size of a match, and fry them a light brown, in butter.

Chop the tongue and sweetbreads fine, mix them well together, grate the half of an onion and chop a few sprigs of parsley, and add them, with salt and pepper to the rest.

Then add the yolks of the eggs, beaten light, to some of the gravy that the sweetbreads have been cooked in, and thoroughly mix together.

When cool and firm, shape into croquettes, dip them into the egg, and then into bread-crumbs, and fry in smoking hot butter or lard until a golden brown.

Lay them on brown paper to drain, and serve with French canned peas, while still hot.

SWEETBREAD PATTIES

GERMAN

Sweetbreads, 1 pair,
Milk, 1 pint,
Butter, 2 tablespoons,
Eggs (yolks, only), 6,
Flour, 4 tablespoons,
Sherry wine, 2 tablespoons,
Salt, and Cayenne pepper.

Parboil the sweetbreads and let them cool. Melt the butter in a pan, and to this add the milk and flour, mixed together, and stir briskly until boiling.

Season with salt and Cayenne pepper to taste.

Cut the sweetbreads into small pieces, put them into the mixture, and cook for 5 minutes.

Take off of the fire, add the beaten yolks of the eggs, and the sherry, and serve in patty shells.

PÂTÉ DE FOIE GRAS, NO. 1

Calf's liver, 1,
Calf's tongue, 1,
Melted butter, ½ cup,
Cayenne, ¼ teaspoon,
Ground cloves, ¼ teaspoon,
Worcestershire, 1 tablespoon,
Made-mustard, 1 teaspoon,
Onion juice, 1 teaspoon,
Boiling water, 1 tablespoon.

Boil the liver until very tender, in slightly salted water; and in another vessel boil the tongue. They should both be cold and firm when later used.

Pound the liver in a mortar, moistening it gradually with the melted butter. When it is a smooth paste put into it all the seasoning, and the water, and pack it firmly into jars, inserting here and there, bits of the tongue, which have been cut and pared for this purpose.

When the jars are firmly packed, cover the tops with melted butter. Cover lightly, and set in a cool place.

PÂTÉ DE FOIE GRAS, NO. 2

Calf's liver, 1 pound,
Olives, 6,
Peppercorns, 6,
Butter, 4 ounces,
Salt, ½ teaspoon,
Bay leaf, 1,
Parsley sprigs.

Place the liver, olives, parsley, and bay leaf in a saucepan, and cover with boiling water. Only use 1 bay leaf and

2 sprigs of parsley. Add the salt and peppercorns. Simmer for two hours, gently. Set off, and when cool, cut the liver into thin slices.

Place in a bowl, strain the broth over it, and let it stand overnight. Next morning take out the meat, pound it to a pulp, adding gradually the 4 ounces of butter beaten to a cream.

Press all through a sieve, add more salt if needed, then pack in glass jars, and keep closely covered until needed for use.

CASSEROLE OF LIVER AND RICE

>Rice, 1 cup,
>Calf's liver, 1 pound,
>Butter, 2 tablespoons,
>Milk, or stock, 2 cups,
>Browned flour, 1 tablespoon,
>Salt, pepper, kitchen bouquet.

Boil the rice, add the butter. Line a well-greased casserole with this, pressing it against the sides and leaving a hollow in the center. Boil the liver, drain it and chop fine. Heat in a saucepan, the milk or stock, add to it the flour and kitchen bouquet, then the minced liver; and put this mixture into the casserole of rice. Sprinkle with bread-crumbs, and set in the oven to brown.

CHILLI CON CARNE
MEXICAN

>Round steak, 2 pounds,
>Flour, 4 tablespoons,
>Garlic bud, 1,
>Melted butter, or drippings, 2 tablespoons,
>Dried Chilli peppers, 4 pods,
>Salt.

Remove all seeds from the pepper pods. Soak the pods in a pint of warm water until they are soft, then scrape the pulp from the skin into the water, discarding the skins and saving the pulp and the water.

Cut the steak into small pieces, and cook in a hot frying-pan with 2 tablespoons of melted butter, or drippings, until well browned.

Add the flour and mix thoroughly, then add the sliced garlic and the pint of chilli water. Simmer about 2 hours; or until the meat is tender; adding hot water if needed. When done, the sauce should be of good consistency. Season to taste, with salt.

CHILLI CON CARNE

Lean beef, 2 pounds,
Onion, 1,
Green, or red pepper, 1,
Tomato juice, 1 quart,
Flour, 1 tablespoon,
Butter, 1 tablespoon.

Cut the meat into small pieces and fry; take it from the pan and arrange on a platter. Over it put a sauce made from the onion, tomato juice and pepper. The onion and pepper should be cut into thin slices, and when put into the tomato juice, the whole must be thickened with butter and flour.

TONGUE IN ASPIC

Pickled beef-tongue, 1,
Aspic jelly,
Stoned olives.

Soak, boil and skin, and then cool, the tongue. Trim it, and cut it into thin slices and press them together again, to retain the shape of the tongue.

Rinse an oblong mold in water and drain. Put a layer of aspic jelly in the bottom, and on it place a layer of stoned olives. Cover with aspic. Place the tongue in the center, and pour aspic about it until it is covered. Chill it, and remove it from the mold, and serve with a vegetable mayonnaise.

CHICKEN MOUSSE

>Cold chicken, finely minced, 1 cup,
>Milk, ½ pint,
>Eggs, 2,
>Gelatin, ½ box,
>Salt and pepper.

Scald the milk, beat the yolks of the eggs, and season with salt and pepper. Add these to the milk, and if milk is not to be had, use an equal amount of water. Place in a double boiler, and cook until it is the consistency of a custard. Take it from the fire and mix it with half a box of gelatin which has been soaked in cold water.

Pour it over the minced chicken-meat, and stir in the whites of the eggs which have been well beaten. Beat all until smooth, and beginning to form, and then pour it into small molds.

RICED CHICKEN IN SHELLS

>Cold, minced chicken, 1 cup,
>Boiled rice, 1 cup,
>Egg (white only), 1,
>Salt, 1 salt-spoon,
>Sweet cream,
>Celery-salt,
>Browned bread-crumbs
>Nutmeg.

Mince the chicken fine, and mix with the boiled rice; adding a little sweet cream, a salt-spoon of salt, a little nutmeg, and a pinch of celery-salt.

When thoroughly mixed beat in the white of 1 egg, whipped stiff. Arrange in individual baking shells; sprinkle with browned bread-crumbs, and brown in a quick oven.

Serve garnished with parsley, and toasted bread fingers.

HASSENPFEFFER (SOUR RABBIT)

GERMAN

Rabbit, 1,
Vinegar,
Pepper,
Laurel leaves,
Onions,
Cloves,
Salt, and browned flour.

Clean, cut up, and wash the rabbit nicely, then put it into a deep dish and cover it with vinegar. Add pepper, laurel leaves, onions, cloves and salt, and put it aside for 2 days.

Then stew it in enough slightly salted water to cover it. When it is done, thicken the gravy with browned flour.

LOBSTER PATTIES

GERMAN

Lobster, 1, medium (2 pounds),
Dry bread-crumbs (rolled fine), 4 tablespoons,
Milk, 1 cupful,
Butter, 2 tablespoons,
Salt and Cayenne pepper.

Boil the lobster, and pick the meat up fine. Dry the bread-crumbs in the oven and roll them fine. Put the lobster in a stewpan, add to it 1 tablespoon of the bread-crumbs, and mix well together, and season highly with salt and Cayenne pepper. Add to this the butter, and the remaining 3 tablespoons of bread-crumbs mixed with the milk.

Put all on the fire; cook for about 5 minutes, constantly stirring, and serve in patty shells.

LOBSTER A LA CREOLE

Lobster meat (fresh or canned), 1 heaping pint,
Butter, 1 tablespoon,
Clear chicken broth, 1 cup,
Chopped onion, 1 tablespoon,
Green pepper (chopped fine), 1,
Rich tomato sauce, ½ cup.

Heat the butter, add the onion and the pepper, which should be seeded and cut fine; add also a cup of rich tomato sauce, and cook all for 5 minutes. Then add 1 cup of clear chicken broth, and cook for 5 minutes longer; then add the lobster, and salt to taste. As soon as the lobster is heated through it is ready to serve.

LOBSTER CROQUETTES

Lobster, 1,
Eggs, 2,
Melted butter, 2 tablespoons,
Bread-crumbs,
Pulverized cracker, mace,
Salt and pepper,
Parsley for garnish.

Boil the lobster. Chop up the meat, and add pepper, salt, and powdered mace. Use about one-fourth as much bread-crumbs as you have lobster meat. Mix all the ingredients together, and form into pear-shaped balls. Roll these in the beaten egg, then in the cracker-crumbs, and fry in butter, first removing the hot-water pan.

Lift out, and serve immediately, using parsley to garnish.

SPINACH LOAF WITH SARDINES

Boiled spinach, 1 cup,
Sardines, 6, large,
Bread-crumbs, ½ cup,
Melted butter, 2 tablespoons,
Lemon juice, 1 teaspoon.

Chop the fish and spinach together, add the crumbs, seasoning, butter and lemon-juice. Shape in a loaf, and set in the oven for 10 minutes. Garnish with slices of hard-boiled eggs and lemon.

TOMATO SOUFFLÉ

Tomatoes,
Garlic, or onion,
Eggs,
Salt and pepper.

The tomatoes must first be stewed as follows: Scald the tomatoes, remove the skins and cut off the blossoms. Cut the tomatoes into quarters. Put them into the saucepan and simmer for about 1 hour, uncovered—then drain off the juice —keeping it for soup or sauce. Add 1 bud of garlic, or 2 slices of onion to the tomatoes, and simmer for another hour.

Drain off the liquid, press the pulp through a sieve, and measure it. To every cup of juice (pulp) allow 2 eggs. Beat the yolks until light and add them to the tomato-pulp. Season with salt and pepper. Beat the whites stiff, and dry, and mix them with the other mixture lightly. Butter and fill the soufflé cases about three-quarters full.

Bake in a hot oven for 10 minutes, and serve at once.

STUFFED TOMATOES WITH BAKED EGGS

> Tomatoes, 6,
> Grated cheese, 4 tablespoons,
> Bread-crumbs, 2 tablespoons,
> Melted butter, 1 tablespoon,
> Raw mustard,
> Salt and cayenne,
> Eggs, 6.

Cut off the tops and scoop out the middles of as many tomatoes as may be required, allowing 1 for each person—the above allows for 6 persons. Make a stuffing with the ingredients: the grated cheese, bread-crumbs, melted butter, salt, cayenne, and raw mustard, the seasoning added to suit the taste.

Stuff the tomatoes with this mixture, and cover the tops with buttered bread-crumbs. Stand them in a baking-tin and bake in a hot oven for half an hour.

Melt a teaspoon of butter in a pie-tin, and carefully break 6 eggs over it. Bake them for 5 minutes, or until the whites are set.

Have ready neat rounds of buttered toast. Slip an egg carefully on each piece of toast, and arrange the baked tomatoes around the eggs and toast, and serve immediately.

This is an excellent dish for breakfast or lunch, and quite a substantial one.

NUT CROQUETTES

> Ground English Walnuts, 1 pound,
> Salt, 1 teaspoon,

Lemon, the juice of ½,
Chopped parsley, 1 tablespoon,
Flour, 2 tablespoons,
Butter, 1 tablespoon,
Milk, 1 cup,
Egg, 1, well beaten.

Mix the ground walnuts, the salt, and the lemon-juice together, and add the parsley.

Put together the flour and butter, and with this, thicken 1 cup of boiling milk. Season, and mix it with the nut mixture, and add a well-beaten egg. Set it to cool. Form into small rolls, dip in egg and cracker-crumbs, and fry till light brown.

NUT AND CRUMB CROQUETTES

Pecans,
Dried toast-crumbs,
Cream sauce.

Pass through the chopper enough pecan-meats to make 1 cupful. Add to the nuts an equal amount of dried toast-crumbs, also passed through the chopper. Moisten with a highly seasoned cream sauce, and form into croquettes in the usual way.

Fry in deep fat. A green pea sauce is delicious served with the croquettes.

SOMERSET CLUB CROQUETTES

Cheese, 1½ cups,
Eggs, 2 yolks,
Butter, 3 tablespoons,
Flour, 3 tablespoons,
Milk, 1 cup (scant),
Salt and cayenne.

Melt the butter and rub in the flour. Then add the milk, stirring constantly. When boiling, add ½ cup of grated cheese, and allow this to melt. Then take from the fire and stir in the remaining cup of grated cheese, and also the eggs, which have been cut into small pieces.

Season with salt and cayenne. Spread on a shallow pan to cool. Shape, and dip into egg and crumbs, and fry in deep fat until light brown. Serve on a folded napkin, garnished with green, with a salad course.

GERMAN GLOBES

Potatoes, medium, 7,
Flour, ½ pound,
Eggs, 4,
Melted butter, 3 tablespoons
Milk, ½ cup,
Salt,
Chopped boiled ham,
Thick sour cream.

Bake the potatoes in their skins, and rub them through a sieve. Put into a bowl a little salt, ½ pound of flour, ½ an yeast-cake, the 4 yolks of the eggs, the melted butter, the potatoes, and ½ cup of milk.

Mix all thoroughly, cover with a clean napkin and leave for an hour to rise. Roll the dough thin on a board, and cut it out with a plain round cutter or with a wine-glass.

Wet the edges with a little white of egg, put in the middle of each a teaspoon of chopped boiled ham and 1 teaspoon of thick sour cream. Place a second cake on top of this, press the edges together, and put in a warm place covered with a napkin for about 2 hours.

Fry in deep hot lard like dough-nuts. Serve with mushroom sauce.

CURRY

This, the great dish of the East, originated in India. Rice, any kind of meat, fish, or game may be used; but the accompaniments or sauces are really what make the dish.

The rice should be well boiled and served in a separate dish.

Place in a stewpan a pint of finely cut (not chopped) meat, one gill of milk, or stock, and to this add soft peppers and two teaspoons of curry powder. Let this simmer for 10 or 15 minutes. This should be served in a separate dish.

The rice should be put on the plates and the curry later over it.

With this should be served the following: Dried fish, or "Bombay duck" (in America a good substitute for "Bombay duck" is dried herring)—sweet, sour, and spiced pickles of all kinds, grated cocoanut, finely chopped hard-boiled eggs, and chutney sauce.

The best body for curry is made from chicken, lamb or lobster. Curry powder, itself, is compounded of turmeric, coriander seed, ginger and Cayenne pepper, to which salt, cloves, cardamons, pounded cinnamon, onions, garlic and scraped cocoanut are added—the latter, "coprath," being only the vehicle or body to carry the various other condiments.

HAWAIIAN CURRY

Grated cocoanut, 1,
Milk, 1 quart,
Chopped onions, 1 tablespoon,
Butter, 1 tablespoon,
Curry powder, 1 (scant) tablespoon,
Ground ginger-root, 1 teaspoon,
Fish (or chicken, or lamb), etc.

Grate the cocoanut, and soak in the milk for 1 hour. Fry the onions in the butter until brown, then add to them the curry and the ginger.

Strain off the milk from the grated cocoanut, and pour it over the mixture in the frying-pan.

Put in, the raw fish, chicken, or other meat, and cook slowly until done.

CHESTNUT PATTIES

> Chestnut meats, 1 cupful,
> Flour, 5 tablespoons,
> Pulverized sugar, 1 cup,
> Baking-powder, 1 teaspoon,
> Egg, 1,
> Cinnamon.

Put the chestnut meats through a grinder. Beat the egg and sugar together. Add the ground chestnut meats, also the flour and baking-powder; beat all lightly together, and then drop by spoonful onto buttered tins.

Dust with pulverized sugar and cinnamon, and bake in a quick oven.

MEATS

TIME-TABLE FOR COOKING MEATS

ROASTING

Beef sirloin, rare, per pound......	8 to 10	minutes
Beef sirloin, well-done, per pound..	12 to 15	minutes
Beef rolled, rib or rump, per pound.	12 to 15	minutes
Beef long or short fillet...........	20 to 30	minutes
Chickens, 3, to 4 pounds weight....	1 to 1½	hours
Duck, tame	40 to 60	minutes
Lamb, well-done, per pound.......	15	minutes
Mutton, rare, per pound..........	10	minutes
Mutton, well-done, per pound......	15	minutes
Pork, well-done, per pound........	30	minutes
Turkey, 10 pounds...............	2 to 3	hours
Veal, well-done, per pound........	20	minutes

BOILING

Beef à la mode...................	3 to 4	hours
Corned beef	3 to 5	hours
Fowls	2 to 3	hours
Ham	5	hours
Mutton	2 to 3	hours
Pigeon, potted	2	hours
Smoked tongue	3 to 4	hours
Sweetbreads	20 to 30	minutes
Turkey	2 to 3	hours
Veal, per pound.................	20	minutes

BROILING

Chickens	20	minutes
Chops	8	minutes
Steak	4 to 8	minutes

FRYING

Bacon	3 to 5	minutes
Breaded chops	6 to 10	minutes
Croquettes	5	minutes

WHAT TO SERVE WITH MEATS

Roast lamb (hot or cold)—Serve mint sauce, French salad, new potatoes, cut cucumber.

Braised lamb—Serve peas, young carrots, and turnips.

Roast veal—Serve thick brown gravy, rolled bacon, tomato sauce, horseradish sauce, quarters of lemon, forced-meat balls, French beans.

Stewed veal—Serve parsley sauce, cooked carrots and turnips cut in dice or small balls, peas.

Calf's head (boiled)—Serve parsley sauce, croutons.

Fricasseed veal—Serve sippets of toast, slices of lemon, rolls of bacon, pickle.

Roast pork—Serve sage and onion stuffing, apple sauce, thick brown gravy, piquante sauce, turnips.

Grilled pork cutlets—Serve mustard sauce, fried potatoes.

Baked ham—Serve orange salad, Madeira sauce.

Boiled ham—Serve champagne sauce, purée of spinach, horseradish.

Roast saddle of mutton—Serve red currant jelly, cranberry jelly, baked potatoes.

Boiled mutton—Serve parsley, caper sauce, carrots and turnips, leeks.

Mutton cutlets—Serve mashed potatoes, brown sauce, or tomato sauce, green peas, sorrel sauce, strips of truffle, gherkins, ham.

Roast neck of mutton—Serve braised carrots.

Grilled breast of mutton—Serve brown sauce, caper sauce, grilled tomatoes, grilled mushrooms.

Roast loin of mutton—Serve brown sauce, caper sauce, piquante sauce, baked potatoes.

Grilled mutton kidneys—Serve potato chips, maitre d'hôtel butter, grilled tomatoes.

Stewed mutton kidneys—Serve croutons, grilled mushrooms.

Roast beef—Serve horseradish sauce, Yorkshire pudding, tomatoes stuffed with mushrooms.

Stewed fillet of beef—Serve macaroni, or spaghetti.

Roast turkey—Serve cranberry jelly.

Grilled steak or grilled fillet of beef—Serve maitre d'hôtel butter, fried potatoes, horseradish, grilled mushrooms, grilled tomatoes, fried onions, mushroom sauce, champagne sauce.

ROAST TURKEY WITH OYSTERS

Turkey, 1 (10 pounds),
Oysters, 1 pint,
Bread-crumbs, 1 quart,
Butter, 2 tablespoons,
Salt, 1 teaspoon,

Pepper, 1 teaspoon,
Thyme, a pinch.

Work the butter into the bread-crumbs. Add a teaspoon of salt, a teaspoon of pepper, and a pinch of thyme. Mix these well together and moisten with 2 tablespoons of the oyster liquor.

Drain the oysters and stuff the turkey with alternate tablespoons of the bread-crumbs and of the oysters. Sew up the opening.

Boil the oyster liquor and skim it; put it into the baking-pan hot, and frequently baste the turkey with it, while roasting.

Rub the turkey with salt and pepper, and dredge with flour, before putting it into the oven.

TURKEY STUFFING

Two quarts of stuffing is generally needed for a good-sized turkey. The foundation is stale bread, finely crumbled. When the crusts are used they should be soaked in water until they are soft, and then squeezed as dry as possible. To this may be added a high seasoning, and at least half a cupful of melted butter, or other shortening.

Additions may be made at will, of chopped celery, raw oysters, drained and quartered, raw sausage-meat, chopped raw veal, boiled chestnuts, chopped or rubbed through a sieve, chopped hard-boiled eggs, chopped parsley, and truffles.

TURKEY DRESSING, NO. 1

Bread, ½ loaf,
Milk, 2 cups,
Pecans, or English walnuts, ½ cup,
Butter, 2 tablespoons,

Onion juice, 1 tablespoon,
Celery, 1 stalk,
Worcestershire, 1 tablespoon,
Salt and pepper.

Cut the crust from the bread, and soak the bread in the milk 1 hour. Use as much of the milk as the bread will take up.

Melt the butter, and add it and the seasoning to the dressing. Chop the nuts and the celery, and mix the whole well together.

TURKEY DRESSING, NO. 2

GERMAN

Baker's bread, ½ loaf,
Milk, 2 cups,
Butter, 1 tablespoon,
Eggs, 2,
Sugar, 1 tablespoon,
Dried currants, 3 tablespoons,
Sweet almonds, 12, cut fine,
Citron, salt, pepper.

Take half a loaf of baker's bread and remove the crust. Soak in a cup of milk. Squeeze the bread out, stir in stock, if you have it, also a tablespoon of butter, 2 or 3 eggs, 3 tablespoons of dried currants, about 2 dozen sweet almonds which have been pounded, or cut very fine, and also some finely cut citron. Season to taste with salt and pepper.

CHESTNUT STUFFING FOR TURKEY

Chestnuts, 1 pint,
Stock, 1 cup,
Fowl's liver, 1,
Ham, 1 slice,

Onion juice, 1 teaspoon,
Bread-crumbs, 2 tablespoons.
Butter, 1 tablespoon,
Salt, 1 teaspoon,
Eggs, 2 yolks,
Grated lemon-peel, Cayenne and black pepper.

Roast and blanch the chestnuts, boil for about 20 minutes in strong chicken or veal stock. Drain, and put through a vegetable press, or through a meat-chopper. Add to this, the boiled liver of the fowl, a slice of ham, both ground fine. Also add the onion juice, bread-crumbs and butter, a pinch of grated lemon-peel, the salt, a dash of Cayenne, and a salt-spoon of black pepper.

Moisten all with the yolks of 2 eggs, and use as a stuffing. This is a delicious stuffing for turkeys, ducks, or chickens.

BOILED HAM

Put the ham in a bucket of tepid water, and let it stand all night. In the morning put it into a pot of cold water and allow it to come to a simmer—not boiling; and let it stew thus for 5 hours. When it has boiled until tender, take it from the fire, and let it cool in the water in which it has been boiled.

Take off the skin, and rub the ham with bread-crumbs and sugar. At intervals sprinkle spots of black pepper; and in the center of each spot stick a whole clove. Then let it brown in the oven.

BOILED HAM

CHAMBERLIN'S METHOD

Put the ham into a tub of cold water the night before you intend to cook it. Place it in the tub with the fleshy part downward, and the skin partly up.

Next morning put it into a large kettle or pot, with cold

water, to boil. Let the water get hot gradually, and continue to cook the ham in a slow boil, scarcely more than a simmer. At the end of 5 hours take it out of the pot, and fill the pot with fresh cold water, then put back at once, and let it simmer 5 hours more. Add, according to your purse, a gallon of vinegar, claret, or champagne.

Simmer 3 hours longer. Take it off, and put it in a cool place. In the morning trim it neatly before serving.

To prevent the ham from tearing, or the water from suddenly boiling too fast, it is best to sew a piece of cotton cloth tightly around the ham, so as to fit it closely. This will keep the meat firm, and guard against the neglect of the cook, in letting the water boil too fast.

SPANISH STEAK

Ham,
Mustard,
Sugar,
Bread-crumbs.

Cut a slice of ham 3 inches thick, and boil until tender. Then place it in a baking-pan, and cover thickly with mustard and sugar. Put bread-crumbs on the top, and bake until brown.

PIGEON PIE

Pigeons, 6,
Clams, 12,
Oysters, 12,
Butter, 1 tablespoon,
Flour, 2 tablespoons,
Stock (pigeon), 1 pint,
Minced parsley, 1 teaspoon,
Onion juice, 1 teaspoon,

Eggs, 2,
Salt and pepper.

Line a deep dish with pie crust, and place it in the oven to bake. Stew the pigeons until tender, then remove the meat as whole as possible from the bones.

Drop 12 clams and 12 oysters into the pigeon stock, and stew until the edges curl; then remove them and chop them coarsely.

Boil the pigeon stock down, until it is only 1 pint, then add to it the butter, flour, onion juice, and parsley.

Place the pigeons, clams, and oysters in the crust. Pour the hot pigeon stock over 2 beaten eggs, stirring constantly to prevent coagulation; then pour this over the pigeons, and cover with the top crust.

Place it in the oven, and bake until it is a light brown.

BRAISED BEEF HEART

The beef heart should be first thoroughly washed, running a knife well down into the cavities, and cutting through the adjacent walls, that all blood-clots may be removed. Trim off the rough "ear" at the top, and dry on a cloth.

Make a savory stuffing with equal parts of sausage meat and fine stale bread-crumbs; adding a large spoonful or more of finely chopped parsley. Fill all the cavities with this, and if any of the stuffing remains, roll it into small balls and place them together with the beef heart into a shallow greased pan.

Fasten the top of the heart with a couple of stitches or skewers. Then brown the entire outside of the heart in a spoonful or two of hot fat in the pan.

Transfer to a deep earthen casserole, or baking-dish having a tightly fitting cover, laying it in, with the point downward. Pour round it a scant pint of either a thin tomato- or savory brown sauce. Lacking either of these, use soup-stock, or plain boiling water—these variations giving different results in the flavor of the finished dish.

Cover the casserole or dish closely and place in a moderate oven for 4 hours. When an earthen dish is used, the evaporation will be less than with a metal one, the latter usually necessitating the addition of more sauce during the cooking.

It is well to have an extra amount of the sauce, that there may be sufficient to fill the gravy-boat.

With this meat a dish of spiced or pickled peaches, or a tart jelly, will harmonize admirably.

Pork tender-loin may be prepared and braised in the same manner.

BAKED LIVER

Take one calf's liver; wash and wipe it dry. Lard it with strips of pork. Dredge flour over it, salt it, and bake for half an hour in a hot oven.

BAKED CALF'S LIVER

Wipe the liver and cut into 1-inch cubes. Sprinkle it with salt and pepper, cover with thin slices of lemon and sprigs of parsley. Cover and let it stand 2 or 3 hours. Sauté in butter until well browned on both sides, turning frequently.

Serve with slices of lemon.

TONGUE RAGOUT

GERMAN

Tongue, 1, fresh,
Sweetbreads, 1 pair,
Forced meat-balls, 1 dozen,
Sherry, 1 wine-glass,
Flour, 1 tablespoon,

Butter, 1 tablespoon,
Mushrooms, or champignons,
Salt and pepper.

Cook the tongue with a good beef-bone, and a soup bunch. This should be done the day previous, and the tongue allowed to cool in the stock in which it has been cooked.

Brown the flour and butter in a pan and add to this a pint of the stock in which the tongue has been cooked. Skin the tongue and cut it into small pieces. Also cut up the sweetbreads, which have been previously boiled. Put these and the mushrooms into the brown sauce, and add the forced-meat balls, and the sherry.

(The forced-meat balls are made of bread-crumbs, marrow, and chopped parsley, or they may be made of chopped sausage and a little egg.)

Put all together in a large stewpan, and let it get thoroughly heated. Serve in a large dish, or in individual patties.

OX TONGUE, À LA JUIVE

Fresh tongue, 1,
Seeded raisins, 1 cup,
Brown sugar, 1 pint,
Lemons, 2,
Allspice, 12 grains,
Peppercorns, 12.
Salt, 1 teaspoon,
Mace, 1 teaspoon,
Nutmeg, 1 teaspoon,
Vinegar, 2 tablespoons.

Boil the tongue 2 hours, and leave it in the water until perfectly cold. Skin it and rub it with salt and ground spices, mace, and nutmeg. Put it back into the water where it was boiled, add the sliced lemons, raisins, sugar, and allspice. Stew slowly 1 hour, and then put in the vinegar.

Serve cold, garnished with parsley. This is most palatable and can be served at luncheon, or for late supper, or with a salad.

KIDNEYS AND BACON

Cut the kidneys in halves, lengthwise, remove all the fat, and skin them. Wash them and lay them in cold water for half an hour and then cut them crosswise, in thin slices.

Slice the bacon thin, and cut each slice into 2 pieces. Place a piece of bacon on a skewer, then a piece of kidney, and thus alternate them until you have 5 pieces of each on a skewer. Dip the pieces of kidney into melted butter before they are put on the skewer.

Place the skewer on a broiler and hold it over a bright fire, turning frequently until all sides are cooked. When the kidneys are broiled, place each skewer on a finger of toast and sprinkle lightly with pepper. Put a tiny bit of butter on each piece of kidney and serve immediately.

STEWED KIDNEY, À LA CREOLE
NEW ORLEANS

Veal kidneys, 3 (or 1 fresh beef-kidney),
Butter, 1 tablespoon,
Sherry, 1 wine-glass,
Chopped parsley, 1 teaspoon,
Bay leaf, 1,
Salt, pepper, thyme.

Boil the kidneys for 10 minutes in 1 cup of water. Let them cool. Slice them thin, and return them to the water in which they were boiled. Season with salt and pepper.

Put the butter into a saucepan, and when melted, add the

herbs and the sherry. Then put the kidneys into the same pan and allow the whole to simmer for a few moments—just long enough for the pieces of kidney to become thoroughly heated.

Kidneys do not require long to cook. The longer they cook the tougher they become. At no time should they be allowed to boil hard.

STEWED RABBIT

Wash the rabbit in cold water, and joint it. Make a brown sauce and stew the rabbit in it for about 1 hour, or until it is tender. Remove the rabbit, and to the gravy add 12 French chestnuts, which have been boiled and chopped.

Garnish with lemon and parsley, and serve with currant jelly.

FRICANDEAU OF VEAL

Fillet of veal, 4 pounds,
Larding pork,
Onion, 1, small,
Carrot, 1, small,
Turnip, 1, small,
Bay leaf, 1,
Parsley, 1 sprig,
Celery, 1 stalk,
Hot stock, 1 quart.

Sauce

Butter, 1 tablespoon,
Flour, 2 tablespoons,
Gravy (strained from the pan), 1 pint,
Tomato catsup, or mushroom catsup, 1 tablespoon,
Pepper, or Worcestershire.

Trim the veal round and skewer into shape. Lard the upper side. Cut the onion, carrot, and turnip into shapes with a vegetable cutter, and put them in the bottom of the braising-pan with one bay leaf, one sprig of parsley, and one stalk of celery.

Lay the fillet on top of this, with the larded side up, and pour over it 1 quart of hot stock. Put the lid on the braising-pan and bake in a moderate oven for 2 hours. When done remove the fillet, and strain the gravy from the pan.

Garnish with cut vegetables and parsley, and serve with a sauce made as follows:

Brown 1 tablespoon of butter, add 2 tablespoons of flour, and stir until smooth and brown. Add 1 pint of the gravy which has been strained from the fricandeau, and stir continually until it thickens. When ready to serve the sauce, add to it 1 tablespoon of tomato- or mushroom-catsup.

Season the sauce if necessary, but pepper is rarely needed when Worcestershire sauce is used.

In summer, peas or other seasonable vegetables may be used.

BOUDINS OF VEAL

Cold, chopped veal, 1 pint,
Butter, 1 tablespoon,
Cream, or milk, ½ cup,
Eggs, 2 (whites, only),
Chopped parsley, 1 tablespoon,
Salt and pepper.

Melt the butter and pour it over the chopped veal. Add the cream or milk, and the seasonings, and then pound the mixture well with a potato-masher. Add the whites of the eggs beaten stiff, and to a dry froth.

Fill custard cups two-thirds full of the mixture, and stand

them in a baking-pan, surrounded with hot water, and bake in a moderate oven for 20 minutes.

When done, put them carefully onto a heated dish and serve with a brown sauce.

CHICKEN IN CASSEROLE, NO. 1

>Chicken, 1,
>Butter, 1 tablespoon,
>Carrot, 1,
>Onion, 1,
>Consommé, or stock, 1 pint,
>Sherry, 1 tablespoon,
>Mushrooms, 1 dozen,
>Thyme, 1 sprig,
>Bay leaf, 2,
>Salt and pepper.

Dress the chicken as for roasting. Place in the casserole the butter, the carrot, and the onion, all these being cut fine. Also put in the thyme and the bay leaves.

Set the casserole on top of the stove for about 10 minutes, or until the vegetables are browned in the butter. Then pour in about a pint of well-seasoned consommé, or stock, and place the chicken in it. Cover the casserole closely, and put it in the oven and braise for about 1 hour.

Ten minutes before the time is up, add the sherry and cover again. When the chicken is done, add the mushrooms to the gravy.

CHICKEN IN CASSEROLE, NO. 2

>Chicken (about 4½ pounds), 1,
>Fresh mushrooms, 2 cupsful,
>Cooked peas, ½ cupful,
>Salt and pepper,

Butter and flour,
Cream, 1 cup.

Wipe the fowl and cut in pieces for serving. Sprinkle with salt and pepper, spread generously with butter, and place in the casserole. Add 1 cup of boiling water, put on the cover, and bake until the chicken is tender. Then add the cream, the mushrooms (cut in pieces), and the cooked peas.

Again cover, and cook for 15 minutes. Thicken the sauce with 1 tablespoon of flour diluted with cold water to pour easily.

FRICASE DE POLLOS

SPANISH

Chicken, 1,
Onions, 2,
Garlic buds, 2,
Green olives, ½ pint,
Stuffed olives, 6,
Chopped parsley, 1 tablespoon,
Tomato juice, 1 cup,
Toasted bread (ground fine), 2 tablespoons,
Spanish sage, ¼ teaspoon,
Salt, pepper, lard.

Clean the chicken and cut it into small pieces. Chop the onion and garlic fine and fry all in fresh lard.

After it is fried add the green and stuffed olives and the parsley. Stir well together, and then add the tomato juice, the ground bread, and the sage. Season to taste with salt and pepper.

Stir well together, and leave on the stove for 10 minutes, or until thoroughly heated.

STEWED CHICKEN, À L'ESPAGNOL

>Chicken, large, 1,
>Butter, ¼ cup,
>Onions, 2,
>Tomatoes, 1 can,
>Olives, stoned and minced, 1 cup,
>Green peppers, 1,
>Peas, 1 can,
>French mushrooms, 1 can,
>Salt, pepper, flour.

Select a large fowl. Joint it, and cut each joint in half, wipe each piece carefully, sprinkle with salt and pepper and roll in flour. Put into a large pot the butter; and when it is melted and hot, lay in the pieces of chicken.

Brown each piece of chicken lightly on both sides, remove, and spread them on a dish. Stir into the butter that is in the pot the two chopped onions and cook them for a minute, and then put in the tomatoes, the olives, the pepper, and onion juice to suit the taste.

Simmer for 10 minutes, then lay in the chicken and pour over it enough cold water to cover well. Put a closely fitting lid on the pot, and set it where the contents will simmer but not boil hard. Cook till the meat of the chicken can be easily pierced with a fork, then add the peas from which the liquor has been drained, and the mushrooms. Simmer for 15 minutes longer, thicken with butter and browned flour, and pour into a deep dish lined with triangles of crisp toast.

CREOLE CHICKEN

>Cooked chicken, cut in cubes, 1½ cups,
>Flour, 5 tablespoons,
>Chicken stock, ¾ cup,

Tomatoes, stewed and strained, 3/4 cup,
Onion, butter, salt, paprika.

Cook the onion and butter 5 minutes, stirring well, then add the flour and stir till well browned. Then pour in gradually, stirring constantly, the chicken stock and the strained tomatoes. Bring to the boiling point, season with 1 teaspoon of salt and 1/8 teaspoon of paprika. Add 1 1/2 cups of the cooked chicken, or other fowl, cut in small cubes, and let it stand 10 or 15 minutes in the top of a double boiler, so that the meat may absorb some of the sauce.

LUAN-ED CHICKEN

HAWAIIAN

Chicken (jointed), 1,
Pork, 1 slice,
Luan or taro tops (broken), 1 pint,
Ti leaves,
Salt and pepper.

Season the chicken, pork, and luan leaves to taste with salt and pepper. Roll them in ti leaves, and bake in an oven or on hot stones.

Fish may be prepared in the same way, omitting the pork.

BRUNSWICK STEW

Chicken, 1,
Onion, 1,
Tomatoes, 4,
Lima beans, 1 pint,
Corn, boiled, cut from the cob, 4 ears,
Butter, 2 tablespoons,
Salt and pepper.

Joint a chicken and stew it with the onion in a little water for 1 hour. Then add the tomatoes, cut in pieces, the beans, corn, butter, and seasoning. Then boil slowly for 1 hour longer.

SPANISH STEW

>Chickens (jointed), 2,
>Salt pork, ½ pound,
>Water, 1 pint,
>Tomatoes, 2 quarts,
>Potatoes (boiled), 4,
>French peas, 1 can,
>Butter, 2 tablespoons,
>Salt, cayenne.

Cut the pork into fine pieces and boil in the water in a stewpan, for 20 minutes. Then put in the chicken and the tomatoes, which have been strained through a colander.

Add a little cayenne and salt and two tablespoons of butter. Stew until tender, and then put in the boiled potatoes and the peas from which the liquor has been drained. Let all simmer for 10 minutes and then serve.

JELLIED CHICKEN, NO. 1

>Veal, 1 knuckle,
>Chicken (6-pound), 1,
>Onion juice,
>Celery seed,
>Salt, pepper, paprika,
>Eggs, hard-boiled.

Wipe the knuckle of veal and put it into a soup-kettle and cover with cold water and bring it gradually to the boiling-point.

Dress and clean a 6-pound fowl and add to the veal-stock,

and cook until the bird is tender. Remove the fowl and cook the stock until it is reduced to 2 cupsful, then season with salt and pepper and onion juice, and clear.

Force 1½ cups of the lean veal through the meat-chopper, add to it 1 cup of stock, and season with salt, paprika and onion juice; then add ½ teaspoon of celery seed, or 1 cup of celery cut in small pieces.

Pour some of the remaining stock into a bread-pan to the depth of ⅓ inch. Set the pan in a larger pan of ice-water, and when firm, garnish with hard-boiled eggs, pimentoes cut fine in fancy shapes, and a few fresh mint leaves.

Cover with the remaining stock, adding it by spoonsful at a time, so as not to disturb the decorations.

When this is firm add a layer of veal, cover with a layer of chicken-meat (also forced through the meat-chopper), and then repeat.

Spread evenly, cover with buttered paper, place a weight on top, and let it stand in the ice-box overnight.

Garnish with fresh water-cresses.

JELLIED CHICKEN, NO. 2

Chicken (young roasting fowl), 1,
Eggs,
Salt, 1 level teaspoon,
Peppercorns, 6,
Mace, 1 blade,
Parsley, 2 sprigs,
Celery, 2 stalks,
Lemon, ½,
Onion, sliced, 1,
Gelatin, 2 tablespoons.

Dress the chicken and cut as for fricassee; put it in a deep saucepan over the fire. Nearly cover with cold water, and add the salt, peppercorns, mace, parsley, celery, half a lemon, onion, cut in slices, and cover closely, and as the scum arises, skim it off with a skimmer. Then let the chicken gently cook till the bones may be easily removed.

A quart of broth should be left when the chicken is done. With a skimmer remove the chicken, strain the broth, return it to the saucepan, add the gelatin (dissolved in half a pint of water) and let simmer for about 10 minutes. Remove the bones, and cut the fowl in small dice. Line a bowl or oval dish with alternate slices of hard-boiled eggs and sliced lemon. Stir the pieces of chicken through the broth; stand the pan in a cool place. When the mixture begins to stiffen, pour it into the mold, distributing the pieces evenly through the broth. Let the mold stand in a cool place for a day, turn out on a platter, and ornament it with parsley.

To serve, cut the chicken in thin slices, and lay on a plate with celery mayonnaise.

CADILLAC CHICKEN

Chicken-fat, 1½ tablespoons,
Cornstarch, 1 tablespoon,
Chicken-stock, ¾ cup,
Milk, ½ cup,
Cream, ¼ cup,
Boiled chicken (cut up), 1 cup,
Sautéd, sliced mushrooms, ½ cup,
Egg, yolk, 1,
Canned pimentoes, ¼ cup,
Butter, 2 tablespoons,
Salt.

Melt the chicken-fat, add the cornstarch, and stir until well blended. While continuing to stir, gradually pour on the chicken-stock, the milk, and the cream. Bring it to the boiling-point, then add the cold fowl, which has been cut in thin strips, also the sliced mushroom-caps, the pimentoes, and the yolk of 1 egg.

Season with salt, and just before serving, add the 2 tablespoons of butter.

This may be prepared either in a chafing-dish, or on a range. It is a delicious filling for patties, *vol-au-vents*, or Swedish timbale cases.

SOUR CHICKEN
GERMAN

Chicken,
Vinegar,
Bay leaves,
Cloves,
Onion,
Browned flour.

Cut the chicken in pieces, stew it in salted water, until tender; and when the water has somewhat boiled down, pour in the vinegar, add a few bay leaves, cloves, and a small sliced onion.

Boil until tender, and thicken the gravy with browned flour.

FRENCH CHICKEN

Chicken, 1,
Cabbage, 1,
Carrots, cut small, 3,
Sausage meat, ½ pound,
Onions, 3,
Salt pork (fat), ¼ pound,
Salt and pepper.

Brown the pork, onions, and carrots in a pot; cover with cabbage leaves, then put in the chicken, either whole or cut in pieces. On it put the remainder of the cabbage, and add just enough water to cover.

Let it cook slowly for 2 or 3 hours (from time to time it may be necessary to add a little water).

Place the chicken on a platter surrounded by the vegetables, and use the water in which it has been boiled as a gravy.

CHICKEN TERRAPIN

Chickens, 2,
Cream, 2 pints,
Butter, ½ cup,
Flour, 3 tablespoons,
Currant jelly, 2 tablespoons,
Made mustard, 1 tablespoon,
Eggs, hard-boiled, 4,
Lemon juice, 2 tablespoons,
Sherry, 2 tablespoons,
Parsley, finely chopped, 1 tablespoon,
Pimolas, or small olives, ½ pint.

Roast the chicken without stuffing. When cold cut the meat into small pieces. Put the meat into a stewpan with 1 pint of cream, add the butter, flour, mustard, currant jelly, salt, and pepper. When boiling add the other pint of cream, and the hard-boiled eggs chopped fine.

Just before serving add the lemon-juice, sherry, and parsley, and garnish with toast-points and pimolas.

HUNGARIAN GOULASHE

Flank steak, 2 pounds,
Fresh, or canned tomatoes, 1 quart,
Small potatoes, 1 quart,
Onions, medium size, 4,
Salt and pepper.

Cut the steak into small cubes and arrange it on the bottom of a flat-bottomed kettle. Season with salt and pepper, and cover it with a layer of sliced onion, then more meat, and so on, until the dish is as full as desired.

Add sufficient cold water to show just above the meat, and then put the kettle over the fire and let it come to a boil.

Have at hand either canned or fresh tomatoes, allowing a pint of tomatoes to every pound of meat. Pour the tomatoes on top of the kettle, but do not stir. Now push the kettle back on the stove, and let it simmer gently for 2 hours or longer, if necessary, to make the meat perfectly tender.

The potatoes should be small, and peeled and put into the kettle, pushing the meat aside, if necessary, to make room for them.

Cook 15 minutes longer after you put in the potatoes, and then serve.

MEXICAN CHILLI CON CARNE

Lean meat, 1½ pounds,
Kidney beans, 1 can,
Red peppers, 3, cut fine,
Olive oil, 4 tablespoons,
Onions, cut fine, 3,
Flour, 1 tablespoon,
Worcestershire, 1 large tablespoon.

Cut the onions fine. Put the oil in a spider, and when it is smoking hot put the onions into it, and also the peppers cut fine.

The beef should have been already cut into dice. When the onions turn yellow add the meat gradually, so as to avoid cooking the oil too much. Stir occasionally, to sear the beef.

In about 5 to 10 minutes add a cup of hot water, and cover. Let it stew for about 2 hours.

Heat the beans in a separate kettle. Mix the flour with some water for thickening, and before adding it, pour 1 large tablespoon of worcestershire over the meat.

Keep plenty of water on the meat to prevent its scorching. Cook all for 10 minutes, and then drain the beans, and add to the beef.

CHINESE CHI LO

Lamb, 2 pounds,
Onions, 2 (sliced),
Lettuce, 1 small head,
Dried flageolets (black beans), 1 cup,
Cold water, 1 pint,
Salt and pepper.

Soak the beans overnight. Cut the meat into small pieces, and put it, with the flageolets and the sliced onions, into a stewpan.

Add a pint of cold water, cover closely and let it simmer for about 3 hours.

About half an hour before it is done, add salt and pepper, and also the lettuce leaves. It may need a little more water from time to time when cooking.

COLLOPS IN BATTER

Cold roast beef or veal,
Butter, 1 tablespoon,
Stock, ½ pint,
Flour, 1 teaspoon,
Onion, 1,
Salt and pepper.

Batter

Flour, 1 cup,
Milk, ⅔ cup,

Egg, 1,
Baking-powder, 2 teaspoons,
Salt.

Cut the meat in pieces 1 inch thick and 2 inches wide and 3 inches long. Put a tablespoon of butter, or of beef-dripping in a frying-pan; shred the onion and brown 1 tablespoon of it in the hot fat. If there is gravy left from a previous meal add half a pint of it to the onion in the pan. Should no gravy be at hand, pour in half a pint of water, and thicken it with a teaspoon of flour rubbed smooth with cold water. Season with salt and pepper. When it boils put the meat in a baking-dish, pour the gravy over, and cover with batter.

To make the batter mix 1 cup of flour with ⅔ cup of milk; stir in 1 egg, beaten light, also pinch of salt, and 2 teaspoons baking-powder. Bake 20 minutes, or until the batter is light, and delicately browned.

MACEDOINE LOAF

Soft stale bread-crumbs, ½ cup,
Cold, cooked fowl, ½ cup,
Butter, melted, 1 tablespoon,
Flour, ½ tablespoon,
Milk, ½ cup,
Eggs, 2,
Macaroni (cooked, and cut small), 1 cup,
Fresh mushrooms, ½ cup,
Canned pimentoes, cut small, 1 tablespoon,
Cream, beaten till stiff, ½ cup,
Salt, 1½ teaspoons,
Parsley, finely chopped, 1 teaspoon,
White sauce, or tomato sauce, parsley sprigs.

Melt the butter, add the flour, and stir till well blended. Then gradually pour on the milk, stirring constantly. Bring to the boiling-point, then add the bread-crumbs and the yolks of the eggs which have been beaten until thick and lemon-colored. Also add the macaroni and fowl. The fowl should be cut in strips. The breast is preferable. Add 1 tablespoon of canned pimentoes cut in small pieces, the mushrooms cut in strips, cream, beaten till stiff, salt, and parsley.

Stir until well mixed, then put in the whites of the eggs beaten until stiff, and stir them lightly in. Turn into a pan or mold lined with buttered paper, and bake in a moderate oven until firm.

Remove to a hot serving dish, and pour round it a tomato sauce or a white sauce, to which sautéd mushroom-caps have been added.

Garnish with sprigs of parsley.

SUBSTITUTES FOR MEATS

VEGETARIAN'S LOAF, NO. 1

Stale white bread-crumbs, 1½ cups,
Nut-meats, 1 cup,
Onion, 1,
Green pepper, 1,
Tomato, 1,
Lemon, 1 (juice, only),
Apple, 1,
Butter, 2 teaspoons,
Egg, 1,
Salt, 1 teaspoon,
Milk.

Soak the bread in all the milk it will take up. Chop all fine, shape in a loaf and put into a greased pan and bake for 20 or 30 minutes. Chicken or beef gravy may also be used to moisten. This may also be used for croquettes. Garnish with slices of orange, and sprigs of parsley.

VEGETARIAN'S LOAF, NO. 2

Stale white bread-crumbs, 3 pints,
Milk, 1 pint,
Nut-meats, 3 cups,
Eggs, 3,
Melted butter, 1/3 pound,
Celery, cut fine, 1 pint,
Salt, 1 1/2 teaspoons,
Ground black pepper, 1/2 teaspoon,
Cayenne, 1/4 teaspoon,
Dried sage leaves, 1 teaspoon,
Summer savory, 1/8 teaspoon,
Minced parsley, 1 tablespoon,
Sour apple (cut fine), 1.

Crumble the inside of stale white bread, and cut the crust fine. Dry it all for 2 hours in a warm oven. Use a granite pan for this, and stir the crumbs often, to dry without browning.

To 3 pints of the crumbs (measured before drying), add a teaspoon and a half of salt, the parsley, minced fine, the sage leaves, crumbled fine before measuring, and the black and Cayenne peppers. Also add the celery finely chopped, and the sour apple chopped in bits.

Melt the butter and fry the chopped onion in it for 5 minutes, and pour over this the other ingredients and mix them together. Beat the 3 eggs and add them to the milk and pour over the bread-crumb mixture. Let it stand to soften the crumbs, while the nut-meats are ground fine. Reserve 1 tablespoon of the nut-meats for the sauce. Mix the rest of the nut-meats with the crumbs.

Mix and shape the loaf to be about 4 inches wide, and 3 or more inches thick. Butter a perforated tin sheet, set the loaf on it, and place it to cook in a slow oven. Bake it for one and a half hours, basting often with butter which has been melted over hot water.

Serve on a hot platter, garnished with slices of orange and sprigs of parsley. Serve the sauce in a separate dish.

This loaf will be sufficient for 12 persons. The sauce for it should be made as follows:

Melt 3 tablespoons of butter in a hot omelette pan, add a teaspoon of chopped onion, half a sour apple cut in bits, and add 2 rounding tablespoons of flour and cook till a clear brown. To this add a pint of milk, a cup of hot water in which some of the gravy from the baking-pan has been melted, and stir till boiling, add the chopped nut-meats that have been left, and a half teaspoon of salt.

VEGETARIAN CUTLET

Eggs, hard-boiled, 4,
Mushrooms (field), ½ pound,
Water, 3 tablespoons,
Butter, 1 ounce,
Salt,
Rice flour.

Peel the mushrooms, and cook them for 10 minutes in the water. Drain, and chop them with the eggs.

Add butter to the liquid, and thicken with a little rice flour, stirring constantly, and stir in the chopped egg and mushrooms.

Press the mixture into cutlet-tins, and when cool turn them out and fry.

Serve with peas and mint sauce.

VEGETABLE ROAST

Cooked beans, or peas,
Chopped nut-meats,
Zwieback,
Sweet cream,
Salt and pepper,
Cranberry sauce,
Sage.

Take a quantity of cooked beans or peas, and pass them through a colander to remove the skins. Mix with them an equal quantity of finely chopped nut-meats, and season to taste.

Put half of the mixture into a buttered baking-dish and spread over it a dressing made as follows:

Pour some boiling water upon four slices of zwieback; cover, and let it stand for a few minutes, then break them up with a fork, and pour over them a half cup of sweet cream. Season this with salt and sage.

Pour this dressing over the nuts and vegetables in the buttered dish, and then cover with the remainder of the nut-mixture. Over all pour half a cup of cream, and bake for 1½ hours.

Serve in slices, with cranberry sauce.

RICE AND MACARONI

BOILED RICE

When properly boiled, the grains of rice should each one be perfect, and stand apart. The following method will ensure this result:

Pick over, and wash 1 cup of raw rice, rubbing it hard, and changing the water until it runs off clear, and then drain.

Have fully 4 quarts of water boiling rapidly in the kettle. Add the rice, and a half-teaspoon of salt, and cover until it boils again, then uncover, or it will boil over. Keep the water at a galloping boil. In 10 minutes begin to test, lifting out a few grains with a fork, and rubbing them between the thumb and finger.

When tender to the center, which will take about 20 minutes, the rice is done.

Turn it into a colander, cover it with a cloth, and let it steam in the oven for 5 or 10 minutes.

RIZOTTO

Rice, 1 cup,
Butter, 1½ tablespoons,
Salt, 1 tablespoon,
Stewed tomatoes, 1 cup,
Chopped onion, 1, small,
Grated Parmesan cheese.

Carefully pick and wash the rice, and put it into a saucepan of boiling water, add the salt, and boil until tender.

Drain, and cover, and set at the side of the fire to steam for 5 minutes.

Put the butter and chopped onion into a saucepan and cook slowly until well browned. Add the stewed tomatoes, season to taste, and simmer for half an hour. Then take it from the fire, pour it over the rice, sprinkle over thickly with grated Parmesan cheese, and send to the table.

MEXICAN RICE

Boiled rice, 2 cups,
Lard, 1 tablespoon,
Onion, minced, 1,
Green pepper, minced, 1,
Tomato, chopped fine, 1.

Put the rice with the lard in a deep frying-pan, and let it get hot; add the tomatoes, pepper, onion, and salt, and stew all, with a quart of boiling water. Let it cook till most of the water is absorbed. Garnish with hard-boiled eggs, cut in quarters.

SPANISH RICE

Rice, 1 cup,
Small, fresh tomatoes, 4 (or, ½ a can),
Green pepper, 1, large,
Onion, chopped, ½.

Chop the onion fine, and cut the pepper into quarters. Add the tomatoes, either canned or fresh, and place all together in a spider well greased with olive oil.

Put in the rice, and just enough hot water to keep the mixture moist. Salt it, and cook slowly for 1 hour or more.

RICE AND HAM

SPANISH

Boiled rice, 2 cups,
Chopped ham, 1 cup,
Tomato sauce, 1 pint,
Chopped parsley, 1 tablespoon.

Spread the rice on a dish, and cover it over with the ham, moisten with the tomato sauce, and place it in the oven until well heated. Take it out, and sprinkle the whole with chopped parsley, and then serve.

RICE AND CHINESE PUDDING

Boiled rice, 2 cups,
White sauce, 1½ cups,
Eggs, well beaten, 2,
Grated cheese, ½ cup,
Butter, 1 tablespoon.

Add the eggs and cheese to the white sauce, and place in a pudding dish alternate layers of the rice and the sauce. Over the top sprinkle grated cheese and butter, place in the oven, and bake for half an hour.

WEST INDIA PILAU

Green peppers, 3,
Onion, 1, small,
Boiled rice, 1 cup,
Stock, or gravy, 1 pint,
Butter, 2 tablespoons.

Seed the peppers, cut them in pieces, and fry in the butter. Take them out, and fry the sliced onion in the same butter.

Chop the peppers and onion, add the rice, and add the stock. Place it all in a deep dish and allow it to remain in the oven until very hot, when it is then ready to serve.

TURKISH PILAU

> Boiled rice, 1 cup,
> Tomato juice, 1 pint,
> Onion, 1, cut fine,
> Almonds, or other nuts, a handful.

After the rice has been boiled and removed from the fire, add to it the above ingredients, and let the whole boil slowly for 1 hour longer. The almonds must not be cut, or crushed, but put in whole.

MACARONI

The wholesome, nourishing qualities of macaroni have never been fully appreciated by the average housewife. As a nourishing food it offers much the same nutrition as white bread; but unless it is eaten to excess it is less apt to cause indigestion than the so-called staff of life.

Its flavor depends largely upon the manner in which it is cooked; whether it is offered alone, or in combination with some vegetable or meat.

To prepare macaroni properly, boil it rapidly for 30 minutes, in boiling, salted water. To keep the tubes of the macaroni from sticking together, the water must be kept at a galloping boil, as with rice.

When it is done, it should be turned into a colander, and thoroughly rinsed under the cold-water tap, to remove the loose, pasty starch on the outside of the tubes. After draining it can be creamed, or finished in any desired way.

Each nation has a different way of preparing macaroni. Here are a number of desirable receipts:

ITALY

Macaroni, 1 pound,
Tomato sauce, 1 gill,
Madeira, 1 gill,
Parmesan cheese, ¼ pound,
Nutmeg, pepper.

Cook the macaroni in salted water for 30 minutes, without breaking it. Drain, and put into a saucepan with the tomato sauce and the Madeira, and add the cheese and seasoning, and cook slowly for 10 minutes, tossing frequently. Serve with the grated Parmesan cheese.

ITALIAN METHOD, NO. 2

Macaroni, ½ pound,
Chopped meat, 2 pounds,
Tomatoes, 1 quart,
Onions, chopped, 3,
Butter, ½ cup,
Cream, ½ cup,
Grated cheese.

Cook the meat, tomatoes, and onions together with ½ pint of water, for 3 hours. Then pass it through a colander. After the macaroni has been boiled and blanched, put it into the mixture, and add salt, and allow it to simmer for half an hour.

Then add the butter and cream, and serve hot, accompanied by grated cheese.

SPAIN

Boiled macaroni,
Flour, 1 tablespoon,
Butter, 1 tablespoon,
Stock, or thin beef juice, 1 cup,
Salt, 1 teaspoon,

Chopped onion, Chilli sauce,
Chopped meat.

Make a sauce from the flour, butter, and stock, and season with salt. In the bottom of a baking-dish place a layer of cold, chopped meat, then a layer of boiled macaroni, a sprinkling of Chilli sauce and chopped onion, and continue this order till the dish is full, the last layer being of macaroni. Pour the sauce over, and bake in a hot oven for 40 minutes.

MEXICO

Macaroni, ½ pound,
Lard, 1 tablespoon,
Pork-chops, 2,
Tomatoes, 1 pint,
Green pepper, cut fine, 1,
Onion, 1, large,
Salt.

Heat the lard in a frying-pan, lay in the pork-chops, and turn frequently till seared. Continue to cook, till very brown. Add the vegetables, and the salt. Cover the pan, and stew slowly till the meat is in rags. Then put it through a coarse sieve, and keep hot till needed.

Boil the macaroni for 30 minutes and when drained, and blanched, place in a colander over hot water for 10 minutes, or till steaming, then turn it into a deep dish, and pour over it the sauce.

FRANCE

Macaroni, ½ pound,
Sage cheese, ½ pound,
Chopped ham, ½ pound,
Onion, chopped fine, 1,
Butter, 1 tablespoon,
Sour milk, or cream, 1 pint.

MACARONI   AROUND-THE-WORLD COOK BOOK

After the macaroni has been boiled, place it in a deep dish, and add to it, the ham, cheese, onion, butter, and cream. Then bake for 45 minutes.

AMERICA

Macaroni, ⅔ cup,
Grated cheese, ⅓ cup,
Melted butter, 1 tablespoon,
Flour, 2 tablespoons,
Hot milk, 1 pint,
Salt and pepper.

Paste for above

Melted butter, ⅓ cup,
Rolled cracker-crumbs, ⅔ cup,
Grated cheese, ⅓ cup.

Cook the macaroni in boiling salted water until tender. Drain, and blanch. Put it into a baking-dish and sprinkle with the grated cheese.

For the sauce, melt the butter in a double boiler, and slowly add the flour, milk, and salt and pepper. Stir constantly while making this sauce, until it is a smooth gravy, and then pour it over the macaroni and cheese.

Over the top of this the following paste should be spread:

Mix together, one-third of a cup of butter, melted, two-thirds of a cup of rolled cracker-crumbs, and one-third of a cup of grated cheese. When this paste has been made and spread over the macaroni and cheese, place all in the oven and bake until brown.

VEGETABLES

Great difference in result may be obtained in cooking vegetables, according to the method employed in preparing them.

When cooking such vegetables as cabbage, sprouts, seakale, lettuce, spinach, cauliflower, etc., they should be "blanched," by either soaking in hot water for from 10 to 15 minutes, or scalded by a short but rapid boiling. This is in some cases for the purpose of whitening them, and in others for the purpose of making them firmer.

The best results will be obtained by combining the two methods, first soaking the vegetables in *salted* water for from 10 to 15 minutes, and then quickly boiling for 2 minutes in *fresh* water. Next drain as completely as possible, and then cook in fresh water, to which, in the case of such vegetables as spinach, etc., where it is desired to preserve the color of the greens, a pinch of soda has been added. Otherwise, as with cauliflower, etc., do not add soda.

Keep covered while cooking, as this retains the strength of the juices. Take care not to overcook, as that is liable to make the vegetables too soft, and certainly less tasteful. Strain off the water as soon as the vegetables have been cooked. Leaving them in the water makes them soggy and tasteless.

After draining, which should be done as completely as possible, a little butter, or a spoonful of cream may be added, which will moisten and make them more palatable. Then place the pot, covered, where it will keep warm until required.

The water drained off should be saved. It has often been

VEGETABLES AROUND-THE-WORLD COOK BOOK

remarked that a French family can live upon what an American family wastes; or, as some one has more aptly stated it, "the cook can throw more out of the kitchen window with a spoon, than the housekeeper can throw into the cellar with a shovel."

In France, when vegetables are boiled, the water is not thrown away, but is saved, and later used for "maigre" soups, and for stock when cooking other vegetables.

TIMES FOR COOKING VEGETABLES

The following table gives approximately the time for cooking various vegetables. The time will in some cases vary, owing to the quantity to be cooked, the state of the fire, and for other unforeseen reasons.

BOILING

Asparagus	20 to 25	minutes
Beans (string, or shell),	1	hour
Beets, new	1	hour
Beets, winter	4 to 5	hours
Cabbage, young	30 to 45	minutes
Cabbage, winter	1	hour
Carrots	1	hour
Cauliflower	30 to 45	minutes
Celery	20 to 30	minutes
Corn, green	5 to 8	minutes
Hominy, fine	1	hour
Hominy, coarse	2	hours
Macaroni	20	minutes
Oatmeal, rolled	30	minutes
Onions	30 to 45	minutes
Parsnips	45	minutes
Peas	15 to 20	minutes

Potatoes	20 to 30 minutes
Rice	15 to 20 minutes
Spinach	20 to 30 minutes
Squash	20 to 30 minutes
Tomatoes	15 to 20 minutes
Turnips, new	35 to 45 minutes
Turnips, winter	1 to 2 hours

LYONNAISE POTATOES

Cold boiled potatoes, 1 quart,
Butter, 1 tablespoon,
Salt, ½ teaspoon,
Pepper, ½ teaspoon,
White onion, 1,
Parsley, 1 tablespoon (chopped fine).

Peel and cut the potatoes into inch cubes. Put a tablespoon of butter in the frying-pan, and when hot add the onion, minced fine, and cook until soft, but not brown. Then add the potatoes and toss them with a fork until they are of an even color.

Sprinkle the salt, pepper, and parsley over them, and again stir with the fork.

Serve at once, with broiled steak.

POTATO SOUFFLÉ

Hot mashed potatoes, 2 cups,
Milk, ½ cup,
Eggs, 4 (whites only),
Butter, 1 tablespoon,
Chopped parsley, 1 tablespoon,
Salt and pepper.

Season the potato with butter, salt, pepper, and parsley. Then beat in the milk and stir the mixture until it is smooth.

Stir in the beaten whites of the eggs, then turn it into a buttered dish, and bake for about 10 minutes.

When the soufflé is puffed and brown, serve it immediately or it will fall.

Grated cheese is sometimes sprinkled over the top, just before serving.

FRIED POTATO BALLS
GERMAN

Mashed potatoes, 2 cups,
Egg, 1,
Milk, 1 tablespoon,
Bread-crumbs,
Lard,
Salt and pepper.

Beat the egg, and mix with the potatoes and milk, seasoning to taste with salt and pepper. Roll into small balls, and then roll them in bread-crumbs and fry in deep lard.

SWEET POTATO CROQUETTES

Mashed sweet potatoes, 1 pint,
Hot milk, 1 cup,
Butter, 2 tablespoons,
Salt, 1 teaspoon,
Eggs, 2 (used separately),
Bread-crumbs,
Lard.

Mix the potatoes with the milk; stir in the butter, salt, and one of the beaten eggs. Shape into desired-sized croquettes, dip into beaten egg, and then roll in bread-crumbs.

Fry in hot lard until a delicate brown. Drain on brown paper, and serve hot.

SPINACH SOUFFLÉ

Cooked spinach, 2 cups,
Eggs, 2 (whites and yolks beaten separately),
Melted butter, 1 tablespoon,
Cream, ½ gill,
Salt and pepper.

Chop the spinach fine, add the beaten yolks, and the butter. Season with salt and pepper, and beat in the cream and the whites of the eggs.

Turn it into a buttered dish, and bake in a hot oven until light brown. Serve at once, or it will fall.

SPINACH PUDDING

GERMAN

Spinach, 2 quarts,
Onion, small, 1,
Rolls of bread, 2,
Eggs, 6,
Sweetbreads, 1 (or ham may be used),
Milk, salt and pepper,
Butter, 2 heaping tablespoons.

Put the spinach in boiling water, salted, and after it has wilted cool it and wring it out, and chop fine with 1 small onion. Season to taste with salt and pepper.

Soak the 2 rolls in milk, then press out the milk and cook the bread with the butter, and then mix it with the spinach.

When cool add the yolks of the eggs, and 1 blanched and chopped sweetbread, or the same amount of chopped ham. Then add the beaten whites of the eggs, and put into a mold and boil for 1 hour.

Serve it with melted butter sauce, or with a mushroom sauce.

This is enough for 8 or 10 persons.

CREAMED ONIONS

> Onions,
> Salt and pepper,
> Cream sauce.

Select onions of medium size. The white variety is milder than the red. Peel the onions, cover with boiling water, and let them stand 5 minutes, then drain; this makes them less rank in flavor. Boil the onions in a saucepan, add a teaspoon of salt, barely cover with water, and let them boil slowly until tender through and through.

Unless the onions are very small this will require about an hour and a half.

Serve them with a cream sauce.

SCALLOPED ONIONS

> Onions,
> Fine bread-crumbs,
> Butter.

Boil the onions for 10 minutes in hot salted water, then drain this off, and cover with cold water, slightly salted. Bring quickly to a boil and cook until soft, but not until they break to pieces.

Sprinkle the bottom of an earthenware baking-dish with fine bread-crumbs, moisten with some of the water in which the onions were cooked. Dot the surface with butter, and set aside until about 30 minutes before wanted for serving, then place them in the oven and cook.

STUFFED BERMUDAS

Large Bermuda onions, 6 or 8,
Minced cold chicken,
Butter,
Fine bread-crumbs,
Salt and pepper,
White sauce.

Peel and wash the onions and arrange them in a bake-dish; cover with boiling water slightly salted. Cook for half an hour, or until a wire will easily pierce them. Transfer the dish to the table, and with a sharp thin blade extract the hearts of the onions without breaking the outer walls.

Fill the cavity with forced meat made of minced cold chicken and fine bread-crumbs seasoned with pepper and salt, and moistened with melted butter. The forced meat should be very soft.

Strew crumbs over the top, pour a rich white sauce into the dish until it almost touches the tops of the onions, cover, and bake for half an hour, then brown delicately.

BAKED ONIONS

Boil the onions in 2 waters, until well done; then drain. Butter a baking-dish and sprinkle bread-crumbs over the bottom of it, then put in a layer of onions, seasoned with salt and pepper, bits of butter, and more bread-crumbs, covering the onions.

Add another layer of onions, more bread-crumbs and seasoning, and so continue until the dish is full. Then pour in enough sweet milk to thoroughly moisten the whole. Put bits of butter on top, and bake until brown.

RED CABBAGE

GERMAN

Red cabbage, 1,
Sour apples, 4,
Red peppers, small, 2,
Cloves, whole, 12,
Allspice, 12,
Vinegar, 1 cup,
Sugar, ½ cup,
Lard, 2 tablespoons.

Cut the cabbage as for cold-slaw, and put it in a kettle with the lard, and also just enough water to cover. Add the apples peeled, quartered and cored, also the spices and sugar.

When these have boiled for 2 hours add the vinegar, and let the whole boil for 1 hour longer.

SCALLOPED CAULIFLOWER

Cauliflower, 1,
Bread-crumbs, 1 cup,
Butter, 2 tablespoons,
Milk, 6 tablespoons,
Egg, 1.

Boil the cauliflower until it is tender, and cut it into pieces and pack the pieces in a buttered pudding-dish with the stems downward.

Beat the bread-crumbs into a soft paste with the milk and melted butter, and season with salt and pepper. Add the egg, well beaten.

With this mixture cover the cauliflower; place it in the oven and bake until it is brown.

STUFFED CUCUMBERS

Cucumbers,
Cold boiled rice,
Finely chopped meat,
Onion-juice, curry powder,
Salt, pepper, beef-stock.

Pare large cucumbers, and cut them in 3-inch lengths; scoop the centers and save them. Add the chopped meat to the cucumber pulp, season with the salt, pepper and onion-juice and curry, add an equal amount to that of the mixture of cold rice, and fill the cavities with this mixture.

Pour into a pan half an inch of seasoned beef-stock, cover, and simmer till tender. Serve on squares of toast, and at the last moment pour over, the gravy from the pan.

CUCUMBER FRITTERS

Large cucumbers, 4,
Eggs, 4,
Butter, 1 teaspoon,
Flour, enough to make a thick batter,
Salt and pepper,
Baking-powder.

Measure the flour, and allow 1 level teaspoon of baking-powder for each cup of flour you use. Peel and grate the cucumbers, press out, and discard the juice; to the pulp add the egg and seasoning, also the butter and flour—the latter containing the baking-powder.

Drop, in tablespoonsful at a time, into a deep kettle of hot fat, and cook until puffed and brown.

BROILED EGGPLANT
FRENCH

Small eggplants,
Salt and pepper,
Tomato sauce,
Oil, lemon-juice, anchovy, onion, parsley.

Cut the eggplants in two, score the cut sides, season with salt, pepper, and oil, and broil until tender.

Serve with a tomato sauce, seasoned with a little fried onion, or garlic, a little lemon-juice, and a sprinkling of shredded anchovy and parsley.

TURKISH EGGPLANT

Eggplant,
Olive oil,
Chopped meat,
Onion,
Tomatoes,
Salt and pepper.

Cut the eggplant in slices, cover with salt, weight it, to draw out the bitter juice. At end of 2 hours, fry in oil, arrange in layers around the sides of a cooking-pot. Lay some of the slices one side. Fry in the same drippings, the chopped meat and onion. Put a layer of the meat and onion on top of the sliced eggplant in the saucepan. Next should come a few slices of fresh tomatoes, seasoning all with pepper and salt. Over this put the other layer of slices of eggplant, then more meat and tomato, and so on, until all the ingredients are used.

Add a little stock, or hot water to partially cover, put on the lid, and cook gently on top of the stove, until the water is almost gone.

EGGPLANT À LA CREOLE

Eggplant, 1,
Tomatoes, 4,
Spaghetti, 1 cup,
Green peppers, 1,
Grated cheese, 1 cup,
Butter, 2 tablespoons,
Cream, 1 cup,
Salt and black pepper.

Cook the spaghetti in boiling water until tender, and then drain it well. Peel and slice thin the eggplant and place a layer of it in a deep earthenware dish or casserole, and sprinkle it well with salt.

Slice the tomatoes and put half of them in a layer on top of the eggplant, next a layer of spaghetti, using all of it, and cover it with grated cheese and bits of butter.

Then add another layer of sliced tomatoes, cover with chopped green pepper, and next a top layer of eggplant, which thickly cover with grated cheese.

Pour over all the cream, place in a moderate oven, and bake for about 1½ hours, or until well browned on top.

FRIED GREEN TOMATOES

Green tomatoes,
Flour,
Boiling fat,
Salt and pepper.

Wash and dry the tomatoes, and cut in rather thick slices, without peeling. Cover with boiling water, and set on the back of the range, so that the water will keep hot, but will not boil. Keep there for 15 minutes, or until the tomatoes turn a pale golden color. Then drain, dip in flour, season with salt and pepper, and fry in hot pork fat or bacon drippings, and serve hot, arranging in little piles of two or three, and putting a piece of butter on each slice as dished.

These are good accompaniments to lamb chops, or veal croquettes.

FRIED RIPE TOMATOES

>Ripe tomatoes,
>Cornmeal,
>Milk or cream,
>Butter,
>Flour,
>Salt and pepper.

Slice large ripe, but firm fruit into medium thick slices, season with salt and pepper, sprinkle plentifully with fine cornmeal, and then fry in smoking hot fat until browned on both sides.

Take up carefully with a broad-bladed knife, and arrange in little piles on a hot platter. Put another spoon of butter or pork-drippings into the pan, add flour and stir till frothy, then add cream or milk, to make the desired consistency, season to taste with salt and pepper, pour it over the tomatoes, and serve.

STEWED TOMATOES AND OKRA

>Tomatoes, chopped, 1 quart,
>Okra, sliced, 1/3 quart,
>Salt and pepper.

Scald and skin the tomatoes, then cut rather fine. Slice the okra, and mix together, seasoning with salt and pepper. Stew the mixture for about half an hour, or till tender.

DEVILED TOMATOES

Tomatoes, 1 quart,
Hard-boiled eggs, 3,
Melted butter, 3 tablespoons,
Vinegar, 3 tablespoons,
Raw eggs, 2,
Sugar, 1 teaspoon,
Made mustard, 1 teaspoon,
Cayenne, a pinch,
Salt.

Mash with a fork, the yolks of the eggs, and rub in the butter and seasoning, add the vinegar and beat all till it is light.

Heat until almost boiling, then take from the fire, and stir in the 2 raw eggs, which have been well beaten together.

Cut the tomatoes into slices nearly an inch thick, broil them over a clear fire.

Lay the broiled slices on a hot dish, and pour over the hot sauce just made.

STUFFED TOMATOES

Tomatoes, 6,
Flaked sardines, 1 cup,
Bread-crumbs, ½ cup,
Salt, ½ teaspoon.

Remove the centers from the tomatoes, add to the chopped centers the sardines and bread-crumbs, season with the salt, and fill the tomatoes with this mixture, and bake for 20 minutes.

FRIED GREEN PEPPERS

>Green peppers,
>Butter.

Cut the peppers open lengthwise, taking care not to let the seeds touch the sides. Take out the seeds, slice the peppers crosswise, and lay in boiling water until they are cold.

Drain and wipe the sliced peppers, and fry in butter. Serve dry, as an accompaniment to fish.

STUFFED GREEN PEPPERS

>Green peppers,
>Chopped meat,
>Tomatoes,
>Bread-crumbs,
>Chopped onion,
>Salt.

Cut off the tops of the peppers with a sharp knife, remove carefully the seeds, make a filling of two parts chopped meat, one part bread-crumbs, and one part tomatoes, season this with salt and chopped onion, and moisten with a little gravy or with milk.

Fill the peppers with this mixture, placing a small lump of butter on top of each pepper. Also sprinkle a few bread-crumbs over it.

Pour into a pan soup-stock to the depth of about one-fourth of an inch, stand the peppers upright in the pan, and bake for 20 minutes, or until they are tender, moistening or basting frequently.

The peppers are best stuffed after being first put in the pan.

When done, place them on a heated dish, thicken the gravy

left in the pan, and pour it about the base of the peppers.

Stuffed tomatoes may be prepared in the same manner, using green peppers as a part of the filling.

STUFFED PEPPERS

>Peppers,
>Bread-crumbs,
>Minced shrimps,
>Worcestershire, and lemon-juice,
>Butter, milk.

Take equal parts of shrimp and bread-crumbs, moisten with milk, flavor with the sauce and lemon-juice, mix and fill the peppers with this. Put a lump of butter on top of each, sprinkle with bread-crumbs, and bake for 30 minutes.

PEPPERS À LA CREOLE

>Minced cold meat,
>Bread-crumbs,
>Onions,
>Peppers,
>Tomatoes,
>Mushrooms,
>Tomato sauce,
>Boiled rice, milk, butter.

Take equal parts of the cold meat, bread-crumbs, onions, tomatoes, and mushrooms, and chop all fine together, and stew in half a cup of butter, with sufficient milk to moisten.

Fill the peppers with this mixture, and bake in stock, flavored with tomato sauce. Garnish with cold boiled rice.

MEXICAN STUFFED PEPPERS

Green peppers, 6,
Sardines, 12,
Bread-crumbs, 1 cup,
Grated cheese, 1 tablespoon,
Tomato sauce, 3 tablespoons.

Cut the tops from the peppers, and remove carefully the seeds and white membranes. Lay the peppers in a bowl and pour over them enough boiling water to cover, and set them aside till the water is cold.

Drain the peppers, and wipe them out. Remove the skins from the sardines, rub them smooth, add to them the cup of bread-crumbs, and the grated cheese, and moisten all with well-seasoned tomato sauce.

Stuff the peppers with this mixture, and stand them side by side in a deep dish. Pour a little tomato sauce, or soup over them and bake in a good oven until tender.

Transfer the peppers to a hot dish, thicken the gravy in the pan, and pour it about them.

STUFFED PEPPERS
SPANISH

Green peppers,
Grated cheese,
Salt, pepper and paprika,
Egg,
Flour,
Tomato juice,
Onion and chilli pepper,
Lard.

Slit the peppers on one side, but leaving the stems intact. After carefully taking out all the seeds, and cores, place the peppers in boiling water, and then remove the skins.

Stuff them *very* full with grated cheese highly seasoned with salt, pepper, and paprika. Roll them in beaten egg, and then in flour; then a second time roll them in egg and flour.

Make ready a sauce composed of 1 quart of tomato juice, 2 tablespoons of chopped onion, and 1 chopped chilli pepper.

Now place on the stove a pan of deep lard and drop the stuffed peppers into this, and fry till a light brown. Then put them into the tomato mixture, and simmer for 2 hours.

PEPPERS SCALLOPED WITH FISH

Cold fish, minced,
Fine bread-crumbs,
Tomato sauce,
Peppers.

Open, empty, and scald the peppers, and when cold fill the halves with the mixture, well seasoned, and wet with rich tomato sauce. Strew over with fine bread-crumbs, arrange in a deep dish, pour more tomato sauce about them, and bake.

GREEN CORN OMELETTE

Corn, 4 good-sized ears,
Eggs, 5,
Cream, 2 tablespoons,
Salt, ¼ teaspoon,
Butter, 1 tablespoon,
Pepper.

Score lengthwise and scrape out the pulp of the corn. Beat the yolks and whites of the eggs separately; mix the corn, cream, yolks, and the seasoning all together, and give it a brisk beating for 1 or 2 minutes.

Put the butter in the omelette-pan, and while it is heating

add the stiffly beaten whites, stirring in lightly. Pour the whole mixture into the hot butter, raising the center with a hot knife, and tipping the pan so as to let all the uncooked part reach the hot pan.

As soon as nicely browned, and evenly cooked, fold it over, turn out on a hot platter, and serve at once.

FRIED CORN

Fresh corn, 6 ears,
Butter, 1 heaping tablespoon,
Salt, ½ teaspoon,
Pepper, 1 salt-spoon,
Cream, ½ cup,
Nutmeg.

Cut the corn from the cob; put it, with the butter, in a saucepan. Sprinkle with salt, pepper, and a few gratings of nutmeg. Cook 10 minutes, stirring well. Put in the cream and cook one minute longer. Serve hot.

CORN FRITTERS

Sweet corn, 12 ears,
Eggs, 3,
Milk, 2 tablespoons,
Flour, 2 tablespoons,
Salt, 1 teaspoon,
Pepper.

Bake in small cakes on griddle, with plenty of butter. Serve hot.

CORN PUDDING

Corn, 1 pint,
Eggs, 2,

Flour, 1 tablespoon,
Melted butter, 2 tablespoons,
Milk, 1 pint,
Salt, sugar, pepper.

If canned corn is used, press it through a colander; if fresh corn, cut very fine from the ear. Add the eggs, flour, butter, and season with salt and sugar in such proportions that it will be neither salt nor sweet to excess, and also add pepper.

Bake in a greased dish until the custard is set, or the handle of a silver spoon will come out clean. Serve with broiled steaks or chops, or with roast lamb.

GERMAN TURNIPS

Yellow turnips (medium), 3,
Sugar, 1 tablespoon,
Butter, 1 tablespoon,
Salt and pepper.

Peel, and cut the turnips small. Brown the sugar and add to it the butter and the turnips. Add enough water to partly cover the turnips, and season with salt and pepper.

Cook slowly, for about 2 hours.

MASHED CARROTS

Carrots,
Butter,
Salt and pepper.

Scrape the carrots and cut in thin slices. Cover with boiling water, and cook gently until tender. Drain, and rub through a sieve, or put through a potato press.

To each pint of carrots add a tablespoon of butter, and salt and pepper to taste. Mix well, press the mixture into small greased cups, or molds, pressing down well.

Set in a hot place for 2 or 3 minutes, then turn out, on a flat dish, and serve with or without a sauce.

BROWNED CARROTS

>Carrots,
>Butter,
>Sugar,
>Salt and pepper,
>Chopped parsley.

Scrape and wash the carrots and cut them into 3-inch lengths, then downward in thin slices, then each slice into strips.

Drop into boiling water, salted, and simmer until tender. If finely cut, this should not take over 25 or 30 minutes.

Put a tablespoon of butter in the frying-pan, and when very hot, add the drained carrots. Dredge lightly with salt and pepper, and a little sugar, and fry until lightly colored.

Sprinkle with chopped parsley, and serve.

CARROT BALLS

>Large carrots, 4 or 5,
>White sauce, 1 cup,
>Seasoning.

Four or 5 carrots will make a dozen small balls. After boiling the carrots drain them and put them through a ricer. Add the white sauce (a thick white sauce, made with 2 tablespoons of flour to one of butter), mix, season highly, and when cold and firm, shape in balls, and finish as for other croquettes.

SQUASH PUDDING

Squash,
Melted butter, 2 tablespoons,
Milk, 1/4 cup,
Eggs, 2,
Cream sauce,
Salt, pepper, celery-salt, mace.

Press the cooked squash dry through a sieve. To a half pint of the pulp add 2 tablespoons of melted butter, 1/4 cup of milk, season with salt and pepper, 2 beaten egg-yolks, and mix all thoroughly; next stir in the beaten whites, turn the whole into a buttered mold, set in a pan of hot water, and bake in the oven till the center is firm.

Serve turned from the mold, accompanied by rich cream sauce, seasoned with salt, pepper, celery-salt and mace. This can be baked in individual timbale molds if so desired.

CELERY FRITTERS

Celery, 1 bunch,
Eggs, 2,
Milk, 1 cup,
Baking-powder, 1 teaspoon,
Flour, 1 cup.

Cut the celery into 4-inch lengths, stand them in boiling water for about 10 minutes, then wipe dry, and dip them in the batter made from the eggs, milk and flour, and then fry, in a deep pot, to a golden brown. It may be that more than a cup of flour will be needed.

CELERY CUTLETS

Cold baked beans, 1 cup,
Chopped celery, 1 cup,

Melted butter, 2 tablespoons,
Bread-crumbs, 2 tablespoons,
Eggs, 2,
Lemon-juice, salt, pepper.

Mix together, shape into oblong balls, roll in bread-crumbs, and fry in deep fat.

HOMINY CROQUETTES

Boiled hominy, 1 pint,
Milk, ¼ cup,
Melted butter, 1 tablespoon,
Chopped parsley, 1 large tablespoon,
Eggs, beaten, 2,
Dry bread-crumbs,
Salt, pepper, onion-juice.

Heat the milk and hominy in a double boiler, add the eggs, and season to taste with salt, pepper and onion-juice, then cook until thick.

When cold, mold into croquettes, dipping each lightly into dry bread-crumbs, then fry golden brown in smoking hot fat.

STEWED MUSHROOMS

Fresh mushrooms, 1 pint,
Butter, 2 tablespoons,
Flour, 1 tablespoon,
Salt and pepper.

Peel the tops of the mushrooms, scrape the stalks, cutting off the roots. Throw the mushrooms into cold water as they are peeled.

Put the mushrooms into the saucepan over the fire, with 1 tablespoon of the butter, and then rub the other tablespoon of butter with the flour.

When the mushrooms commence to stew, add the flour and butter, stirring it well in. Stew gently for about 15 minutes. Season with salt and pepper, and serve.

FRENCH CHESTNUTS

French chestnuts, 1 pound,
Butter, 1 tablespoon,
Sugar, 2 tablespoons,
Bouillon, or stock, 1 tablespoon,
Salt, ½ teaspoon.

Slightly boil, and shell the chestnuts, and let them stand about 10 minutes in hot water to loosen the skins, which remove. Brown the sugar and butter in a saucepan, and add the stock or bouillon.

When well mixed, add the chestnuts, cover, and stew slowly until the nuts can be pierced with a straw. Salt while cooking.

This is a very good accompaniment to roast turkey, veal, saddle of mutton, or chops.

CHESTNUTS IN WHITE SAUCE

Chestnuts,
White sauce,
Onion-juice, celery-salt.

Shell and blanch the chestnuts, boil them in salted water, for 10 minutes. Make a white sauce, and add to it, a teaspoon of onion-juice, a dash of celery-salt, and pepper and salt to taste.

In this sauce lay the chestnuts, and let them simmer for half an hour. Serve very hot.

CHESTNUTS IN BROWN SAUCE

>Chestnuts,
>Butter, 1 tablespoon,
>Browned flour, 1 tablespoon,
>Chicken gravy (well seasoned), 1 cup,
>Onion juice,
>Salt and pepper.

Shell and blanch the chestnuts, boil them in salted water for 10 minutes. Make a brown sauce of the other ingredients, and should the gravy be not highly seasoned, add to it a tablespoon of good catsup. Good stock for this may be made from giblets.

Lay the chestnuts in this sauce, and let them cook half an hour. This is an excellent dish to serve with fowls, roasted or broiled.

STEWED CHESTNUTS

>Chestnuts, 3 pints,
>Butter, 2 tablespoons,
>Minced onion, 1 tablespoon,
>Chopped celery, 1 tablespoon,
>Tomato catsup, 3 tablespoons,
>Milk, 1 pint,
>Flour, 1 tablespoon.

Shall and blanch the chestnuts. Fry in the butter the minced onion and the chopped celery.

Put the chestnuts with this, add the tomato catsup and the milk, into which has been stirred the flour, and cook over a slow fire in a double boiler for about 1 hour, stirring often.

Serve hot.

CHESTNUT CROQUETTES

Spanish chestnuts, 1 quart,
Onion juice, ½ teaspoon,
Butter, 2 tablespoons,
Bread-crumbs, 2 tablespoons,
Egg, 1 yolk,
Salt and pepper.

Boil and blanch the chestnuts, cook until tender, rub them through a colander, and work into them the onion juice, butter, bread-crumbs, salt, pepper, and egg-yolk. Heat in a double boiler till hot, set aside, and when cold form into croquettes, roll in egg and crumbs, and fry in deep fat. They are better when small.

BAKED APPLES

Apples,
White Sugar,
Lemon rind,
Cinnamon,
Blanched almonds,
Crabapple jelly.

Wash and core large apples. Put them in a pan and fill each hole with plenty of white sugar. Sprinkle more sugar over them and add a little lemon rind, grated, and a little powdered cinnamon.

Pour in enough water to fill the bottom of the pan to about ½ inch, then put them in the oven and bake until tender without falling to pieces. Baste them often.

If the apples are done before the syrup is thick enough, place the apples on a dish, and cook the syrup on top of the stove until it thickens, and then pour it over the apples.

Garnish with blanched almonds and fill the tops of the apples with crabapple jelly.

STEAMED APPLES

Apples, 2 quarts,
Sugar, 1 cup,
Butter, ½ cup.

The apples should be cut in quarters and cored (not peeled), then put the butter and sugar in a deep cooking-pan and when melted add the apples, and cover, and slowly cook for 1 hour.

Serve with meat.

EGGS

OMELETTES

The omelette, like the pie, can be made of anything which "takes kindly to flavoring." Eggs may be combined with good results with fish, meat, vegetables, cheese, etc., and the variety of sweet omelettes is endless. Sugar, jam or any kind of preserves, or fruits, and also rum, can be used in combination to make very tasteful omelettes.

A simple method of making an omelette is to break four eggs into a bowl, season with salt and pepper, and beat lightly until well broken. Place on a fire, which while glowing is yet not too fierce, the omelette pan, and dissolve in it 2 level tablespoons of butter—you should always allow half a tablespoon of butter for each additional egg you may use.

Let the butter froth up well, or, as the cooks say, "fritter in the pan." When you pour in the egg mixture let it cook for a few seconds—not minutes—until a film of cooked egg has formed in the bottom of the pan. Then with a flexible knife lift the edge of the omelette, and if a puff of steam escapes at this point, near the knife, tilt the pan, so as to let as much of the egg as is still liquid run under the omelette, repeating this process until there is no liquid left.

Loosen the omelette on all sides, fold it over, slide it from the pan onto a platter, and serve at once.

The above is for a simple omelette. Any omelettes requiring seasoning should have the seasoning mixed with the eggs before they are placed in the omelette pan; and in case of a sweet omelette, in which there is a sauce, filling, or fruit, this should be placed in the center of the omelette, just before it is folded over, and the outside of the omelette dusted with sugar.

The following is a partial list of materials which are suitable for combination with eggs, for making omelettes:

Fish (cold boiled), ham, chicken, veal, oysters, shrimps, onions, lamb, etc., tomatoes, green beans, peas, mushrooms, cheese, etc., etc.

With sweet omelettes: Jams, preserves of any kind, fruits, and rum.

The same combinations may be used with eggs for a scramble, but while the same results may be obtained as regards flavor, the omelette is more attractive, and seems more inviting. However, eggs scrambled with meats or vegetables may be served on toast, and thus make a more finished dish.

OYSTER OMELETTE

Oysters, stewed and chopped fine, 12,
Eggs, 6,
Butter, 3 tablespoons,
Milk, 1 cup,
Salt and pepper.

Chop the oysters fine; beat the yolks and whites of the eggs separately. Heat the butter while mixing the omelette. Stir the milk into a deep dish with the beaten yolks of the eggs. Season with salt and pepper, and next add the chopped oysters, beating hard as you gradually add them.

Pour in the melted butter, and lastly stir in the whites lightly. Melt some more butter in a skillet, pour the omelette mixture into it, and leave over the fire until the omelette is set.

Fold it over, place on a dish, and serve hot.

OMELETTE AUX HARICOTS

Cooked string beans, 2 tablespoons,
Eggs, well beaten, 4,
Grated Parmesan cheese, 2 tablespoons,
Melted butter, 2 tablespoons,
Salt and pepper.

Cut the beans fine, and stir them into the eggs which have been well beaten together; then add the cheese, and season with pepper and salt to taste.

When perfectly mixed, put the whole with the butter, into the omelette pan, and fry a pale brown. The time varies from 3 to 5 minutes.

TOMATO OMELETTE

Tomatoes, 3,
Chopped onion, 1 teaspoon,
Chopped parsley, 1 teaspoon,
Eggs, 3,
Butter, salt, pepper.

Scald and skin the tomatoes, melt a small piece of butter in a saucepan, and to it add the onion and parsley. Season with salt and pepper; put in the tomatoes and let them remain in the butter for 2 minutes.

Turn out the mixture and set it aside until it is quite cool. Beat up the eggs, together, and mix them in with the tomatoes. Place a lump of butter about the size of a walnut in a frying-pan and when the butter dissolves pour the omelette mixture into the frying-pan, leaving it over the fire until the omelette rises to the top.

It should be served at once.

BAKED CHEESE OMELETTE

Stale bread-crumbs, 1 cup,
Grated cheese, 1 cup,
Milk, 1 pint,
Melted butter, 1 tablespoon,
Eggs, 2,
Salt, ¼ teaspoon,
Baking-soda, 1 salt-spoon,
Cayenne.

Soak the bread-crumbs in the milk, to which has been added the baking-soda which has been dissolved in 1 teaspoon of hot water.

When thoroughly soaked, add the eggs, beaten until very light, the salt, a dash of cayenne, the grated cheese, and the melted butter.

Turn quickly into a greased baking-dish, and place in a very hot oven. Serve as soon as it is well puffed up and pale brown, as it quickly falls.

OMELETTE CELESTINE

Eggs, 6,
Thick whipped cream, 1 tablespoon,
Powdered sugar, 1 tablespoon,
Butter, 1 teaspoon,
Macaroons (stale and crumbled), 6,
Apple (or other acid jelly), 3 tablespoons.

Place the crumbled macaroons and the acid jelly in the whipped cream. Beat the eggs without separating. Add 1 tablespoon of warm water, and the powdered sugar.

Drop the butter into a very hot pan, and tilt until the bottom is evenly greased. Pour the eggs into it, and shake and stir with a spatula. When the omelette is ready to fold, pour the cake mixture in the center, fold over, and turn out on a hot dish.

Dredge with a little powdered sugar, and brown quickly by holding it close to a clean red-hot shovel, or a stove-lid.

Send it quickly to the table, and pass with it, a bowl of whipped cream.

SCRAMBLED EGGS, WITH TOMATOES

Tomatoes, 1/2 can,
Butter, 1 large tablespoon,
Eggs, well beaten, 6,
Chopped onion,
Salt, pepper, herbs,
Thin buttered toast.

Stew the tomatoes with some chopped onion; salt and pepper herbs to season; then rub through a sieve.

Return it to the fire, and add 1 large tablespoon of butter. When bubbling add the eggs which have oeen well beaten, and stir until the mixture is thickened, and then dip out by spoonsful, and spread on hot thin buttered toast.

SCRAMBLED EGGS WITH CHEESE

Eggs, 6,
Grated cheese, 1/2 cup,
Butter, 2 tablespoons,
Salt, 1/2 teaspoon,
Cream, 6 tablespoons,
Pepper.

Beat the eggs well, and add the salt, pepper, and cream. Melt the butter in a pan, and when hot, turn into it the egg mixture. Stir it as it thickens. When almost done, sprinkle in a half-cup of grated cheese. Stir for a moment longer, and then turn it into a hot dish, and serve.

TOMATO-AND-EGG-TOAST

> Tomatoes, fresh, 2 (or, 4 tablespoons of pulp),
> Finely chopped ham, 1 tablespoon,
> Butter, 1 tablespoon,
> Eggs, well beaten, 2,
> Chopped onion,
> Buttered toast.

If fresh tomatoes, put them in boiling water, then peel and chop them. Melt the butter in a small pan, add the tomatoes, ham, and some chopped onion. Cover, and cook gently for 10 minutes, or till the tomatoes are quite soft. Make buttered toast. When the contents of the pan are cooked enough, add the eggs, stir till thick, and serve hot, on the toast.

SWISS EGG TOAST

> Grated cheese, 3 tablespoons,
> Chopped parsley, 1 dessert-spoon,
> Melted butter, 1 tablespoon,
> Eggs, 3,
> Salt, pepper, toast.

Melt the butter on a plate or platter, and spread over it one-half of the cheese. Break 3 eggs on the platter, taking care not to break the yolks. Sprinkle with a little fine salt and pepper, and the rest of the cheese, and some chopped parsley, all mixed together.

Set the platter in the oven and bake until set. Cut out each egg with a cutter, and serve on rounds of toast.

CREAMED EGGS

Take hard-boiled eggs, cut a slice from the base of each, so that it will stand. Then cover the eggs with a cream sauce, and garnish with sprigs of parsley and with olives.

This may be served individually for luncheon.

STUFFED EGGS

Eggs, 12,
Mayonnaise, 2 tablespoons,
Chopped ham, or Bologna, 3 tablespoons,
Worcestershire, 1 tablespoon.

Boil the eggs hard and peel them. Cut in halves, and take out the yolks, and with a fork put in mayonnaise, chopped parsley, meat, and seasoning and return them to the whites and put the whites together, securing them with an orange-wood toothpick. Then they are ready for serving.

EGGS IN MOLDS

Eggs,
Chopped ham, tongue,
Cream- or tomato-sauce, parsley.

Butter small molds, or little cups, sprinkle the sides with finely chopped ham, tongue, or parsley. Break 1 egg at a time into a saucer, and slide it into the mold.

Stand the molds or cups in a pan filled with boiling water, and cover and place in a hot oven until the eggs are set.

Loosen the edges and turn out carefully. Pour over them a cream- or a tomato-sauce, and serve at once.

MEXICAN EGGS

Eggs,
Green peppers,
Hot butter,
Ham,
Toast.

Take 3 sweet green peppers, split them lengthwise, and remove the core and seeds. Fry them 2 minutes in hot butter. Fry very thin slices of ham and place each piece on a slice of toast. Then on each slice of ham put a poached egg, on top of both.

VENETIAN EGGS

Eggs, 4,
Strained tomatoes, 1 cup,
Grated cheese, 1 cup,
Butter, 1 tablespoon.

Put the butter and tomatoes into a double boiler, and when hot add the cheese and seasoning (salt and pepper).

When this is dissolved put in the beaten eggs, and cook until it thickens, and then serve on toast.

JAPANESE EGGS

Eggs, 6,
Boiled rice, 1 cup,
Milk, 1 cup.
Butter, 1 tablespoon,
Flour, 1 tablespoon.

Boil the eggs hard; cut them in half and press them into the bed of rice. Over this pour a cream made from the milk, flour, butter, and seasoning of salt and pepper.

HUEVOS
SPANISH EGGS

Eggs, 6,
Onions, 2,
Tomatoes, 3,
Green chilli peppers, 2,
Chopped parsley, 1 salt-spoon,
Melted butter, 1 tablespoon.

Chop together the onions, tomatoes, and chilli peppers; add a salt-spoon of chopped parsley, and put all into a frying-pan with a tablespoon of melted butter, and cook for 5 minutes.

Fry the eggs on both sides, and then pour the sauce over the eggs, and serve hot.

FRIED SAVORY EGGS

Eggs, 7,
Bread-crumbs,
Ham, chopped fine,
Parsley, minced,
Pepper,
Tomato-sauce.

Six of the eggs should be previously hard-boiled. Shell them and beat up the seventh egg, and dip the shelled eggs in it. Then roll the eggs in a mixture made of fine bread-crumbs, chopped ham, minced parsley, seasoned with pepper and salt if desired.

Fry them in boiling fat to a good brown, and place on a hot dish and serve with a hot tomato-sauce poured round them.

EGGS WITH SPAGHETTI

Spaghetti, boiled and chopped fine, 1 cup,
Butter, 1 large tablespoon,

Fresh mushrooms, 1 cup,
Milk, 1 cup,
Eggs, well beaten, 6,
Salt, 1 teaspoon,
Chopped parsley, 1 teaspoon,
Pepper, and toast-points.

Melt the butter in a saucepan, add the mushrooms and cook first for 5 minutes. Pour in the milk and spaghetti and heat slowly. When beginning to simmer, add the eggs, salt, and a dash of pepper.

Stir till the eggs have thickened, then add the parsley, and turn into a hot dish and garnish with toast-points.

EGG TIMBALES

Eggs, 4,
Milk, 2½ cups,
Salt, ½ teaspoon,
Pepper, butter, chopped parsley.

Break the eggs into a bowl and beat them enough to mix them thoroughly. Add the milk, salt, a dash of pepper, and strain.

Butter small molds and sprinkle the sides with chopped parsley and fill the molds with the liquid. Stand the molds in a pan of warm water, and place them in a moderate oven until set in the center, like a baked custard.

SAUCES

Much of the former superiority of French cookery over that of other nationalities was due to their ingenious methods of preparing appetizing sauces for their various dishes.

Some of these sauces are quite simple, and readily made, while others are more elaborate, and require more time in their preparation.

Most sauces are made by cooking together equal quantities of butter and flour for the body of the sauce, and then adding a seasoning and a liquid, cooking these together also with the thickening, or body, until well corporated.

White sauces are the simplest, and most frequently used; and derive their name from the fact that the flour in the thickening is not allowed to color. Milk is always used in white sauces, while in brown sauces, stock or gravy is used, which also tends to make the sauce a darker color.

For white sauces the ingredients are, butter, flour and milk, in the proportion of 1 tablespoon each of flour and butter to half a pint of milk.

To make a white sauce, first put the milk in a stewpan, and let it heat to the scalding point. In another pan put the flour and butter, and let them melt, stirring occasionally until the flour and butter are well mixed together. Bring it to a bubble, and then add the hot milk gradually, and stir all together, until the whole is smoothly thickened. Then season and set aside and allow it to simmer for a few minutes.

Brown sauces are made by cooking the butter and flour together, constantly stirring all the while to prevent burning, but until the flour is well browned. As browned flour does not have the thickening effect that unbrowned flour has, it is necessary to use a heaping tablespoon of flour to a tablespoon of butter and half a pint of the gravy or stock used as a liquid.

"Piquante" sauces are those which contain vinegar in some form. For example, a tablespoon of vinegar added to finely chopped pickles makes a "poivrade" sauce, and this, or finely chopped pickles with mustard are good sauces to serve with pork chops or with mutton cutlets.

Various other sauces, most of which start with either a white or a brown sauce, derive their names from the manner in which they are prepared, or the ingredients which they contain.

When milk cannot be had for a white sauce, water may be used instead, in which case the sauce becomes known as a drawn-butter sauce. Using cream instead of milk, makes a cream sauce; while a béchamel sauce is composed of equal parts of cream, and either chicken stock, or veal stock.

Breaking the yolks of eggs into a white sauce makes it a "polette"; while a good sauce for fish is made by adding to a white sauce, either a few chopped oysters, or hard-boiled eggs, or capers, or chopped parsley. Capers added to white sauce makes a good sauce for boiled mutton. Chopped mushrooms added to white or brown sauce, makes a mushroom sauce. An olive sauce is made by adding chopped olives to a brown sauce; etc., etc.

In making sauces do not simply stir the flour and butter into an already hot liquid, but first combine the flour and butter together, and then add the hot liquid, gradually to the mixture. This prevents the sauce from being lumpy.

The following will be of use in determining the sauces to be served with various meats:

Apple sauce—Serve with roast pork, pork chops, roast duck, or roast goose.

Bechamel sauce—Serve with cutlets, or with small broiled meats.

Black currant jelly—Serve with venison.

Bread sauce—Serve with roast chicken, or with game.

Caper sauce—Serve with boiled mutton, or with boiled fish.

Cranberry jelly—Serve with roast turkey.

Cream, or White sauce—Serve with fried chicken, croquettes, cauliflower, stewed carrots, and various vegetables.

Grape jelly—Serve with venison, or with roast meats.

Hollandaise sauce—Serve with boiled, or broiled fish.

Horseradish sauce—Serve with boiled ham, roast beef, roast veal, roast pork, grilled steak, fillet of beef.

Lemon butter—Serve with fried fish, or with broiled meats.

Maitre d'hotel sauce—Serve with broiled steak, chops, cutlets, or baked fish.

Mint sauce—Serve with roast lamb.

Mushroom sauce—Serve with broiled steak, fillet of beef.

Mustard sauce—Serve with roast beef, corned beef, roast ham, or boiled ham.

Parsley sauce—Serve with boiled, broiled or baked fish.

Red currant jelly—Serve with roast mutton, stewed rabbit, or with game.

Tartare sauce—Serve with cold boiled tongue, fried smelt, cod, or halibut.

Tomato butter—Serve with broiled meats.

Tomato sauce—Serve with chops, croquettes, cutlets, or with fried oysters.

Vinaigrette sauce—Serve with fish or with calf's head.

WHITE SAUCE

Butter, 1 tablespoon,
Flour, 1 tablespoon,
Hot milk, ½ pint,
Onion juice, or lemon juice, 1 teaspoon.

Cream the butter and flour together, and put into them the hot milk. Let it boil for 10 minutes, and then take it off the fire, and stir in the seasoning. It should be strained before serving.

BROWN SAUCE, NO. 1

Butter, 2 tablespoons,
Flour, 1 tablespoon,
Onion, 1, small,
Turnip, ½,
Carrot, ½,
Stock, 1 pint,
Salt and pepper.

Cut the vegetables into thin slices, and with the butter, put into a stewpan to cook until brown, taking care not to burn.

Shake in the flour, and add the stock. Stir them all together until the sauce boils, then simmer slowly for half an hour.

Strain after seasoning with salt and pepper.

BROWN SAUCE, NO. 2

Soup stock, or gravy, ½ pint,
Butter, 1 tablespoon,
Flour, 1 large tablespoon,
Seasoning.

Heat half a pint of good soup stock or gravy, and when neither of these are on hand use water, though the result is naturally not quite so good. In another saucepan melt and slowly brown 1 tablespoon of butter or clarified fat. Add to this, 1 slightly heaping tablespoon of flour and stir until browned.

Gradually add the hot liquid, stirring continuously until it is smoothly thickened. Season according to left-overs which are to be used; salt, pepper, onion-juice, herbs, spices, etc., can all be used for the seasoning.

BROWN BUTTER SAUCE

Butter, 2 tablespoons,
Flour, 2 tablespoons,
Boiling water, 1½ cups,
Vinegar, or lemon-juice,
Salt and pepper.

Place the butter and flour in a saucepan and heat them until the mixture becomes a rich brown color, taking care, however, that it does not burn. Add a little vinegar, or lemon-juice, and pour over the fish or joint with which it is to be served.

PARSLEY SAUCE

GERMAN

Parsley, 1 small bunch,
Anchovies, 8,

Onion, 1, small,
Mixed mustard, 2 teaspoons,
Salad oil, 6 teaspoons,
Vinegar, 3 teaspoons,
Salt and pepper.

Chop finely together, the parsley, anchovies, and onion. To this add the mustard, vinegar, oil, pepper, and salt.

This is an excellent sauce to serve with fish.

MUSTARD SAUCE

Mustard, 1½ tablespoons,
Flour, 1 tablespoon,
Vinegar, 2 tablespoons,
Cold water, 3 tablespoons,
Boiling water, ½ pint,
Butter, 1 tablespoon.

Mix together the mustard, flour, butter, and cold water until it makes a smooth paste. Then add the hot water and boil for 5 minutes. Remove it from the fire and when nearly cold, add the viengar.

CUCUMBER SAUCE, NO. 1

Cucumber, 1 small,
Butter, 1 tablespoon,
Salt, pepper.

To be later added,
Butter, ½ cup,
Flour, 1 tablespoon,
Milk, ½ cup,
Cold water, 1 teaspoon,
Salt, a pinch.

Remove the peel from a small cucumber, cut it into moderately thin slices and then into small squares. Melt 1 tablespoon of butter in a small saucepan, put in the cut cucumber, and pour in sufficient water to cover.

Season with salt and pepper. Place a buttered paper over the top, and allow it to simmer until it is tender. Prepare some drawn butter by melting half a cup of butter over a slow fire. Then sprinkle in a tablespoon of flour and add a half a cup of scalded milk, and a pinch of salt.

Boil for a few minutes, stirring well and adding 1 teaspoon of cold water. Stir this well into the cucumbers, and serve as a sauce for fish.

CUCUMBER SAUCE, NO. 2

Cucumber, 1,
Eggs, 2,
Vinegar, 1 dessert-spoon,
Salt, pepper, olive-oil.

Put the yolks of 2 raw eggs into a basin and mix together. Add seasoning of salt, pepper, and a few drops of oil, and whisk them together thoroughly. Add more oil, drop by drop, whisking all the time, and blend the oil with the eggs, in the same way, till the mixture is about the consistency of mayonnaise. As soon as this result is obtained, pour in the vinegar, slowly, and a dessert-spoon of cucumber vinegar, if at hand. Add a few more drops of vinegar if necessary.

Lastly, stir in 2 tablespoons of cooked cucumber, cut into small dice-shaped pieces, and place the sauce on ice until it is required.

VINAIGRETTE SAUCE

Salt, ½ teaspoon,
Paprika, ¼ teaspoon,

White pepper, a dash,
Tarragon, or plain vinegar, 3 tablespoons,
Oil, 6 tablespoons,
Gherkins, 1 tablespoon,
Parsley, 1 teaspoon,
Chopped onion, or chives, 1 teaspoon.

Mix all thoroughly together. A tablespoon of minced green peppers is an addition which improves it.

HOLLANDAISE SAUCE, NO. 1

Butter, ½ cup,
Eggs, 4 yolks,
Lemon juice, 1 tablespoon,
Boiling water, 1 cup,
Salt, cayenne, nutmeg.

Put the butter into a double boiler and cream it with the egg-yolks, adding them one by one. Stir in the lemon-juice, and add a pinch of salt, a dash of cayenne, and a little grated nutmeg. Stir it until it is thick, then add the boiling water gradually, and continue to stir until the mixture is creamy, then serve.

HOLLANDAISE SAUCE, NO. 2

Butter, 1 tablespoon,
Flour, 1 tablespoon,
Brown sugar, 1 tablespoon,
Stock, ½ pint,
Lemon-juice, 1 teaspoon,
Egg, 1 yolk, well beaten,
Salt, pepper.

Heat all the ingredients together. Boil for 5 minutes, and take from the fire. Last of all add the beaten yolk of 1 egg.

SAUCE TARTARE, NO. 1
FRENCH

Mayonnaise, 1 pint,
Onion-juice, 1 teaspoon,
Capers, finely chopped, 1 tablespoon,
Olives, chopped, 1 tablespoon,
Cucumber pickle, chopped, 1 tablespoon,
Parsley, chopped, 1 tablespoon.

Stir the other ingredients into the mayonnaise. This is a suitable sauce to serve with fish, or where a cold sauce is desired.

SAUCE TARTARE, NO. 2

Mayonnaise, ½ pint,
Onion-juice, 1 tablespoon,
Capers, 1 tablespoon,
Chopped olives, 1 tablespoon.

Mix well, and serve with fish, crabs, cold meats, etc.

MAÎTRE D'HÔTEL SAUCE, NO. 1

Butter, 4 tablespoons,
Lemon-juice, 2 tablespoons,
Chopped parsley, 1 tablespoon,
Salt, pepper, cayenne.

Cream the butter, and mix thoroughly.

MAÎTRE D'HÔTEL SAUCE, NO. 2

Butter, 1 tablespoon,
Flour, 1 tablespoon,
Chopped parsley, 1 teaspoon,
Onion-juice, 1 teaspoon,
Stock, ½ pint.

Put the butter and flour in a pan and melt. Add the stock, the parsley, and onion-juice, and boil for 5 minutes.

This is suitable to serve with almost any roast meat, or with baked fish.

MINT SAUCE

Chopped mint, 4 tablespoons,
Sugar, 2 tablespoons,
Vinegar, ½ cup,
Salt, ½ teaspoon,
Cold water, ½ cup.

Mix all together, and serve cold.

PEPPER SAUCE

Onions, 2, small,
Tomatoes, 2,
Green peppers, 2.

Chop the vegetables all together, put them in a stewpan with water to cover. Boil until perfectly soft, and add salt. Serve cold with meat.

BECHAMEL SAUCE

Hot butter, 2 tablespoons,
Flour, or arrowroot, 2 tablespoons,
Salt, 1 teaspoon,
Nutmeg, a dash,
Cayenne, a dash,
Hot stock, 1 cup,
Hot cream, ½ cup,
Egg, 1 yolk,
Lemon-juice, 1 tablespoon.

Cook the butter and flour together until smooth, and then add the seasoning. Then gradually add the hot stock and the cream. When boiling add the egg and the lemon-juice.

This is a good sauce for meats, poultry, and vegetables.

ESPAGNOL SAUCE

Hot butter, 2 tablespoons,
Ham, chopped, 1 tablespoon,
Onions, chopped, 1 tablespoon,
Celery, chopped, 1 tablespoon,
Parsley, chopped, 1 tablespoon,
Flour, 3 tablespoons,
Salt, ¼ teaspoon,
Paprika, ½ teaspoon,
Stock, 2 cups,
Cloves, 2,
Mace, bay leaf.

Chop the ham and vegetables fine, and cook them with the butter, flour, salt, and paprika, until brown. Then add the stock, 1 bay leaf, 1 blade of mace and 2 cloves, and let simmer gently for 2 hours.

Strain and serve.

BORDELAISE SAUCE

Espagnole sauce,
Red Bordeaux wine,
Sweet herbs,
Beef-marrow.

Prepare an espagnole sauce as given above, and when this is heated add some minced sweet herbs, and a half of a cup of red Bordeaux wine.

Scald a beef bone, and remove the marrow and cut it into

small cubes and add them to the sauce when it is well heated.

Serve very hot, because the marrow chills easily.

BREAD SAUCE

> Milk, 2 cups,
> Bread-crumbs, ½ cup,
> Butter, 2 tablespoons,
> Onion, ½,
> Cloves, 2,
> Parsley, 1 sprig,
> Mace, 1 blade,
> Salt, ½ teaspoon,
> Paprika, ½ teaspoon.

Simmer all the ingredients together except the butter and the bread-crumbs. Strain, return to the fire, add the butter and crumbs, and simmer for ½ hour.

HORSERADISH SAUCE

> Horseradish, 4 tablespoons,
> Bread-crumbs, 4 tablespoons,
> Powdered sugar, 1 teaspoon,
> Vinegar, 2 tablespoons,
> Salt, ½ teaspoon,
> Made mustard, ½ teaspoon,
> Hot cream, or white sauce, ½ cup.

Mix all except the cream, or the white sauce, thoroughly, and put in a double boiler. Then add the cream, or the white sauce, and let it all heat together.

TOMATO SAUCE

> Tomatoes, 6, ripe, peeled,
> Green peppers, 2,

Onions, 4,
Vinegar, 2 cups,
Salt, 1 tablespoon.

Chop the tomatoes, peppers, and onions, and place them, with the vinegar and salt on the fire.

Boil until perfectly soft. This should take about 3 hours. Then press through a colander.

CHESTNUT SAUCE FOR FOWLS

Chestnuts, 2 cups,
Chicken stock, 1 cup,
Mushrooms, 1 tablespoon,
Tomato catsup, 1 tablespoon,
Butter, 2 tablespoons,
Flour, 2 tablespoons.

Shell, blanch, boil, and put through a vegetable press, the two cups of chestnuts. Add to them the chicken stock, mushrooms, and tomato catsup, and set to one side.

Cook together in the frying-pan, the butter and flour. If there is good sweet fat from fowls this may be used in place of the butter.

When the fat and the flour bubbles, add the purée of chestnuts already prepared. Season to taste with salt and pepper, and serve very hot, in a sauce-boat.

TOMATO BUTTER

Tomatoes,
Cooking apples,
Brown sugar,
Cinnamon.

Peel and cook tomatoes. When cool, put them through a sieve, and cook again until it begins to thicken; then add one-third as many cooking apples as you have taken tomatoes. The apples should be finely cut before being placed in the tomato-pulp. Sweeten to taste with brown sugar and season with cinnamon. Cook thoroughly, and put into cans.

LEMON BUTTER

Butter, 1 tablespoon,
Salt, ½ teaspoon,
Lemon-juice, ½ tablespoon,
Minced parsley, ½ tablespoon,
Pepper, ½ salt-spoon.

Mix well, and spread on hot broiled steak or chops. This may also be used with hot fried or broiled fish.

CITRON SAUCE

GERMAN

Eggs, 4,
Sugar, ½ cup,
Lemon, 1 (using juice and rind),
White wine, sherry or rum, ½ wine-glass.

To the yolks of the eggs add the sugar, wine, and lemon, using both the juice and the rind of the lemon. Place on the fire, and stir briskly with a wooden spoon until it comes to a boil. Then remove from the fire, and when cool mix this with the well-beaten whites of the eggs. This is to be served with cornstarch, rice, or any cold pudding.

CLARET SAUCE

GERMAN

Claret, 1 cup,
Water, 1 cup,

Cinnamon, 1 stick,
Sugar, 4 tablespoons.

Put all of the above ingredients on the fire, and let it get hot, but not boil.

This sauce is for puddings and may be served either hot or cold.

SALADS

Salads are economical dishes, and in many cases furnish opportunity to utilize remnants, or "left-overs" of cold cooked meats, fish and vegetables, where these have flavors which will harmonize.

The different foods should be kept apart until about to make the salad. All raw greens, such as lettuce, cabbage, etc., should be well washed in clear cold water to make them crisp, then dried on a cloth. Remove all bone, gristle and fat from the meats, and flake cold fish into fine bits. Vegetables should not be chopped fine, but diced with a sharp knife. All green vegetables, and some other vegetables, are much improved if they are marinated, or sprinkled with French dressing and allowed to remain an hour before preparing the salad.

Vegetable salads may be made of lettuce, cauliflower, green string beans, celery, cold boiled potatoes, cucumbers, tomatoes, cabbage, etc. Nuts may be also used with almost any vegetable or fruit combination.

Lettuce, celery, cabbage, etc., should be placed in cold water to make crisp. Asparagus should be boiled, then cooled, cut into small lengths, and the tougher parts of the stalks removed, then served with mayonnaise or with French dressing.

Cold boiled potatoes cut in dice, may be used, flavored with onion or with parsley, and served with either a French dressing or with mayonnaise. Potatoes may also be combined with other vegetables such as beets, beans, peas, carrots, and green peppers. Vegetable salads are particularly appropriate to serve at luncheon with cold meats.

Cold boiled cauliflower, the flowers picked apart, and the tender parts of the stems cut in small pieces, mixed with olives or tomatoes, may be served with mayonnaise or with French dressing.

Cabbage, white, raw and tender, cut in fine strips, and mixed with celery, or with strips of green pepper, is served with either French dressing or with mayonnaise.

Cooked green beans, cut in 2-inch lengths, flavored with finely chopped onion, and put on lettuce leaves, may be served with French dressing.

Young dandelion, mixed with either lettuce leaves or with watercress, may be served with a French dressing.

Tomatoes, raw, should have the skins removed, then either sliced, or served whole. If sliced, add onion and green peppers and serve with a French or a mayonnaise dressing; but if served whole, the tomatoes should have a filling of celery, nuts, vegetables or fish, and should always have a mayonnaise dressing.

CHEESE BALLS

Grated cheese, 1 cup,
Whites of eggs, 2,
Worcestershire, ½ teaspoon,
Salt, bread-crumbs.

Beat the eggs well, mix all the ingredients together, and mold into balls. Roll them in fine bread-crumbs, and fry in deep fat.

CHEESE STRAWS

Flour, 1 cup,
Melted butter, 1 tablespoon,
Baking-powder, 1 teaspoon,
Grated cheese, ½ cup,
Salt, cayenne, milk.

Sift the flour and baking-powder together, add a dash of salt, rub in the butter and roll out thin, using enough milk to make it roll. Sprinkle thickly with the cheese, a dash of cayenne, and cut in strips, and bake in the oven till brown.

SALAD DRESSINGS

Dressings for salads are both cooked and raw. The simplest uncooked dressing is called a French dressing. Another well-known dressing is called a mayonnaise.

A cooked dressing may be made with cream, eggs, or butter, for those who do not care for the taste of oil.

FRENCH DRESSING, NO, 1

> Oil, 4 tablespoons,
> Vinegar, 1 tablespoon,
> Salt, ½ teaspoon,
> Pepper, ¼ teaspoon.

Put the salt, pepper, and oil in a bowl, and mix well by stirring; add slowly the vinegar, and stir vigorously, and continue to stir it until the mixture looks slightly grayish, which is the sign that the vinegar and oil are blended.

This dressing should be used at once, for the ingredients will soon separate.

FRENCH DRESSING, NO. 2

> Oil, 6 tablespoons,
> Vinegar, 3 tablespoons,
> Worcestershire, 1 teaspoon,
> Salt, ½ teaspoon,
> Pepper, ¼ teaspoon.

Mix the oil, salt, and pepper together, add the vinegar slowly and when well blended together, last add the worcestershire, and stir it well in.

It may be well to state here that a bit of ice put into the oil and vinegar for a French dressing results in its being surprisingly thickened and remaining the consistency of cream for some time.

MAYONNAISE DRESSING, NO. 1

>Eggs, 2 yolks,
>Olive oil, 1 pint,
>Vinegar, 4 tablespoons,
>Made mustard, 1 teaspoon,
>Salt, ½ teaspoon,
>Cayenne, a dash.

Beat the yolks and put them in a bowl with the mustard and the dash of cayenne. Mix well together; and add, slowly, drop by drop, the oil. When the mixture is well beaten then add the vinegar, the salt being last put in.

Much of the success depends on the ingredients being cold; and a silver fork is best to do the beating.

MAYONNAISE DRESSING, NO. 2

>Olive oil, 1½ cups,
>Vinegar, ½ cup,
>Made mustard, 1 teaspoon,
>Egg, 1 (yolk),
>Salt, 1 teaspoon.

Place the yolk of the egg in a bowl and to it add the mustard. Mix well together, then add the oil, drop by drop, stirring constantly. When thick add slowly the vinegar, and lastly the salt.

If the dressing is to be kept for any length of time omit the salt until just before putting over the salad.

The yolk of a hard-boiled egg may be used instead of the

raw egg. Also lemon-juice may be used in place of vinegar.

To obtain the best results the bowl and the ingredients should be cold. When the oil is added to the egg and mustard, should it curdle, then take another yolk, and to it add the mixture and beat until smooth.

MAYONNAISE WITHOUT OIL

>Butter, 1 tablespoon,
>Vinegar, 3 tablespoons,
>Eggs, 2,
>Dry mustard, ½ teaspoon,
>Salt and pepper.

Put all the ingredients in a granite saucepan, salt and pepper to taste, place the saucepan over a kettle of boiling water, and stir till it begins to thicken, but not boil. Then when cool put it in the ice-box, and when needed pour it over the salad.

GREEN MAYONNAISE

Green mayonnaise is prepared in the following manner: First make a mayonnaise in the usual way, then at the last, add 2 or 3 tablespoons of finely chopped parsley, which has been cut to almost a powder.

BOILED DRESSING, NO. 1

>Eggs, 3,
>Vinegar, ½ cup,
>Butter, 3 teaspoons,
>Salt, ½ teaspoon,
>Warm water, ½ cup,
>Cayenne, a dash.

Beat together the eggs, warm water, and vinegar, and stir over the fire in a double boiler until it begins to thicken—cook slowly or the mixture will curdle.

Take from the fire, add the butter, and stew again till blended, then put in the salt and cayenne. This will keep for some time, and is improved by adding a little whipped cream, later, when just about to be used.

BOILED DRESSING, NO. 2

>Eggs, 2,
>Vinegar, ½ cup,
>Butter, 1 tablespoon,
>Milk, ½ pint,
>Salt, ½ teaspoon,
>Made mustard, 1 teaspoon.

Melt the butter, add the eggs well beaten, then add the milk and the vinegar. Pour into a double boiler, and place over the fire and let it boil slowly, constantly stirring until it thickens to the consistency of a custard. Take it from the fire, as soon as possible after this, for it is apt to curdle.

This may be kept in a cool place for a fortnight.

CREAM DRESSING

>Sour cream, 1 cup,
>Vinegar, 2 tablespoons,
>Salt, ½ teaspoon,
>Cayenne, a dash.

Beat the cream until it thickens, then add the vinegar, salt, and pepper. Lemon-juice may be used instead of the vinegar.

JAPANESE SALAD DRESSING

Eggs (yolks only), 2,
Lemon-juice, 1 teaspoon,
Salt, a pinch,
Oil, and paprika,
Whipped cream.

Beat together the egg and oil, seasoning with salt and paprika to taste, till thick, and thinning with the whipped cream and lemon-juice.

MEAT SALADS

CHICKEN SALAD

Cold chicken, 1 quart,
Celery, 1 pint,
Lettuce leaves,
Mayonnaise.

Cut the chicken in ½-inch dice, and to each quart of the cut meat allow a pint of celery cut in ½-inch pieces. Mix in a bowl with mayonnaise, and garnish with lettuce leaves and celery tips. Cover the top with mayonnaise. This receipt may also be adapted for cold veal or cold pork.

Cucumbers may also be used to garnish.

LAMB SALAD

Take equal parts of cold chopped lamb and celery, covered with mayonnaise and garnished with mint-jelly and capers.

SWEETBREAD SALAD

Take equal parts of sweetbread and cucumber (cut in dice), arrange on individual plates on leaves of lettuce, and cover with mayonnaise and garnish with asparagus tips.

DUCK AND ORANGE SALAD

Cut cold roast duck in dice, arrange on lettuce leaves, with thin slices of orange. Use French dressing.

TONGUE SALAD

>Tongue, cold boiled, 1 pound,
>Chopped olives, 1 dozen,
>Lettuce, 1 head,
>Cold string beans, sliced, 1 cup,
>Tomato, chopped, 1,
>Mayonnaise, 1 small cup.

Cut the tongue in dice, chop the olives fine, shred the lettuce leaves, slice the string beans, and chop the tomato, then mix the ingredients lightly together, and blend all together with 1 small cup of mayonnaise.

FISH SALAD

SPANISH

>Cut celery, 1 quart,
>Flaked fish, boiled, 1 pint,
>Tomato, cut small, 1,
>Chopped onion, 1 tablespoon,
>Chopped green pepper, 1 tablespoon.

Mix with mayonnaise, and serve on lettuce leaves.

OYSTER SALAD

>Oysters,
>Vinegar,
>Cloves and allspice,

Salt and pepper,
Lettuce leaves and cut celery.

The oysters should be cooked in their own liquid, till they ruffle. Take them from the fire, and lay them in vinegar, in which has been mixed, salt, cloves (whole), and allspice.

When cold, put them on lettuce leaves (four oysters to each), and allowing 2 tablespoons of cut celery to each 4 oysters.

Cover the whole with mayonnaise.

SHAD-ROE SALAD

Shad-roe, 1,
Onion, cut fine, 1,
Salt and bay leaves,
Cucumber,
Mayonnaise.

Boil the roe for 20 minutes, wrapped in a cloth, and in the water put 1 onion, chopped fine, 6 bay leaves, and a tablespoon of salt.

Serve on a platter, with a border of cucumber, and with mayonnaise sauce.

LOBSTER SALAD WITH CREAM DRESSING

Lobster, 1 large, or 2 small,
Salad oil, 1 cup,
Cream, ½ cup (whipped very light),
Lemon (juice only), 1,
Eggs (yolks only), 2,
Vinegar, 4 tablespoons,
Powdered sugar, 1 tablespoon,
Mustard (wet with vinegar), 1 teaspoon,

Salt, 1 teaspoon,
Lettuce leaves.

Beat the eggs till light, adding to them while beating, the sugar, salt, mustard, and pepper, and then very gradually, the oil. When the mixture is quite thick, whip in the lemon-juice, and beat about 5 minutes more before putting in the vinegar.

Just before the salad goes to the table, add half of the whipped cream to this dressing, and stir in well the cut lobster-meat.

Line the salad bowl with lettuce leaves, and put in the seasoned meat, and cover all with the remainder of the whipped cream.

HERRING SALAD, NO. 1

GERMAN

Cold tongue, or ham, ½ pound,
Cold veal, or beef, ½ pound,
Herrings (small), 3,
Green apples (chopped), ½ cup,
Cold boiled potatoes, 3,
Onion, 1,
French dressing.

For the garnishing

Red beets (chopped), 2,
Hard-boiled eggs (yolks and whites cut separately), 3,
Parsley, chopped, 3 tablespoons,
Cucumber pickles, cut fine, ½ cup,
Olives, 12,
Lettuce leaves.

Soak the herrings overnight, and when about to make the salad, pick the fish in small flakes, removing all bones. Also chop the meats coarsely and the onion, potatoes, and apples, and place all in a salad-bowl and mix well. Moisten plentifully with French dressing, and garnish as follows:

In the center of the bowl of salad place an olive; and from that, trace radiating lines, forming as many sectors as you have colors for garnishing; then cover these sectors over with the garnishing materials; one sector covered with red beets, the next with chopped yolks, the next with chopped whites of egg, the next with chopped parsley, etc.

Place 1 or 2 of the whole olives in each sector; put lettuce leaves about the edge of the bowl, and it is ready for serving.

HERRING SALAD, NO. 2

GERMAN

Boiled beets, 2 quarts,
Milker herring, 8,
Large boiled potatoes, 8,
Boiled or roasted veal, 3 pounds,
Salad oil, 3 tablespoons,
Vinegar, 5 tablespoons,
Pepper.

A few days before making the salad, boil 2 quarts of beets, and when soft, slice them and put them into vinegar seasoned plentifully with sugar.

The potatoes should be boiled with their skins on, and without scraping; if they are scraped before boiling their flavor is lost.

Wash the herring thoroughly in cold water, and remove the milker and bones. Then cut the herring, beets, veal, and potatoes in $\frac{1}{4}$-inch cubes.

Dressing

Cut the milker in pieces and strain through a sieve, thereby dispensing with the skin. Then add the 3 tablespoons of fine salad-oil, the 5 tablespoons of vinegar, and a pinch of pepper.

If you find as you proceed that the salad after finishing will be too dry, add some of the vinegar of the beets, and some white wine, which will greatly improve the flavor.

Season according to taste.

TOMATO AND CRAB SALAD

Tomatoes, 6,
Boiled crabs, 6,
Mayonnaise,
Lettuce,
Seasoning.

Skin the tomatoes carefully and remove the centers. Fill the hollowed tomatoes with the chopped and seasoned meat of the crabs.

Set the stuffed tomatoes on the ice for several hours. Lay them on crisp lettuce leaves for serving and pour a spoonful of mayonnaise dressing upon each tomato.

In the same manner tomatoes may be filled with shrimps, chopped celery, cucumbers, potatoes, etc., covered with mayonnaise, and served on lettuce leaves.

SALMON ASPIC

Cooked salmon,
Aspic jelly,
Mayonnaise,
Mixed vegetables (chopped).

Line a china mold with the aspic jelly, and when the jelly is firm, cover it with flakes of the salmon, dipping each flake separately into cold liquid aspic, to make it adhere. Have ready cooked mixed vegetables, cut these in small pieces, and dress them with mayonnaise.

Fill up the mold with these pieces, and cover over the cut vegetables with more aspic jelly.

VEGETABLE SALADS

Vegetable salads are delicious when one needs something piquante, to encourage the appetite. These salads may be made of tomato, celery, green peas, dandelion, cauliflower, potato, cucumber, asparagus, and cabbage, besides the ever popular lettuce.

Cold potatoes cut in dice, and laid on a bed of lettuce may be covered with cream dressing.

Dandelion salad is made of the young leaves of the plant thoroughly washed, soaked in cold water for an hour, shaken dry, and saturated with French dressing.

Lettuce should be put in cold water to make it crisp, and shaken dry in a napkin, before being dressed.

Green beans are cooked, cut in 2-inch pieces, laid on a bed of lettuce, and covered with French dressing and chopped onion.

Asparagus is boiled, the tough part removed, the remainder cut in short lengths, and covered with mayonnaise.

Cauliflower is separated into sprigs, the tender part of the stalk cut fine, and covered with mayonnaise. It must not be boiled too long, or it becomes dark.

Cabbage is eaten raw, shredded fine, soaked in French dressing, and covered with boiled dressing.

Cucumbers are thinly sliced, soaked in ice-water, and then in French dressing.

Tomatoes are scalded to remove the skin, when cold are cut in slices, and served with a spoonful of mayonnaise, or boiled dressing on each slice.

GERMAN POTATO SALAD

>Potatoes, 6,
>Onions, 1,
>Bacon, 2 slices,
>Vinegar, 3 tablespoons,
>Salt and pepper.

Boil the potatoes with the skins on. Peel them while hot, and slice thin. Add to them the onion, finely cut.

Cut the bacon into squares, and fry it until nicely browned, and then mix it with the potatoes.

Place the vinegar in a frying-pan, heat to the boiling point, and then pour it over the potatoes and bacon.

Season to taste with salt and pepper, mix all thoroughly, and place in a warm oven for 10 minutes, to blend the flavors.

ALLIGATOR PEAR SALAD
HAWAIIAN

>An alligator pear,
>Lettuce leaves,
>Small red tomatoes,
>Small white onions,
>Mayonnaise.

Peel the tomatoes. Peel the alligator pear, cut it around in rings, and slip these from the seed. Lay each ring on lettuce leaves. Put a spoonful of mayonnaise on top of each tomato, and on the top of all, the small onion.

CHESTNUT SALAD, NO. 1

>Chestnuts,
>Lettuce leaves,
>French dressing.

Boil and blanch the chestnuts, cook until tender, in boiling water; take them out, throw into cold water, drain, and dry on a soft cloth.

Arrange on lettuce leaves, and pour over them a French dressing.

CHESTNUT SALAD, NO. 2

Prepare the chestnuts as before, cut each one in two, and cover them with the grated rind of an orange. Arrange on lettuce leaves, garnish with small pieces of orange, and serve with mayonnaise.

BEAN SALAD

GERMAN

Beans,
Chopped onion,
French dressing.

Chop string beans into inch pieces, chop the onion, and cover plentifully with French dressing.

BAHIA SALAD

BRAZILIAN

Watercress, 1 quart,
Stuffed olives, 20,
Onion, 1, small,
French dressing.

Cut the onion fine, mix with the cress and olives, and use French dressing.

POMPADOUR SALAD

This is composed of a whole head of cauliflower, boiled, and is served with a border of tomatoes and a mayonnaise dressing.

PEPPER SALAD

CUBAN

Sliced boiled potatoes,
Shredded red cabbage,
Shredded green peppers,
Cold corned beef,
Hard-boiled eggs,
Mayonnaise,
Lettuce leaves.

Take equal parts of the potatoes, cabbage, and green peppers. To a quart of this add 1 cup of corned beef, cut in pencil strips. Mix with mayonnaise, and serve on lettuce leaves, with a garnish of hard-boiled eggs.

RADISH SALAD

Red radishes,
Cucumbers,
French dressing,
Lettuce leaves.

This is a good summer salad. The red radishes, which are strong in taste, should be cut in thin slices, with a fluted vegetable cutter. Cut an equal number of thin slices of cucumber. Soak them separately in ice-water for half an hour, then drain and dry on a soft cloth.

Arrange in overlapping slices on a bed of lettuce leaves, and sprinkle with a French dressing.

SPANISH SALAD

Bananas,
English walnuts,

Lettuce leaves,
Mayonnaise.

The bananas should be ripe, but not soft. Cut them into thin slices, using a silver knife. Shell the walnuts, of which use one-third the quantity of the sliced bananas. Chop the nuts, mix the fruit and nuts lightly, and heap them on a platter that has been covered with lettuce leaves. The leaves should be crisp.

Pour mayonnaise dressing over the whole, taking care that the mayonnaise has been seasoned quite sharply with cayenne.

TOMATO JELLY

Tomatoes, 1 can,
Onion, 1 slice,
Bird peppers, 1, small,
Tarragon vinegar, 1 tablespoon,
Gelatin, 1 tablespoon.

Boil the tomatoes and strain. Return to the fire, and add the onion, vinegar, pepper, and gelatin. When the gelatin is dissolved take from the fire, and when cool, pour into a ring mold, and let it get perfectly cold.

When served, the ring may be filled with almost any kind of salad, such as chopped celery, cucumber, potatoes, cabbage, etc.

TOMATO-JELLY AND CUCUMBER

Ripe tomatoes, 1½ pounds,
Gelatin, 1 tablespoon,
Onion, a slice,
Tarragon vinegar, 1 teaspoon,
Peppercorns, 2,
Salt, pepper, sliced cucumber.

Make a tomato-jelly by stewing the tomatoes till soft enough to pass through a sieve; strain off the seeds and skins. Put the tomato pulp over the fire, add a clove, onion slice, the peppercorns, vinegar and a pinch of salt. Melt the gelatin and add it also, and stir the mixture till the gelatin is entirely dissolved.

Pour into the ring mold; when ready dip the mold into quite hot water for a moment, so as to loosen the jelly within.

Fill the center of the mold with sliced cucumber, prepared with vinegar, pepper, and salt in the usual manner.

RAW TOMATOES AND CUCUMBERS

Cut off the tops of large firm tomatoes; carefully remove most of the pulp, and keep the pulp and tomatoes in the refrigerator, while you peel and cut into small dice, ice-cold cucumbers.

Mix the cucumber dice with the tomato pulp, fill the shells, set them on crisp lettuce leaves, and pour a large spoonful of mayonnaise dressing over each.

TOMATO FRAPPÉ
HAWAIIAN

Tomato jelly (without gelatin), 1 quart.
Cream, 1 pint,
Lettuce leaves,
Mayonnaise.

Make a quart of tomato jelly, omitting the gelatin. Whip the cream stiffly, beat them together, and place in a freezer and let it freeze.

Cut slices of this and place on lettuce leaves; and on top put a spoonful of mayonnaise.

TOMATO AND CELERY SALAD

Tomatoes, ½ can,
Cloves, 3,
Gelatin, ¼ box,
Salt, 1 teaspoon,
Paprika, 1 salt-spoon,
Bay leaf, ½,
Celery, finely cut,
Lettuce leaves,
English walnuts
Mayonnaise.

Place in a stewpan the tomatoes, cloves, salt, paprika, and a half of a bay leaf, and cook for 15 minutes. Add then one-fourth of a box of gelatin, which has been softened in a half-cup of cold water, and stir till the gelatin is dissolved, then strain into a border mold.

When firm, turn it out on a bed of lettuce leaves, and fill the center with finely cut celery, and broken English-walnut meats, moistened with mayonnaise, or with a boiled dressing.

TOMATO ASPIC

Tomatoes, about 12,
Onion-juice, 1 teaspoon,
Sugar, 1 teaspoon,
Gelatin, ¼ package,
Whole cloves, 2,
Bay leaf, 1.

Stew the tomatoes till soft, then strain through a bag, without squeezing. There should be about 1 pint of the juice. Put the juice over the fire, add the strained onion-juice, a bay leaf, and 2 whole cloves.

Bring to a boil, and skim, and strain again. Boil up a third time, and stir into the liquid, while it is still on the fire, the half-package of gelatin, which has been soaking for an hour in a cupful of cold water.

Wet a mold, and pour in the aspic. Set it away to form. It is useful to serve with lettuce as a dressing, or alone with a mayonnaise, or as a garnish with cold chicken, lamb, etc.

If formed in small cups, or plate-molds, it is a pretty accompaniment to lettuce, and is as palatable as it is pretty.

ASPIC JELLY

Clear consommé, 2 quarts,
Tarragon vinegar, 1 tablespoon (lemon-juice may be used),
Gelatin, 1 tablespoon,
Sherry, 2 tablespoons.

Dissolve the gelatin in half a cup of cold water. Boil the consommé and vinegar, till reduced to 1 quart; add the sherry and the gelatin, strain, and put into shallow molds to cool.

Cut into small pieces, cubes, diamonds, etc., to be used for garnishing.

QUEEN'S ASPIC

Aspic jelly, ¾ pint,
Tomato catsup, 3 tablespoons,
Mayonnaise, ¼ pint,
Sliced fresh tomatoes,
Sliced cucumbers,
Cold boiled potatoes,
Vinegar and oil.

Put the aspic jelly into a basin and add the tomato catsup. Add also a quarter of a pint of stiff mayonnaise, and allow this mixture to set in a round mold, to cool.

Slice an equal quantity of cucumbers and tomatoes, and half that quantity of potatoes, and dress these with oil and vinegar, and arrange around the cold aspic.

FRUIT SALADS

A fruit salad, is as the name implies, a mixture of several kinds of fruit. Grape-fruit, orange, pineapple, grapes, or cherries make the best mixtures.

The dressing for such a salad should be made of sugar, lemon-juice, sherry, or Madeira wine. Sometimes a little grated cocoanut is an improvement.

Fruit salads should be prepared several hours before required, and should be served cold. If vegetables, such as celery, or olives, are added to the fruit, the salad may require a French dressing.

WHITE GRAPES SALAD

> White grapes,
> Eggs, 2,
> Catawba wine, 2 cups,
> Salt, 1 teaspoon,
> Mustard, ⅛ teaspoon,
> Lettuce.

Remove the stems and seeds from the grapes, halve them, then chill them thoroughly. Beat the eggs very lightly, and add slowly to them the Catawba wine, stirring constantly in a double boiler, until thick. Remove the catawba and egg mixture from the fire, and add to it the salt and mustard, and set it aside where it will get very cold.

Serve the grapes on lettuce leaves, with a little of the dressing added at the last moment.

GRAPE-FRUIT AND CHESTNUT SALAD

>Grape-fruit,
>Celery,
>French chestnuts,
>Mayonnaise,
>Tarragon vinegar.

Mix equal bulks of grape-fruit, celery, and boiled French chestnuts which have been boiled in salted water 20 minutes, and blanched.

Serve with mayonnaise dressing flavored with tarragon vinegar.

APPLE, CRESS, AND CELERY SALAD

>Celery,
>Watercress,
>Apple,
>French dressing.

Arrange on individual service plates, a bed of shredded celery and cress. In the center stand a tart tender apple, which has been pared, sliced and cored with a slender knife, so as to retain its original shape.

Tuck a bit of the cress in the top of the apple, and pour over all a French dressing.

Do not pare the apple till almost ready to serve, as it will discolor with waiting.

APPLE AND BANANA SALAD

>Large sour apples, 2,
>Bananas, 2,
>Pineapple, 1 slice,
>Cherries, canned, or fresh, 1 cup,

Blanched almonds, 1 cup,
Cream salad dressing,
Lettuce leaves.

Peel and cut the applies into dice, also slice the bananas, and add the slice of pineapple cut in bits, the canned or fresh cherries, and the almonds chopped. Moisten all with a cream salad dressing, and serve on lettuce leaves.

CELERY AND PINEAPPLE SALAD, NO. 1

Celery,
Pineapple,
Olives and nuts,
Lettuce and mayonnaise.

Cut the celery in small pieces, shred the pineapple in bits, with a fork, allow equal parts of both.

Garnish with olives and nuts, and serve on lettuce leaves, with mayonnaise.

CELERY AND PINEAPPLE SALAD, NO. 2

Chopped celery, 1 cup,
Pineapple, 1,
Red pepper, cut in dice, 1,
Chopped nut-meats,
French dressing,
Mayonnaise,
Lettuce leaves.

This is a very good salad to serve with game. Cut the celery in fine pieces, shred the pineapple with a silver fork, and let both the celery and pineapple get thoroughly chilled.

Allow 1 pineapple to each cup of chopped celery; add 1 red pepper which cut in small dice.

Sprinkle first with French dressing, garnish with grated nut-meats, and finally serve with mayonnaise, on lettuce leaves.

CHERRY SALAD

> Large cherries,
> Chopped nut-meats,
> Cherry-juice and lemon-juice,
> Wine and sugar,
> White lettuce leaves.

Remove the stones of the cherries and fill the cavities with chopped nut-meats. Lay the cherries on white lettuce leaves, and put over it a dressing made of the cherry-juice, lemon-juice, a little wine and sugar.

FLOWER SALADS

These salads, which are said to be of Japanese origin, make very attractive dishes representing different flowers. They are rather difficult to make, and should always, after being prepared, be placed in the refrigerator until wanted for serving, as they are liable to wilt.

CHRYSANTHEMUM SALAD

This is made with a bed of lettuce leaves and a hard-boiled egg to represent the center of the flower. Peel the egg under water, and then cut through the white, lengthwise, in strips, leaving a little uncut at the top and bottom to hold the strips together. Then wrap in a warm damp cloth till required.

Lay small lettuce leaves in a plate, tips outward, so as to represent curled leaves; then take the egg, still covered with the damp cloth, and press it gently together, endwise, causing the strips to open, exposing the yellow. Put the egg in the center of the bed of lettuce, and serve with a French dressing.

LILY SALAD

This requires cold boiled beets, egg and lettuce leaves. For each individual salad make a cornucopia of three or four sizes of lettuce leaves, the largest leaf being outside. Tie these in a roll, at both ends, and let them remain in a cool place for some hours, to set.

Boil an egg hard, and when cold slice it into several rings. Remove all the yellow, and chop it fine, and season it with salt and pepper.

When about to serve, remove the strings, putting one of the rings of egg around the base of each cornucopia, to hold it in shape.

Put some of the chopped beets and chopped yellow of egg into the cornucopia, and serve with a French dressing.

POPPY SALAD

Use red beets, lettuce and hard-boiled eggs. The beets should be boiled, cooled in water, skinned and dried. Then cut from stem upward, forming petals. Gouge out the inner part, leaving half an inch at the bottom, and around the inner sides. Fill the space with yellow and white of egg. seasoned and chopped. Put in the center of a plate, and garnish with white lettuce. Serve with French dressing, or with mayonnaise.

ROSE SALAD

Use white lettuce leaves, celery, and red tomatoes. Wash and dry the lettuce, cut the celery into small lengths, shave these lengthwise, and place in cold water to curl the shavings.

Scald the tomatoes for a few moments, then cool, but do not remove the skins. From the stem side of each, remove a square plug, taking care to leave 1-8-inch or 1-16-inch below the portion removed. Then, commencing at the edges of the square, cut through the skin of the tomato, in rose-shaped leaves, and roll them backward.

Fill the square with a Japanese salad dressing, or with mayonnaise. Place in the center of a plate on a bed of lettuce leaves, and around it, put a circle of the curled celery.

Chop blanched pecans, or almonds, and sprinkle a teaspoon of this like pollen, over the top of the tomato.

TULIP SALAD

Use egg and white cabbage. This, like the chrysanthemum, has a hard-boiled egg to represent the center of each flower.

The eggs, hard-boiled, should be put into cold water until required, to keep them moist. Shave the cabbage into fine threads.

Thrust a long needle through the center of each egg, and draw a coarse thread through, passing it completely around the egg, as a girdle. Then from the top, downward, cut through the white, making four leaves, ending at the thread. Curve these slightly outward, leaving the yolk partly exposed, then withdraw the thread.

Season with salt and pepper, and put in the center of a salad plate, on a bed of the shaved cabbage, and serve with a French dressing, or with mayonnaise.

PICKLES AND RELISHES

GRANDMOTHER HOLT'S CUCUMBER PICKLES

>Small cucumbers, 500,
>Vinegar, 1 gallon,
>White mustard seed (whole), ¼ pound,
>Whole cloves, 1 ounce,
>Whole allspice, 1 ounce,
>Bird peppers, 6,
>Garlic buds, 6,
>Mixed pickle spices, ¼ pound.

Let the cucumbers remain in strong salt and water for 24 hours, then wipe and pack them in jars. Heat the vinegar and spices to the boiling-point, and pour it over the pickles, being careful to see that the jars are filled to overflowing, and that there is in each jar, 1 red pepper, and some garlic.

CUCUMBER CATSUP, NO. 1

>Ripe, yellow cucumbers, 4,
>Small white onions, 24,
>Red peppers, 3,
>Whole cloves, 1 ounce,
>Whole allspice, 1 ounce,
>Vinegar.

Chop the cucumbers, onions, and peppers, and let them stand overnight. Drain, put in jars, and cover with the vinegar and spices while still hot.

CUCUMBER CATSUP, NO. 2

Green cucumbers, chopped, 2 quarts,
Cabbage, chopped, 2 quarts,
Small onions, 12,
Green tomatoes, 1 quart,
Green beans, 1 quart,
Green peppers, 12,
Vinegar, 1 gallon,
Grated horseradish, 2 tablespoons,
Turmeric, 3 tablespoons,
Ground cinnamon, 1 tablespoon,
Ground mace, 1 tablespoon,
Cayenne, 1 tablespoon,
Celery seed, 1 tablespoon,
Olive oil, 3 tablespoons,
White mustard seed, 1 cup,
Sugar, 1 cup.

Chop the cucumbers, onions, peppers, cabbage, and beans, all together, and sprinkle with salt and let it stand for 6 hours.

Drain, and put into jars and cover with the spices and vinegar, which should be made very hot.

PEPPER CATSUP

Red peppers, 24,
Onions, 6,
Horseradish roots, 2,
Whole mustard seed, 2 tablespoons,
Salt, 2 tablespoons,
Brown sugar, 1 cup,
Vinegar, 3 pints,
Water, 1 pint.

Chop the peppers and onions, grate the horseradish, add the spices, sugar, and vinegar, also a pint of water, and let it boil for 1 hour.

GREEN TOMATO AND ONION PICKLE

>Green tomatoes, 1 peck,
>Onions, 24, large,
>Salt, ½ pint,
>White mustard seed, ½ pound,
>Ground black pepper, ¼ pound,
>Ground cloves, 1 ounce,
>Ground cinnamon, 1 ounce,
>Mace, 1 ounce,
>Mustard, ½ pound,
>Strong vinegar,
>Grated nutmeg, ¼.

Cut the tomatoes and onions into thin slices, and strew the salt among them and let them stand for 24 hours. Drain off the water that has formed, and then place in the kettle, a layer of onions, then a layer of tomatoes, then a layer of the spices that have been mixed together. Cover all with strong vinegar, and simmer over a slow fire for 3 hours.

TOMATO PICKLE

>Tomatoes, 1 peck,
>Onions, ½ peck,
>Cabbage, 1 large head,
>Peppers, chopped fine, 12,
>Sugar, 1 cup,
>Salt, 1 cup,
>Ground allspice, 1 tablespoon,
>Ground cloves, 1 tablespoon,

Ground mustard seed, 1 tablespoon,
Celery seed, 1 ounce,
Turmeric, 1 ounce.

Chop all the vegetables together, sprinkle well with salt, and let them remain overnight. Drain, and then place in the kettle; cover all with vinegar, and boil for 1 hour or more.

CHILLI SAUCE, NO. 1

Tomatoes, large, ripe and peeled, 12,
Onions, large, 2,
Green peppers, large, 4,
Salt, 1 tablespoon,
Sugar, 1 tablespoon,
Vinegar, 2 cups.

Chop the tomatoes, onions, and peppers fine, and place all on the stove to simmer for about 4 hours.

CHILLI SAUCE, NO. 2

Ripe tomatoes, 24,
White onions, 4,
Green peppers, 4,
Sugar, 1 teacup,
Salt, 4 tablespoons,
Ground cinnamon, 1 tablespoon,
Ground cloves, ½ tablespoon,
Allspice, ground, ½ tablespoon,
Vinegar, 2 pints.

Peel the tomatoes and onions, chop fine the vegetables, add the spices, salt and sugar, place in a kettle, pour over the vinegar, and let boil slowly for 3 or 4 hours.

MUSTARD PICKLE

Cucumbers, sliced, 1 quart,
Green tomatoes, sliced, 1 quart,
Small onions, 1 quart,
Cauliflower, large, 1,
Green peppers, chopped fine, 4,
Salt, 1 pint,
Flour, 1 cup,
Ground mustard, 6 tablespoons,
Turmeric, 1 tablespoon,
Vinegar, 2 quarts,
Sugar, 1 cup.

Slice the tomatoes and cucumbers, divide the cauliflower into flowerets, and chop the peppers fine. Leave the small onions whole.

Make the brine of 4 quarts of water and 1 pint of salt, and pour it over the vegetables mixed, and let it soak for 24 hours.

Heat it just enough to scald, and turn all into a colander to drain.

Mix the flour, mustard, and turmeric with enough cold vinegar to make a smooth paste, add to it the cup of sugar, and enough more vinegar to make 2 quarts in all.

Boil the mixture till it thickens and is smooth, then add the vegetables, and cook till heated well all through.

RED PICCALILLI

Tomatoes, 1 peck,
Salt, 1 cup,
Onions, chopped fine, 10,
Red peppers, large and chopped fine, 6,

Chilli peppers, chopped, 6 or 7,
Grated horseradish, 1 cup,
Whole allspice, 2 tablespoons,
Cinnamon (whole), 2 sticks,
Whole cloves, 1 tablespoon,
Sugar, 1½ cups,
Vinegar.

Scald and peel the tomatoes, sprinkle over them the salt, let drain overnight in a steamer, or colander; in the morning chop them fine. Put all spices in a lace bag, mix all ingredients together, in a kettle and cover with vinegar. Cook slowly uncovered for about 2 hours. Put in Mason fruit-jars, quart or pint. It is not necessary to be so particular in sealing as in case of fruit.

CHUTNEY

Apples, chopped, 2 quarts,
Tomatoes, chopped, 3 quarts,
Onions, chopped, 1 quart,
Green peppers, chopped, 1 quart,
Raisins, chopped, 1 pound,
Ground allspice, 2 tablespoons,
Ground white mustard seed, 2 tablespoons,
Ground cloves, 1 tablespoon,
Ground cinnamon, 1 tablespoon,
Turmeric, 1 tablespoon,
Brown sugar, 2 cups,
Vinegar, 2 quarts,
Salt, 2 tablespoons.

Mix all well together, the chopped vegetables, and the ground spices, sugar and vinegar, the salt being mixed with the ground spices. Place in a kettle, and boil for about 2 hours.

PICKLED RED CABBAGE

>Red cabbage, 1 large head,
>Vinegar, 2 quarts,
>Salt, 2 tablespoons,
>Whole black peppers, 1 tablespoon,
>Mace, 2 blades,
>Cinnamon, 2 sticks,
>Whole cloves, 1 tablespoon.

The head of the cabbage should be of good size and firm. After removing any straggling leaves, cut it in quarters, and then slice thin. Sprinkle well with salt, and set it aside for 48 hours.

Drain off the liquor which has formed, and pour over the cabbage a pickle of hot vinegar, in which the spices, etc., as given above have been spoiled.

Let it all boil for about 1 hour, slowly. Place in jars and cover; and let it stand until the cabbage is cold, then fasten tightly.

Cauliflower may be pickled in the same manner.

SWEET PICKLED PEACHES

>Peaches, 7 pounds,
>Sugar, 4 pounds,
>Vinegar, 1 quart,
>Whole cloves, 1 tablespoon,
>Whole allspice, 1 tablespoon.

Peel the fruit, and boil with the other ingredients until soft, but not broken. Then put in fruit jars.

Pears may be prepared in the same manner.

SWEET PICKLED WATERMELON RIND

>Watermelon (medium size), 1,
>Vinegar, 1 quart,
>Brown sugar, 3 pounds,
>Alum, 1 ounce,
>Stick cinnamon, 1 ounce,
>Whole cloves, ½ ounce.

Only the rind of the watermelon will be used. Pare it, and cut the rind into thick slices. Boil the alum in a gallon of water, and pour it over the sliced rind, letting it stand on the back of the stove for half a day. Remove it from the alum water, and let it lie in cold water until cold, then drain it.

Have ready the vinegar, sugar, and spices, and boil the sugar and vinegar together, and strain; then add the spices and the rind to the vinegar and sugar, and boil all together, until the rind is soft.

For peaches and pears, use the same proportion of sugar and vinegar, but not quite so much spice as is used for the watermelon rind.

SWEET PICKLED PINEAPPLE

HAWAIIAN

>Pineapple, 14 pounds,
>Brown sugar, 7 pounds,
>Vinegar, 7 pints,
>Whole cloves, 1 tablespoon,
>Peppercorns, 1 tablespoon,
>Stick cinnamon (broken into small bits), 1 tablespoon.

Cut the pineapple into slices or small pieces. Boil together the sugar, vinegar, and spices for 10 minutes, and then add the fruit.

Let all boil together until the fruit is tender, then remove fhe fruit, and place it in jars, or in an earthenware vessel.

Let the syrup continue to boil and thicken for 10 minutes longer, then pour it over the fruit.

SPICED GRAPES

Grapes, 7 pounds,
Sugar, 4 pounds,
Vinegar, 1 quart,
Ground cloves, 1 tablespoon,
Ground cinnamon, 2 tablespoons.

Slip the pulp from the skins, and save the skins. Boil the pulp until soft, and then pass it through a sieve.

Boil the sugar and vinegar together, and then add the pulp, the skins and the spices, and boil all together for 2½ hours.

VENISON JELLY

Grapes, 1 peck,
Vinegar, 1 quart,
Whole cloves, 1 ounce,
Cinnamon (stick), ¼ ounce,
Sugar, 6 pounds.

Boil the vinegar, grapes, and spices together until the grapes are soft. Drain off the juice and boil it for 20 or 30 minutes longer. Add the sugar (which has already been heated) to the juice, and boil for 5 minutes, or until jellied, which in some cases takes as much as half an hour.

TOMATO PRESERVES

Ripe, firm tomatoes, 5 pounds
Sugar, 4 pounds,

Lemons, sliced thin, 2,
Candied ginger, 1½ ounces.

The candied ginger should be cut fine, and the lemons sliced very thin. Mix, and cook for from 2½ to 3½ hours; until quite thick.

Cook very slowly.

CURRANT BAR-LE-DUC

Large currants, or gooseberries, 1 pound,
Currant, or gooseberry juice, 1 pint,
Sugar, 3 pounds.

Select a pound of the largest and finest berries, and stem them without breaking. From the other ordinary berries make 1 pint of juice, first warming, then bruising and then squeezing out the juice.

Put half a cup of this juice in the preserving kettle and add to it the sugar, and bring slowly to a boil. Skim carefully.

After boiling 5 minutes, drop the large berries that have been retained, carefully into the syrup, and let them simmer for 5 minutes. Take them from the syrup without breaking, and then boil the syrup for 5 minutes, or still longer if it is not very thick, as currants are some times less juicy than at others.

When the syrup is thick, skim well, and strain through a hot cloth, over the fruit. Put it in jelly glasses, and when cold, cover with hot paraffin, and paste paper over all. Keep in a dark place.

GINGER PEAR

Candied ginger-root, 1½ pounds,
Pears, 8 pounds,

Granulated sugar, 8 pounds,
Lemons, 4.

Pare the fruit and cut and slice into small pieces. Slice the ginger, and place the pear, ginger, and sugar on the fire, and boil slowly for 1 hour. Do not put water with it unless the pears are very dry.

While this is boiling put on the lemons, in cold water and boil until very tender; then cut them up, taking out the seeds, and cut them fine. After the pears have boiled an hour add them to the lemons, and boil together for another full hour.

Put in jelly tumblers.

RHUBARB MARMALADE

Rhubarb, 7 pounds,
Sugar, 7 pounds,
Figs, 2 pounds,
Ginger-root, 1 large piece.

Cut the rhubarb in ¾-inch lengths, and pour on it the sugar, and then let it stand overnight.

In the morning add the cut-up figs, and boil.

DUNDEE SCOTCH MARMALADE

Oranges, large, 14,
Granulated sugar, 4 pounds,
Lemon, the juice of 2.

Wash and peel seven of the oranges, selecting the largest, taking care not to use any pithy membrane. Put the peelings into a deep kettle, with 2½ quarts of cold water, let stand 36 hours, changing the water 2 or 3 times. The second morning put the soaked peelings with their last water over the fire.

Peel the other seven oranges, discarding the peelings, and slice all the fourteen peeled oranges, and add to them 4 pounds of granulated sugar, and the juice of 2 lemons.

Turn this into the kettle together with the soaked peelings, and simmer for 2 hours, or until clear and thick, stirring often to prevent scorching; and when partly cooled, pour into glass jars, but do not seal until cold.

Lemon marmalade, and grape-fruit marmalade may be prepared in the same manner.

CALIFORNIA ORANGE MARMALADE

Oranges, 12.
Lemons, 5.
Sugar.

Slice the oranges and lemons very thin, and cover with 8 quarts of cold water. Let it stand for 24 hours.

Cook for 1 hour after the boiling-point has been reached, stirring constantly, and then put away for another 24 hours. Measure 1 cupful of sugar to each cupful of the orange mixture, and then cook for another hour.

Put into jelly glasses, or pint jars. This receipt makes 2 dozen glasses.

BAKED QUINCES

Peel and core the fruit, and put into a deep earthen dish, and fill the cavities with sugar and a little grated lemon-rind. Add water in abundance, for the quince is a dry fruit. Cover closely, and bake in a moderate oven until tender and a fine red. This will take several hours.

Serve cold, with whipped cream.

BAKED PEARS

Peel and cut the pears in halves, and pack as tightly as possible in an earthenware jar or casserole, with as much sugar as will be needed to sweeten them to desired taste, add half a teacup of water for each pound of pears, a few cloves, 2 or 3 bits of thinly peeled lemon-rind, and a little cochineal.

Cover the dish carefully, and bake in a cool oven for at least 6 hours. Serve with whipped cream.

SALTED ALMONDS

Almonds, shelled and blanched, 1 pound,
Olive oil, 3 tablespoons,
Salt.

Put the oil in a pan and let it get hot, then put in the nuts, sprinkled generously with salt. Toss them about lightly, until they are all a light brown.

Take them from the pan, and place on paper, sprinkle again with salt, and put them in a warm (not hot) oven, for a few minutes to dry off.

Take from the oven, wipe them with a dry cloth, and they are then ready for use.

Almonds prepared in this way, if kept in a tin box, will remain fresh for some time and can be reheated at any time, to make them crisp.

SALTED PEANUTS

Peanuts, 1 pound,
Butter,
Salt.

Buy the unroasted peanuts and shell, blanch by pouring boiling water over the shelled nuts, let them stand for a few minutes, when the brown inner hulls are easily removed.

Spread the blanched nuts on a platter to dry for several hours, having first dried them on a cloth.

Heat a teaspoon of butter in a frying pan, on top of the stove, put the nuts in it, and then place the pan in the oven. Stir often until brown.

Take from the oven and sprinkle plentifully with salt.

Salted almonds may also be prepared in the same manner.

CHAFING-DISH RECEIPTS.

PANNED OYSTERS

Oysters, 3 dozen,
Butter, 2 tablespoons,
Salt, ½ teaspoon,
Paprika or white pepper, ¼ teaspoon,
Mace, a small pinch,
Lemon-juice, 1 teaspoon.

Place the upper dish, or blazer, directly over the light-lamp; drop in the butter, cut in bits, the salt, and the paprika, or white pepper, and the tiny pinch of mace. Then add the prepared oysters.

Cover, and cook until the oysters are plump, and slightly ruffled, uncovering every half minute to stir.

Slip the lower pan, half filled with hot water, underneath, and add a teaspoon of lemon-juice, and serve on small thin squares of toast.

CURRIED OYSTERS

Oysters, 1 quart,
Curry powder, 1 teaspoon,
Flour, 1 tablespoon,
Butter, 1 tablespoon,
Salt and pepper.

Cook the oysters over a slow fire, in their own juice; if this is not sufficient to cook add a little water. Add salt and pepper, butter and curry powder.

When the oysters are firm, moisten the flour with water to make a paste, and thicken the liquor. It must be watched carefully, and stirred thoroughly, after adding the flour and water.

CREAMED OYSTERS

Oysters, 3 dozen,
Butter, 2 tablespoons,
Milk, 1½ cups,
Salt, ½ teaspoon,
Flour, 2 tablespoons,
White pepper, ¼ teaspoon,
Lemon-juice, 1 teaspoon,
Nutmeg, mace.

Have the hot-water pan underneath. In the upper dish melt the butter, adding to it the salt, pepper, and flour. Stir till all is blended, then gradually stir in the milk, and stir till the sauce is thick and smooth; then add a pinch of nutmeg, or mace, a teaspoon of lemon-juice, and the oysters previously rinsed and drained.

Cover it, stirring occasionally, till the oysters are plump and ruffled. The liquor which exudes from them will thin the sauce sufficiently. Extinguish the lamp as soon as the oysters begin to swell, else they may be overcooked.

Lobsters, shrimps, fish, veal, sweetbreads, chicken, mushrooms, peas, asparagus, and other vegetables, may be cooked and creamed in the same way, using for the sauce the same butter and flour, 1 pint of milk, or thin cream, and such seasonings—onion-juice, parsley, herbs, spices, etc.—as are indicated by the article to be creamed.

OYSTERS À LA PARISIENNE

Cold veal cutlet,
Oyster soup, or creamed oysters,

Paprika,
Tabasco sauce,
Cream, ½ cup,
Butter,
Madeira, or sherry.

Chop the veal and oysters together, mixing in the cream sauce, or soup, as the case may be. Flavor with paprika, salt, and a few drops of tabasco.

Place the cream in the chafing-dish, adding a generous piece of butter, and when boiling hot, stir in the chopped veal and the oysters. Simmer for 5 minutes over the hot-water pan, remove from the fire and add a little Madeira or sherry.

Serve on oblongs of toasted bread.

HARD-SHELL CLAMS

Clams,
Egg, 1 yolk,
Cream, 1 tablespoon,
Sherry, ½ wine-glass.

Put in the liquor of the clams, the cream, egg (stirred by itself). When hot, add the clams, chopped fine, cook a few moments, then add the sherry, and serve on toast.

SOFT-SHELL CLAMS

Clams,
Chopped onions, 1 teaspoon,
Chopped parsley, 1 teaspoon,
Butter, 1 heaping tablespoon,
Egg, 1 yolk,
Cream, 1 tablespoon,
Madeira, or sherry, 1 wine-glass.

Put the liquor of the clams into the chafing-dish, add the chopped onion, parsley, and butter; and when hot, add the yolk, stirred by itself. Then stir in the cream, and next put in the bellies of the clams, only, and also a wine-glass of good sherry or Madeira. When all gets hot it is ready to serve.

LOBSTER À LA NEWBURG
CHAMBERLIN

Lobster meat, 2 pounds,
Butter, 1 tablespoon,
Flour, ½ tablespoon,
Cream, 1 cup,
Salt, 1 teaspoon,
Eggs (yolks only), 2,
Sherry, 2 tablespoons,
Cayenne, ¼ teaspoon.

Melt the butter in the chafing-dish and stir in the flour. When well mixed add gradually the cream, stirring constantly. When hot and smooth add the lobster-meat which has been cut into medium pieces, and cook until the lobster is well heated.

Add the salt, cayenne, sherry, and the beaten yolks of the eggs, stir all well in, and serve at once.

CREAMED SHRIMPS

Eggs, 2 yolks,
Anchovy sauce, 1 teaspoon,
Shrimps, 1 bottle,
Cream, ½ cup,
Toast.

Mix the eggs with the anchovy sauce, in the dish, also the cream. Put in some of the shrimps, let them get hot, not allowing the eggs to curdle. Serve on strips of toast.

SCRAMBLED EGGS AND SAUSAGE

>Eggs, 6,
>Sausages, 2,
>Butter, 1 tablespoon,
>Milk, or cream, 4 tablespoons,
>Salt and pepper.

Cut the sausages in small pieces and warm them over,—pouring off all the fat. Add the butter, eggs, well beaten, and the milk.

Stir constantly, and cook until thick and smooth. Season to taste, and serve.

This egg dish can be varied in ever so many ways; using oysters, cheese, sardines, etc., indeed almost anything goes well with a scramble, if it is well seasoned.

EGG AND TOMATO SCRAMBLE

>Butter, 1 tablespoon,
>Tomato sauce, 1 pint,
>Chopped onion,
>Eggs, 6,
>Seasoning,
>Salt, ½ teaspoon.

Melt the butter, add the tomato sauce which has been previously stewed with a little chopped onion, and a high seasoning and then strained.

When boiling hot, slip the water-pan underneath, and add the 6 eggs which have been slightly beaten, and also a half teaspoon of salt. Stir continually until the mixture is quite thick and creamy, and then serve quickly.

WELSH RAREBIT, NO. 1

American cheese, 1 pound,
Butter, ½ teaspoon,
Paprika, 1 teaspoon,
Beer, ½ cup.
  To add later
Beer, 1 teaspoon,
Salt, 1 salt-spoon,
Cayenne, mustard, a pinch each.

Put the butter in the chafing-dish and let it melt; then add the paprika and beer (½ cup), and when this is hot, put in the cheese, which has been cut in dice, and let it melt slowly.

When the cheese has almost entirely melted begin to stir vigorously for a few minutes till the cheese is smooth.

Then add the later mixture, which has been made in a cup, and well stirred. This is composed of 1 teaspoon of beer, 1 salt-spoon of salt, a pinch of cayenne, and a pinch of mustard, well mixed and stirred together, before being put into the rarebit. When put in, stir, and then serve the rarebit, hot, on thin slices of toast.

WELSH RAREBIT, NO. 2

American cheese, 1 pound,
Butter, 1 tablespoon,
Eggs, well beaten, 2,
Dry mustard, ½ teaspoon,
Cayenne, ¼ salt-spoon,
Worcestershire, 1 tablespoon,
Beer, 1 gill.

Put the seasoning, butter, and beer in the chafing-dish. When the butter is melted, add the cheese, cut in small dice.

Stir all the time, and add more beer if needed to keep moist.

When the cheese is melted and creamy, add the eggs which have been well beaten together, and then serve at once.

SPANISH RAREBIT, NO. 1

>Cheese, ½ pound,
>Butter, 1 tablespoon,
>Tomato soup, 1 can,
>Eggs, 2,
>Onion, chopped fine, 1, small,
>Worcestershire, 1 tablespoon,
>Dry mustard, ½ teaspoon,
>Cayenne, a dash.

Cook the chopped onion in the butter till it is soft, but not colored. Add the tomato soup. When well blended and hot, add the cheese finely cut, and when these are well blended and the cheese is all melted, then add the beaten eggs and the condiments.

Stir a few minutes until it is thick and smooth, and then serve on crackers.

SPANISH RAREBIT, NO. 2

>Cheese (grated or fine), 1 pound,
>Butter, 1 large tablespoon,
>Tomato soup, ½ can,
>Eggs, 4,
>Bermuda onion, medium, grated, 1,
>Worcestershire, 1 tablespoon,
>Dry mustard, 1 teaspoon,
>Salt, ½ teaspoon,
>Tabasco, ½ teaspoon.

Cook the grated onion and the butter till smooth, then add the salt and worcestershire, mustard, and tabasco, then the tomato soup. Allow all to cook thoroughly, then add the cheese, which is either grated, or cut very fine, and stir till soft.

Then add the eggs, well beaten, and stir it and allow it to cream.

Serve on toast or crackers. Only ¼ teaspoon of the tabasco may be used if it isn't wanted so hot.

AMERICAN WOODCOCK

Cream, or rich milk, 1½ cups,
Worcestershire, ½ teaspoon,
Cream cheese, cut fine, ½ pound,
Egg, well beaten, 1,
English walnut-meats, chopped, ¾ cup,
Olives, chopped, ⅓ cup,
Butter (only if milk is used), 1 tablespoon,
Paprika, ¼ salt-spoon.

Put the cream in the chafing-dish, and when hot, add the cheese and stir until it is dissolved. Add the paprika, worcestershire, and the beaten egg, and stir all well together.

Cover, and let it cook for 5 minutes, then spread, first the chopped nuts, then the chopped olives on the top, pressing them in with a fork.

Cook for 5 minutes longer, and then serve.

SCOTCH WOODCOCK

Flour, 1½ tablespoons,
Butter, 3 tablespoons,
Milk, 1 cup,
Eggs, hard boiled and chopped, 4,

Salt, ½ teaspoon,
Cayenne, anchovy sauce.

Melt the butter, add the flour, and stir until well blended, then while constantly stirring, gradually pour on the milk. Bring it to the boiling-point, and season with the salt, cayenne, and anchovy sauce.

Add the eggs, which have been finely chopped, and cook until thoroughly heated, and then serve.

ENGLISH MONKEY

Stale bread-crumbs, 1 cup,
Cold milk, 1 cup,
Butter, 1 tablespoon,
Cheese, cut in dice, ½ cup,
Egg, beaten, 1,
Salt, ½ teaspoon,
Cayenne, a dash,
Toasted crackers.

Soak the bread-crumbs in the milk for 15 minutes. Melt the butter, and add to it the cheese which has been cut in dice, and when the cheese has melted add the bread-crumbs, the egg, well beaten, half a teaspoon of salt, and a dash of cayenne.

Cook for 3 minutes, and serve hot on toasted crackers.

CHEESE FONDUE

Cheese, ¼ pound,
Flour, 1 tablespoon,
Butter, 1 tablespoon,
Milk, ¾ cup,
Bread-crumbs, ½ cup,
Eggs, well beaten, 3,

Dry mustard, ¼ teaspoon,
Baking-soda, ¼ teaspoon,
Paprika, ¼ teaspoon,
Salt, a dash.

Melt the butter in the blazer. Mix, and add the flour, mustard, soda, paprika, and salt. When blended stir in the milk. When the sauce is smooth and thick, slip the hot-water pan under, and add the half cup of fine stale bread-crumbs, and the cheese.

Cover, and stir often, until the cheese melts, and then add the eggs, well beaten, stir them in, and when well heated then serve.

MOCK TERRAPIN

Cooked chicken, or veal,
Butter, 1 tablespoon,
Flour, 2 tablespoons,
Milk, 1 cup,
Eggs, 2,
Sherry, 1 wine-glass,
Cayenne, a pinch.

Rub the flour and butter together, and stir them into a cup of milk that has been made very hot in the cooking-pan. When nicely blended add the eggs, beaten, and at once put in the chicken, or veal, which has been cut in dice. This only needs to get hot in the sauce, as it is sufficiently cooked already.

At the last add a generous wine-glass of sherry and a dash of Cayenne pepper.

BARBECUED HAM

Cold boiled and sliced ham,
Butter, 2 teaspoons,

Tomato catsup, 5 tablespoons,
French mustard, 1 tablespoon,
Sherry, 3 tablespoons.

Make a sauce by stirring together in the chafing-dish, the butter, catsup, mustard, and sherry; and when this is hot, lay the slices of ham in the dish, and let them heat through.

SHRIMP, WITH FRENCH PEAS

Shrimps, 1 small can,
French peas, 1 small can,

Sauce

Milk, 1 cup,
Flour, 2 tablespoons,
Butter, 2 tablespoons,
Salt and pepper.

Turn the shrimps and peas from the cans, and allow them to stand in the air for an hour or so. Make 2 cupsful of white sauce with the above ingredients, season with salt and pepper, and when the sauce is well mixed turn into it the peas and shrimps; let them heat thoroughly, and serve.

SANDWICHES

An almost endless variety of fillings may be suggested for sandwiches: Fruit, vegetables, nuts, eggs, cheese, fish, meat, olives, jams, and preserves,—almost any combination is good if well put together.

The bread should be cut thin and well trimmed. Should mayonnaise or French dressing be used, it is not necessary to spread the bread with butter.

The savory sandwiches are appropriate for a luncheon, or supper. Sweet or fruit sandwiches seem better for afternoon teas.

Sweet sandwiches are variously made. Either chopped nuts or grated cocoanut may be with good results combined with jam, jelly, marmalade, preserved ginger, maraschino cherries, chopped raisins, figs, or dates.

The dried fruits are always improved by the addition of a little sherry or grape-juice. Cream cheese may also be added to either the preserved or the dried fruits.

The following is a good list of fillings for various sandwiches:

Apple and celery—Chopped apples, chopped celery, and grated cheese, moistened with French or mayonnaise dressing.

Baked beans—Beans, tomato catsup, and French dressing.

Caviare—Caviare made into a paste with fresh lemon-juice.

Celery—Chopped celery, olives and nuts, moistened with mayonnaise.

Chicken and almond—Equal portions of cold chicken and blanched almonds, chopped and moistened with cream.

Club sandwich—Thinly sliced chicken and broiled ham, with lettuce leaves, on thin slices of buttered toast.

Club cheese sandwich—Cheese with lettuce on thin slices of bread.

Cucumber sandwich—Chopped cucumber, seasoned with onion, moistened with mayonnaise.

Egg sandwich—Yolks of hard-boiled eggs, salt, pepper, mustard, and olive oil, all forming a paste, add vinegar, and spread on the slices of bread.

Green pepper sandwich—Equal parts of chopped green peppers and chopped onion, moistened with French dressing.

Ham and olive sandwich—Olives and ham, chopped fine, and moistened with mayonnaise.

Lettuce-Mayonnaise—Spread mayonnaise on thin slices of bread, with leaves of lettuce.

Mutton sandwiches—Cold mutton, chopped fine and seasoned with mint sauce.

Nut sandwich—English walnut meats, chopped fine, with mayonnaise dressing and cream cheese.

Sardine sandwich—Sardine and lemon-juice filling.

Watercress sandwich—Watercress and hard-boiled eggs, coarsely chopped, and moistened with French dressing.

DESSERTS

RICE PUDDING

Rice, ½ cup,
Milk, 1 pint,
Eggs, 3,
Sugar, nutmeg,
Salt, vanilla.

Put the milk and rice on the fire and let it cook until the rice has become tender. Set it off and let it stand until nearly cold; then stir in the beaten yolks of the 3 eggs.

Season to taste with sugar, salt, nutmeg, and vanilla, and then add the whites of the eggs which have been beaten to a froth.

Bake for about 1 hour.

COLD RICE PUDDING

Rice, ¼ pound,
Butter, 1 teaspoon,
Vanilla bean, 1 pod,
Preserved peaches or apricots,
Whipped cream,
Salt and milk.

Cook the rice, butter, and vanilla bean together, adding a pinch of salt, and set it to cool. When cold, put a layer of the rice on a dish, then a layer of the preserved peaches, or apricots, then a layer of the whipped cream, and so on; the top layer being a thick layer of the cream.

Put it on the ice, and serve cold. With a quarter of a pound of rice, this should be enough for 8 or 10 persons.

RUSSIAN RICE

> Boiled rice, ¼ pound,
> Sugar, ¼ pound,
> Jamaica rum, or arrack, 1 wine-glass,
> Canned pineapple, or maraschino cherries.

Put the rice, which has been previously boiled, in a glass dish. Take a gill of water, with the sugar, and boil for 20 minutes. When it is somewhat cool, add the spirits to it, and pour it over the rice.

Serve it very cold, with maraschino cherries or with slices of canned pineapple. Apricots can be used instead of pineapple.

TRAUTMANSDORF RICE PUDDING
GERMAN

> Cold boiled rice, 2 cups,
> Granulated gelatin, 2 tablespoons,
> Hot milk, 1 cup,
> Sugar, 1 cup,
> Cream, 1½ cups,
> Vanilla extract, ½ teaspoon,
> Salt.

Soak the granulated gelatin in the cup of hot milk; to this add the sugar and a pinch of salt. Let this cool, stirring occasionally.

Whip the cream, flavor it with the vanilla, and beat into in the gelatin mixture. Then stir in the boiled rice.

One-half cup of raw rice will make the required quantity of boiled rice. Instead of vanilla extract, rum may be used as a flavoring, in which case, use 2 tablespoons of rum.

BREAD PUDDING

Baker's bread, ½ loaf,
Hot milk, 1 quart,
Eggs, 3,
Butter, 1 heaping tablespoon,
Vanilla, or lemon,
Salt and sugar.

Pour the hot milk over the bread, let it stand till partly cold, and then mash fine. Next add the yolks of the eggs, beaten and sweetened and flavored to taste, then add the whites of the eggs, beaten to a stiff froth, and stir in lightly, adding a little salt and a piece of butter about the size of an egg.

Bake in a medium oven.

ST. DENIS INDIAN PUDDING

Indian-corn meal, ¼ pound,
Sugar, ½ pound,
Eggs, 5,
Milk, 1 pint,
Molasses, 2 tablespoons,
Ginger, or nutmeg, 1 tablespoon,
Salt.

Cook the milk and Indian meal together, add the other ingredients, and bake for about 1 hour.

GRAHAM PUDDING

Molasses, 1 cup,
Sweet milk, 1 cup,
Graham flour (not sifted), 2 cups,

Melted butter, 1 tablespoon,
Mixed and chopped, raisin, currants and citron, 1 cup,
Soda, 1 scant teaspoon.

Stir all the ingredients together, into a batter, turn into a mold, and steam for 3 hours.

GERMAN BALLOONS

Flour, 1 cup,
Butter, 1 tablespoon,
Eggs, 3,
Lard,
Lemons, 1½,
Powdered sugar.

Put a cup of water in a saucepan, and when it is boiling, add the butter. When the butter is melted, add the flour, and beat it with a fork or with a wire whip, until it is smooth, and leaves the sides of the pan.

Remove from the fire, and add the eggs, one at a time, beating each one very vigorously before adding the next one.

Let it stand until cold. When ready to cook, drop it, spoonful at a time, into moderately hot lard, and fry for about 15 minutes. Take out with a skimmer, and dry on brown paper.

The batter will puff into hollow balls, if the fat is not too hot.

For the sauce, strain the juice of the lemons, to which add the powdered sugar, and ½ cup of boiling water.

BATTER PUDDING

Milk, 2 cups,
Flour, 2 cups,

Eggs, 4,
Melted butter, 1 tablespoon,
Baking-powder, 1 heaping teaspoon,
Salt.

Sift the baking-powder into the flour, add the salt and butter, then add the milk, gradually, stirring carefully. Next add the eggs, the yolks and whites of which have been beaten separately.

This pudding will bake in 15 minutes. If it is to be boiled make it stiffer than for baking; and if fruit is to be used the batter must be very stiff.

It should not stick to the knife when served. Serve with a rich sauce. The pudding is better if 6 eggs can be used instead of 4.

EGYPTIAN PUDDING

Gelatin, ½ box,
Rice, ½ cup,
Figs, 2,
Dates, 4,
Preserved ginger, chopped, 3 pieces,
Orange juice,
Lemon juice,
Cream, 1 pint,
Pulverized sugar, ⅔ cup.

Cover the gelatin with a cup of cold water, let it soak for half an hour. Boil the rice in plenty of salted water for 25 minutes. Drain.

Cut the figs, dates, and ginger into small pieces, mix and cover them with a little lemon- and orange-juice, and add also a dessert-spoonful of the juice from the preserved ginger, and let the fruit soak for half an hour. Whip the cream to a stiff, dry froth, dissolve the gelatin over hot water, and add it, and also the sugar to the cream. Also add the fruit and the rice.

Stir from the bottom toward the top, till the pudding begins to form; then turn it into individual molds, previously wet with cold water, and put them away in a cool place to solidify.

STEAMED BLUEBERRY PUDDING

>Flour, 2 cups,
>Baking-powder, 4 teaspoons,
>Milk, 1 cup,
>Blueberries, 1 cup,
>Salt, ½ teaspoon.

Stir all together, and after mixing, turn it into a buttered mold, and steam for 1½ hours. Serve it with a cream sauce or with a hard sauce.

CHERRY PUDDING

>Canned cherries, 1 can,
>Milk, 1 cup,
>Sugar, 1 tablespoon,
>Melted butter, 1 tablespoon,
>Sifted flour, 2½ cups,
>Eggs, 2,
>Baking-powder, 1 heaping teaspoon,
>Salt, ½ teaspoon.

Beat together all the ingredients, except the cherries; then stir in the cherries which have been drained from their syrup.

Turn this into a mold and steam it for 2 hours. Serve it with a sauce made with the drained syrup, sweetened, and slightly thickened.

STEAMED BLACKBERRY PUDDING

>Blackberries, 1 pint,
>Flour, 1 cup,
>Milk, 1 pint,
>Eggs, 2,
>Baking-powder, 1 teaspoon,
>Salt.

Sift the flour into a basin, add the salt and baking-powder, and then gradually add the eggs, well beaten, and the milk.

Stir in the blackberries, which have been thoroughly dredged with flour. Pour at once into a greased mold, cover with a greased paper, and steam steadily for 2 hours. Serve with a hard sauce.

FIG PUDDING

>Chopped suet, 1 cup,
>Chopped figs, 1 pound,
>Eggs, 3,
>Bread-crumbs, 2 cups,
>Sugar, 1 cup,
>Milk, 2 cups.
>
>*Sauce*
>Tart wine, or sherry, 1 cup,
>Butter, ½ cup,
>Powdered sugar, 1 cup.

Wash, and pick over the figs and chop them. Chop the suet, beat the eggs light, without separation, and mix all these thoroughly, and turn it into a well-greased mold. Cover and boil for 3 hours and serve it hot.

The sauce for the pudding would be a wine sauce, made as follows:

Beat a half-cup of butter to a cream, add a cup of sugar, gradually, and when light, add, a little at a time, the wine, which has been made hot; stir the sauce for 2 or 3 minutes, till it becomes smooth and foamy.

WASHINGTON PUDDING

Flour, 3 cups,
Molasses, 1 cup,
Butter, ½ cup,
Milk, 1 cup,
Chopped raisins, 1 cup,
Baking-powder, 1 heaping teaspoon,
Cloves, 1 teaspoon,
Cinnamon, 1 teaspoon,
Nutmeg and salt.

Mix the ingredients, and of salt and nutmeg add a pinch. Steam for 2 hours in a pudding-mold, and serve with a hard sauce.

BROWN BETTY

Bread-crumbs, 1 cup,
Sugar, ½ cup,
Chopped sour apples, 2 cups,
Chopped raisins, 1 cup,
Butter, 2 tablespoons.

Butter well, a deep pudding-dish, and put into it a layer of the apples, and raisins, a sprinkle of sugar, a layer of the bread-crumbs, and a few bits of butter.

Proceed in the same order, until all the materials are used, having the last layer one of bread-crumbs. Cover closely, and bake 45 minutes in a moderate oven, then uncover and brown.

Serve hot or cold, with a hard sauce.

PUMPKIN PIE

Pumpkin, 1 cup,
Egg, 1,
Sugar, 1 cup,
Cinnamon, 1 teaspoon,
Ground ginger, ½ teaspoon,
Salt, ½ teaspoon,
Milk, enough to thin as desired.

The pumpkin should be peeled, cubed, stewed till tender, and then passed through a colander. Mix with the other ingredients, line a pie-plate with crust, fill with the mixture, and bake in a moderate oven, until it has a rich brown shade.

APPLE CUSTARD PIE

Tart apple-sauce (strained), 1 quart,
Butter, ½ cup,
Sugar, 1 cup,
Eggs, 4,
Cinnamon.

Beat the eggs, and mix them with the sauce. Melt and stir in the butter, then add the cinnamon and sugar. Line a deep plate with a good crust, and fill it with the pie-mixture and bake in a moderate oven.

CHOCOLATE PIE

Milk, 2 cups,
Eggs, 3,
Sugar, 4 tablespoons,
Grated sweet chocolate, ½ cup,
Vanilla extract, 1 teaspoon.

Make a custard by scalding the milk and pouring over it gradually the eggs, which have been well beaten together, with the sugar. Return it to the fire, and stir in a half-cup of grated sweet chocolate.

Then remove it from the fire, add a teaspoon of vanilla, and pour the mixture into a pie-plate lined with puff paste.

Bake until "set."

INGREDIENTS FOR MINCE-MEAT

Cold boiled fresh tongue, 2 pounds
  (chopped very fine),
Finely chopped suet, 1 pound,
Tart apples, finely chopped, 5 pounds,
Seeded raisins, 2 pounds,
Sultana raisins, 1 pound,
Cleaned currants, 2 pounds,
Shredded citron, 1 pound,
Powdered cinnamon, 2 tablespoons,
Mace, 2 tablespoons,
Cloves, 1 tablespoon,
Allspice, 1 tablespoon,
Salt, 1 tablespoon,
Brown sugar, 3 pounds,
Sherry, 1 quart,
Brandy, 1 pint.

Chop fine the larger ingredients, mix well together, and pack in a stone crock. If sealed in glass fruit-jars it will keep indefinitely.

CARAMEL CUSTARD

Sugar, ½ cup,
Salt, ½ teaspoon,
Vanilla, 1 teaspoon,

Hot milk, 1 quart,
Eggs, 3.

Put the sugar in an omelette pan and stir until it melts and is light brown. Add 2 tablespoons of water to the sugar, and then stir this into one pint of the milk. Beat the eggs lightly and add to them the salt and vanilla, and add this to the sugar and milk.

When well mixed then pour into it the rest of the milk. It is important that you do not pour the milk into the sugar, but the *sugar* into the *milk*, otherwise the mixture will become lumpy.

When the remainder of the milk has been added to the mixture, pour it into a 2-quart mold, and set the mold in a pan of water and bake until it is a light brown.

Make for it a caramel sauce, composed of half a cup of sugar and half a cup of boiling water, allowed to simmer for 10 minutes.

LEMON PUDDING

Sugar, 2 cups,
Butter, 1 cup,
Sweet milk, 1 pint,
Eggs, 5,
Lemons, 2.

Cream the butter and sugar; beat the eggs separately, and put in first the yolks, then the whites. Stir in the milk. Grate the outsides of the lemons, squeeze the juice, and add these, the very last, just before placing in the oven.

Bake about 30 minutes. Cocoanut pudding may be made in the same way, grating the cocoanut, and in this case, leave out a little of the butter.

STRAWBERRY SPONGE

>Gelatin, ½ box,
>Sugar, 1 cup,
>Strawberry-juice, 2 cups,
>Eggs, 4,
>Cream, ½ pint,
>Vanilla, ½ teaspoon.

Soak the gelatin in a half-cup of cold water for half an hour. Then pour on to it 1 cup of boiling water, add the sugar, and stir till it is dissolved. Add 2 cups of strawberry-juice and strain all into a bowl.

Put the bowl into a pan of cold water, and let the mixture become thick, stirring it now and then as it cools.

Then beat it to a stiff froth with a whisk; add the beaten whites of the eggs, and beat all together till smooth. Put it into small molds, or into one large mold, and chill.

Serve with a cold liquid sauce, flavored lightly with vanilla, or a thin custard made with the yolks of the eggs.

Pineapple, raspberry, and blackberry sponge may be prepared in the same way.

SOUFFLÉ CUSTARD

>Flour, ½ cup,
>Sugar, 2 tablespoons,
>Milk, 1 pint,
>Butter, 2 tablespoons,
>Eggs (beaten separately), 5,
>Salt.

Mix the flour, salt, and sugar to a paste with a little cold milk. Turn this quickly into a pint of scalding hot milk on the fire, and stir rapidly until very thick and smooth. Cover, and cook for 10 minutes.

Add the butter, cut in bits, and the beaten yolks of the eggs, and stir for a moment longer, then cover and set it aside for 10 minutes.

Whip the whites to a stiff froth and beat them into the partly made custard. Then bake in a well-greased pudding-dish placed in a pan of hot water, or in cups.

Have the oven very hot, and serve at once, as it quickly falls.

PINEAPPLE SPONGE

Gelatin, 1/4 box,
Pineapple, 1 can,
Thick cream, 1/2 cup,
Eggs, 2.

Cover the gelatin with 1/4 cup of cold water. Drain the syrup from the can of pineapple, measure it, and add enough water to it to make 1 1/2 cups.

Heat this to the boiling point, take it from the fire and add the gelatin to it, and stir until it is dissolved. Strain it and set it aside until it begins to thicken, then add the cream which has been whipped to a solid froth, also the whites of the eggs beaten until stiff and dry.

Stir carefully together, and when quite thick, add 1 cup of the pineapple which has been cut in tiny bits.

Turn into molds previously wet with cold water, and stand them in a cool place until firm.

PRUNE SOUFFLÉ

Prunes, 1 pound,
Eggs, 6 or 7,
Sugar,
Whipped cream.

The prunes should be soaked overnight, and then cooked until they are soft. Put through a sieve, and mix with the whites of the eggs beaten stiff. Sweeten to taste with sugar, bake for 20 minutes, and serve with whipped cream.

APPLE SOUFFLÉ

> Tart apples, 5,
> Melted butter, 2 tablespoons,
> Sugar, ½ cup,
> Eggs, 3,
> Lemon (juice and grated rind), 1,
> Nutmeg.

Pare and grate the apples, add the butter, sugar, lemon-juice, and rind, then the eggs, beaten stiff. Pour the mixture into a buttered dish, grate a little nutmeg over the top, and bake for 30 minutes in a moderate oven.

Serve immediately with a hard sauce.

FRAPPÉED FIGS
HAWAIIAN

> Ripe figs, 1 quart,
> Cream, 1 quart,
> Sugar, 1 cup,
> Sherry, ½ cup.

Whip the cream until very stiff; add the sugar and sherry. Cut the figs in pieces, and put into a freezer, in alternate layers of fruit and cream.

Let it stand until frozen.

GUAVA SHERBET
HAWAIIAN

> Ripe guavas, 24,
> Eggs (whites, only), 3,

Sugar, 1 cup,
Lemon, 1 (juice only),
Sherry, ½ cup.

Pass the guavas through a sieve, add the whites of the eggs, beaten stiff, also the sugar, lemon, and sherry wine. Then freeze.

ROTHE GRUETZE
GERMAN

Currants, 2 quarts,
Raspberries, 1 quart,
Lemon, 1,
Sago, or tapioca, 1 cup,
Sugar.

Mix the berries, currants, and the grated rind of the lemon with enough water to thoroughly cover all, then cook 20 minutes, and strain and sugar to taste. Add the sago, or tapioca, and then cook for 10 or 15 minutes longer, stirring constantly. Serve cold, with thin custard sauce. Cornstarch may be used instead of sago or tapioca.

CHOCOLATE PUDDING
GERMAN

Unsweetened chocolate, ¼ pound,
Gelatin, ½ package,
Milk, 1 quart,
Eggs, 3,
Sugar, 4 heaping tablespoons,
Vanilla.

Cook the chocolate with the milk; stir in the yolks of the eggs, and also the gelatin. When cool, add the whites, beaten, stir through the pudding, and put it in a form.

Serve ice-cold, with a custard sauce, flavored with vanilla.

CHOCOLATE PUDDING WITH CREAMY SAUCE

Chocolate, 2 tablespoons,
Powdered cinnamon, ½ teaspoon,
Hot milk, 3 cups,
Scalded milk, 1 cup,
Stale bread-crumbs, 2 cups,
Eggs, 2,
Sugar, ½ cup,
Salt, a pinch.

Sauce

Butter, ½ cup,
Powdered sugar, 1 cup,
Thick whipped cream, 1 pint,
Vanilla, 1 teaspoon.

Mix the chocolate with the cinnamon and gradually add 1 cup of scalded milk, and simmer for a moment. Add the hot milk and pour all over the bread-crumbs in a bowl. Cover it, and let it stand for 15 minutes, then beat with a spoon to mix thoroughly.

Beat the eggs and sugar together till light, adding a dash of salt, and stir into the prepared bread. Mix well, and turn into a greased pudding-dish, and bake for 45 minutes in a moderate oven. Serve with a creamy sauce, which is made as follows: Cream ½ cup of butter with 1 cup of powdered sugar, and beat till it is light. Whip in, gradually, a teaspoon of vanilla and a pint of thick whipped cream. Set this over a pan of water, and stir well for 2 minutes. It is then ready to serve at once.

LEMON CREAM

Lemon, 1,
Cornstarch, 2 tablespoons (dissolved in cold water),

Eggs (beaten separately), 3.
Sugar, 1 scant cup,

Put the grated rind and the juice of the lemon into 2 cupsful of water, and when it boils, stir the cornstarch into it. When it thickens a little, sweeten it to taste with a scant cup of sugar, and then add the beaten yolks of the eggs.

When taken from the fire, stir in the whites, beaten to a stiff froth. Be careful not to get it too thick, as it should be creamy, and it is thicker when it is cold.

FLORENTINE CREAM
ITALIAN

Lemons, 2 (the juice only),
Oranges, 2 (the juice only),
Gelatin, 1 heaping tablespoon,
Sugar, 1½ cups,
Cream, 1 pint,
Milk, ½ cup.

Boil the fruit juices and the sugar together, for about 5 minutes, and set it away to cool. Dissolve the gelatin in the milk, on the back of the range. Do not let it curdle.

Whip the cream stiff; add the fruit juice to it gradually, and then add the gelatin mixture. Stir until it thickens; pour into a mold, and set it on the ice to harden.

MOLDED FARINA

Milk, ½ pint,
Farina, 1 large tablespoon,
Sugar, 1 tablespoon,
Vanilla, or almond extract, 1 teaspoon,
Egg, 1,
Salt, a pinch.

Scald the milk in a double boiler, add the farina and stir until it has thickened nicely; then add the salt and sugar, and cover it, and cook for half an hour. Add the egg and flavoring just before taking from the fire.

Pour into cups or molds which have been rinsed in cold water. When it has become very cold, turn it out, and serve with cream and sugar.

GERMAN FARINA PUDDING

>Farina, 4 ounces,
>Milk, 1 quart,
>Chopped almonds, 2 tablespoons,
>Grated rind of 1 lemon,
>Eggs, 4,
>Sugar, 4 tablespoons,
>Almond extract, 1 teaspoon,
>Salt, 1 salt-spoon.

The yolks and whites of the eggs must be beaten separately. Beat the farina into the milk. When it begins to thicken, add the grated lemon-rind, chopped almonds, sugar, salt, and the almond extract.

When sufficiently thickened, take from the fire, stir in the yolks of the eggs, and then the beaten whites. Put into a mold, and let it get firm.

Serve with raspberry, or any fruit sauce.

CREAM CHOCOLATE

>Unsweetened chocolate, 2 tablespoons,
>Eggs, 2,
>Cream, ½ cup,
>Milk, ¼ cup,
>Granulated sugar, 4 heaping tablespoons,
>Salt, vanilla, and cinnamon.

Cook the sugar and chocolate together with 4 tablespoons of hot water, till it becomes a smooth shiny paste. Let it boil hard, but be careful that it does not scorch. Add the cream, reserving back 1 tablespoon which will later be used to add to the egg-yolks, to prevent their curdling. Also add a quarter of a cup of milk, and stir it in until it boils.

Set it over a hot-water pan, and add the eggs very carefully, using the reserved cream, and stirring fast all the time

After it thickens, which will be almost immediately, stir in the beaten whites of the eggs, lightly and gently.

Then cover, and leave it over the hot-water pan 10 minutes longer, until light and spongy. Sprinkle powdered sugar over the top, and serve with cream.

ALMOND BLANCMANGE

Powdered gelatin, 1½ heaping tablespoons,
Milk, 2 pints,
Sugar, 3 tablespoons,
Almond extract, ½ teaspoon.

Dissolve the powdered gelatin in a half pint of the milk, add the sugar, the almond extract and the remaining pint and a half of milk.

Strain into a basin, stirring occasionally until cool, then pour into a wet mold, and set off in a cool place. Turn it out when firm, and serve with cream.

ALMOND VELVET CREAM

Gelatin, ¼ box,
Milk, 2 pints,
Eggs, 3,
Sugar, ⅔ cup,
Vanilla and almond extracts.

Soak the gelatin in a cup of the milk for 1 hour. Heat a pint of the milk in a double boiler. Beat the eggs and two-thirds of a cup of sugar together, add a half pint of the cold milk, and then mix this with the scalded milk in the double boiler.

Stir and cook 5 minutes, remove from the fire, and flavor with the almond and vanilla extracts.

Then add the gelatin. Stir until it dissolves in the hot milk, then strain into molds and set away to cool. Serve with sugar and cream.

TUNIS FRUIT CREAM

Cream, 1 pint,
Dates, ½ cup,
Figs, ½ cup,
Sherry, ½ cup.

Cut the fruit into small pieces and stew until soft, in just enough water to cover it. When cool, put it into glasses (six), and over each put 1 tablespoon of sherry. Cover with whipped cream.

CHESTNUT SNOW

Chestnuts,
Orange-juice,
Sugar,
Whipped cream.

Boil, shell, and blanch the chestnuts and pound them in a mortar, moistening them from time to time with orange-juice.

To each pint of chestnut-pulp, add 4 tablespoons of whipped cream, and 1 tablespoon of sugar. Place them in sherbet cups, and garnish with split chestnut-meats.

CHESTNUT CREAM

Chestnuts, 2 quarts,
Powdered sugar, 1 tablespoon.
Brandy, or good sherry, 1 wine-glass,
Vanilla.

Shell and blanch the chestnuts, and put them over the fire in boiling water and cook until tender enough to put through a sieve.

Toss them up lightly with a fork, and add to them the powdered sugar, the brandy, or sherry, and a little flavoring of vanilla.

Place on a dish, and cover with a pint of cream whipped light with a little powdered sugar.

CHESTNUT COMPOTE

Chestnuts, 1 pound,
Granulated sugar, ½ pound,
Water, 1 gill.

Boil, shell, and blanch the chestnuts. Make ready a syrup by cooking together in a saucepan, a gill of water and half a pound of granulated sugar. When it comes to a boil, drop in the chestnuts, and let them remain at the side of the stove where they will be at a very gentle simmer.

JELLIED CHERRIES

Red cherries, 1 can,
Gelatin, 2 tablespoons,
Whipped cream.

This should be made the day before you wish to serve it. Dissolve the gelatin in a little cold water, add to it 1½ pints of the liquid drained from the cherries, and strain this mixture into a ring mold and set it aside to harden.

When ready to put on the table, turn it out on a low dish, and fill the center with the cherries after having removed the pits. Sweeten slightly if necessary, and cover the top with mounds of whipped cream.

GERMAN FRUIT TARTS

Flour, 2 cups,
Sugar, 1/3 cup,
Butter, 3 level tablespoons,
Milk, 1/3 cup,
Egg, 1,
Baking-powder, 1 teaspoon.

Mix all the dry ingredients. Rub the butter in with the finger-tips until it crumbles. Beat the egg into the milk, then stir it into the flour with a fork. Place on a well-floured board and roll it a little thicker than a pie crust.

Line the sides and bottom of deep layer-cake tins, selecting those having movable sides. For filling, use any small fresh fruit that is in season—halved and stoned plums, sliced apples, peaches, etc.

Sugar the fruit liberally, and if desired, pour a custard of 1 egg to half a cupful of rich milk or cream, over it before baking. When ready for serving take off the rim of the tin and leave the tart on the bottom sheet; sprinkle with confectioner's sugar, or if suited to the fruit, heap with whipped cream.

PORCUPINE

GERMAN

Lady-fingers,
Creamed butter, 1 cup,

Eggs, 8,
Sugar, 8 tablespoons,
Strong coffee, 8 tablespoons,
Almonds.

Stir slowly together; spread a layer half an inch thick of the mixture on a plate, then a layer of lady-fingers; and repeat until only enough cream is left to cover the top and the whole outside.

Stick in, on end, all over the outside, quartered almonds. Put on ice for 3 or 4 hours. This quantity is enough for 6 persons.

APPLE CAKE

GERMAN

Flour, 1 pint,
Sugar, 3 tablespoons,
Butter, 2 tablespoons,
Egg, beaten, 1,
Milk, ½ cup,
Salt, ½ teaspoon,
Baking-powder, 1 teaspoon,
Apples, quartered and peeled,
Cinnamon.

Mix together the flour, salt, and baking-powder. Rub in the butter, then mix to a soft dough, or very thick batter with the egg and milk; turn it into a well-greased shallow pan and press partly into it, peeled and quartered apples, arranging them in regular circles or rows, according to the shape of the pan.

Sprinkle them with granulated sugar, mixed with ⅓ teaspoon of ground cinnamon. Bake in a hot oven, and serve hot with cream.

APPLE FLORENTINE

Large firm apples, 12,
Sugar, ¼ pound,
Eggs, 4,
Sherry, 1 gill,
Butter, ¼ pound,
Nutmeg.

Peel, core, and slice the apples, and stew them in as little water as possible. When cooked, mash them through a colander, and let them stand until cold.

Sweeten with the sugar, add ¼ pound of butter, the sherry, a seasoning of nutmeg, and the eggs, which have been beaten until light. Bake 1 hour, and serve hot.

CAKE

REMARKS

Handling cakes—To turn out a cake from a tin without breaking, wrap a damp cloth around it for a few moments. This will prevent its sticking to the tin.

Icing cake—Cake icing will not crack when cut, if a little thick cream is added to it. Allow 1 teaspoon of cream to each white of egg. Before icing a cake, rub the top over with flour. This will make the icing stick more firmly. If you wish the icing to stand up, round the edge of the top, pin a band of oiled paper round it before icing.

Blanching almonds—Put them in a stewpan with enough cold water to cover, and bring quickly to a boil. Strain, rinse them in cold water, and rub them in a clean cloth. The skins will then come off easily.

Pounding almonds—When pounding almonds add a few drops of cold water, or they are liable to oil. Almonds already pounded can be bought in tins, or by the pound. In any case they need to be stored in tins, as any paper left in contact with them absorbs oil.

YELLOW FROSTING

Eggs, 2,
Sugar, ½ cup,
Lemon-extract, ½ teaspoon.

Beat the yolks thoroughly, add half a cup of sugar (powdered), half a teaspoon of lemon-extract. Use on a small white cake.

BLACK FRUIT CAKE

Brown sugar, 2 cups,
Butter, 1 cup,
Eggs, 3,
Molasses, 1 cup,
Soda, 1 teaspoon,
Ground cloves, 1 teaspoon,
Powdered cinnamon, 1 teaspoon,
Flour, 5 cups,
Sour milk, 1 cup,
Raisins, 1 pound,
Currants, 1 pound,
Citron, 1 pound,
Nutmeg.

Cream the butter with the sugar. Beat the eggs thoroughly, and add them to the creamed butter and sugar. Add also the molasses, soda, and spices, and beat well. Next add the 5 cups of sifted flour, and 1 cup of sour milk, beating it in; first adding a little flour, and beating it in, and then a little of the milk, and so on, until all is well beaten in.

Flour lightly, 1 pound of raisins and 1 pound of currants, and 1 pound of finely shaved citron, and stir into the batter, and bake in a slow oven.

This will make 2 loaves. The putting together of the ingredients counts very much in making; and this fruit cake should be put together as directed, in order to insure success.

DARK FRUIT CAKE

Flour, 3 cups, sifted,
Sugar, 1 pound,
Dried peaches, 1 pound,

Dried prunes, 1 pound,
Butter, ½ pound,
Eggs, 5,
Oranges, 2,
Cloves, ½ teaspoon,
Ginger, 1 teaspoon,
Cinnamon, 1 teaspoon,
Salt, ½ teaspoon,
Chopped nuts, ½ pound,
Baking-powder, 2 teaspoons.

The prunes should be washed and soaked for 12 hours; then drained and stoned. Both the prunes and the peaches should be cut up fine. Cream ½ pound of butter, add 1 pound of sugar, 5 beaten eggs and the spices. Add gradually 3 cupsful of sifted pastry flour, the juice and also the grated rinds of two oranges, and the chopped fruit, which should be lightly dusted with flour.

Bake in a moderate oven for about 3 hours.

COMPOSITION CAKE

Flour, 1½ pounds,
Sugar, 1¼ pounds,
Butter, ¾ pound,
Eggs, 4,
Milk, 1 pint,
Soda, 1 (large) half-teaspoon,
Cream of tartar, 1 half-teaspoon,
Brandy, 1 wine-glass,
Sherry, 1 wine-glass,
Raisins, 2 pounds,
Currants, 1 pound,
Citron, ½ pound,
Grated nutmeg, ½ teaspoon,

Ground cinnamon, ½ teaspoon,
Ginger, ½ teaspoon,
Cloves, a pinch.

Mix, and bake slowly in a moderate oven. In lieu of the soda and cream of tartar, 1 teaspoon of baking-powder may be used.

FRUIT CAKE

Browned flour, 1 pound,
Sugar, 1 pound,
Butter, 1 pound,
Seeded raisins, 2 pounds,
Eggs, 12,
Stemmed currants, 2 pounds,
Candied orange-peel, ¼ pound,
Citron, ¾ pound,
Shelled almonds, 1 pound,
French brandy, 1 gill,
Curaçao cordial, 1 wine-glass,
Maraschino, 1 wine-glass,
Allspice, 1 tablespoon,
Cloves, ¼ tablespoon,
Mace, ½ teaspoon,
Molasses, 1 cup,
Soda.

First get the fruit ready; raisins seeded and chopped, currants washed, stemmed and dried, almonds blanched and cut in thin slices, citron and orange-peel cut in long thin slices, and mix all together. Flour very lightly all that is put in, as that prevents the fruits from settling at the bottom of the pan.

Cream the butter and flour, stir until very light the yolks of the eggs with the sugar. Then add the whites of the eggs which have been well whipped. Next the seasoning and after that the fruit must be added, in small quantities at a time, and finally add the molasses, to which a little soda is added just as it is put in.

Bake in a deep pan for 4 hours. Be sure it does not bake too long else it will be too dry. This cake will keep a year; and is at its best when 4 weeks old.

WHITE FRUIT CAKE

Butter, 1 pound,
Granulated sugar, 1 pound,
Eggs, 10,
Grated lemon-rind, 1,
Seeded raisins, 1 pound,
Citron, thinly sliced, 1 pound,
English walnut kernels, ½ pound,
Flour, 1 pound,
Soda, ½ teaspoon,
Nutmeg, ½ teaspoon,
Brandy, or rum, ¼ cup.

Mix the same as a pound cake, beating long and hard before adding the fruit. It is better to use pastry flour, and sift it twice. Reserve a part of the sliced citron to stick in the top of the batter after it is in the pan.

SPICE CAKE

Flour, 2 cups,
Granulated sugar, 1 cup,
Sour milk, 1 cup,
Seeded raisins, 1 cup,
Soda, 1 teaspoon,
Egg, 1 yolk,

Butter, a piece size of an egg,
Cinnamon, ½ teaspoon,
Cloves, ½ teaspoon,
Nutmeg, a pinch,
Allspice, a pinch.

Chop the raisins and mix with the sugar and ground spices. Beat the egg yolk, and stir it into the butter. Dissolve the soda in the milk, and stir it into the egg and butter. Then add a little flour and stir this mixture into the raisins and sugar.

COFFEE CAKE

Flour, 2 cups,
Sugar, 1 cup,
Butter, ½ cup,
Molasses, ½ cup,
Eggs, 2,
Seeded raisins, 1 cup,
Cinnamon, 1 teaspoon,
Cloves, 1 teaspoon,
Mace, 1 teaspoon,
Baking-soda, 1 teaspoon,
Cold coffee, ½ cup.

Mix well. The baking-soda must be dissolved in the coffee. Bake in a loaf, and when done, turn out, and ice the bottom and sides with white frosting.

POUND CAKE, NO. 1

Flour, 1 pound,
Butter, 1 pound,
Sugar, 1 pound,
Eggs, 12,

Brandy, 1 tablespoon,
Mace, 1 salt spoon.

Cream the butter and sugar; beat the whites and the yolks of the eggs separately, and very light. Add the brandy and mace to the creamed butter and sugar. Stir in the yolks, and after beating hard for a couple of minutes, then add the flour and the beaten whites of the eggs, alternately, whipping them lightly, but not stirring after they have gone in.

A pound-cake batter should be as stiff as it can be stirred. Bake in brick tins, or in small pans, in a steady oven, covering with paper to prevent too quick browning.

POUND CAKE, NO. 2

Butter, ¾ pound,
Sugar, 1 pound,
Eggs, 10,
Flour, 1¼ pounds,
Rosewater, 1 teaspoon,
Brandy, 2 teaspoons.

Beat the butter and sugar until very light. Add the yolks of the eggs, and beat them together. Whip the whites of the eggs and stir them in, gently, with the flour, into the mixture.

Use 1¼ pounds of flour, and if too soft, add more. Add 1 spoonful of rosewater, and 2 of brandy. Bake slowly.

WHITE CAKE

Flour, 2 cups,
Sugar, 1 cup,
Baking-powder, 2 teaspoons,
Egg, 1 (white only),
Milk, 1 cup,

Butter, 2 tablespoons,
Salt.

Sift the flour, sugar, baking-powder, and a pinch of salt together twice. Take the white of the egg in a cup, and fill the cup with milk. Add to it, 2 tablespoons of soft butter, and then put all together, and stir well, as therein lies the secret of good making.

This cake is as equally well baked in a sheet, or in a loaf, or in layers; and is very cheaply made.

BRIDGET CAKE

Butter, 1 cup,
Sugar, 2 cups,
Flour, 3½ cups,
Milk, 1 cup,
Baking-powder (mixed with the flour),
    1 teaspoon.

Stir well, bake in a loaf in a slow oven.

DRIED APPLE CAKE
GERMAN

Dried apples, 3 cups,
Molasses, 3 cups,
Sugar, 1 cup,
Sour milk, 1 cup,
Flour, 3 cups,
Eggs, 2,
Butter, ¾ cupful,
Stoned raisins, 1 cup,
Soda, 2 teaspoons,
Ground cloves, 1 teaspoon,
Ground cinnamon, 1 teaspoon.

Soak the apples overnight. Chop them fine and simmer in the molasses for 2 hours, and let them cool.

When cold, add all the other ingredients, the eggs being well beaten; stir all thoroughly together and pour into a large tin, and bake in a slow oven.

GERMAN LOAF CAKE

> Flour, 4 pounds,
> Butter, 1¾ pounds,
> Sugar, 1½ pounds,
> Sweet almonds, ½ pound,
> Bitter almonds, ¼ pound,
> Citron, 6 ounces,
> Eggs, 4,
> Raisins, 1 pound,
> Currants, 1 pound,
> Warm milk, 1 quart,
> Seasoning, spices, and rosewater.

Make the dough with flour, etc., and set it to rise with yeast. The butter and other ingredients are worked in afterwards.

SOFT GINGERBREAD

> Flour, 4 cups,
> Sugar, 1 cup,
> Molasses, 2 cups,
> Butter, 1 cup,
> Sour milk, 1 cup,
> Eggs, 3,
> Soda, 1 teaspoon,
> Ginger, 1 teaspoon,
> Ground cloves, 1 teaspoon,
> Mace and salt.

Mix all together, and bake in a moderate oven.

MEASURED ANGEL CAKE

Flour, 1 cup,
Sugar, 1½ cups,
Eggs, 9, or 11, according to size,
Cream of tartar, 1 teaspoon,
Salt.

Take 1 glassful of the whites of the eggs, which will be 9, or 11, according to the size of the eggs, and add to it, 1 teaspoon of cream of tartar and a pinch of salt.

Beat until so stiff that the dish can be turned upside down and the eggs will stay firm. Then season.

Stir together 1 cup of flour and 1½ cups of sugar; into this stir the eggs lightly—so lightly that particles of the beaten eggs can be seen as the mixture is turned into the baking-pan.

Bake in a moderate oven until a nice light brown.

CAKES WITH FILLINGS

MINNEHAHA CAKE

Butter, ½ cup,
Sugar, 1½ cups,
Eggs, 3,
Milk, 1 cup,
Flour, 2½ cups,
Baking-powder, 2 teaspoons,
Vanilla.

Mix all the dry ingredients. Cream the butter and the sugar together, and add to it the beaten yolks of the eggs.

Add next some vanilla, and then add, alternately, the milk and the flour, beating well in, and bake in 3 layers in a quick oven.

Put the cake together with a fruit filling in which the whites of the eggs are used.

CARAMEL CAKE

Eggs, 6,
Sugar, 2 cups,
Flour, 2½ cups,
Milk, 1 cup,
Baking-powder, 1 teaspoon,
Vanilla, 1 teaspoon.

Bake in 3 layers, and when cool fill and ice with Caramel mixture.

Caramel Filling

Brown sugar, 1 pound,
Butter, ¼ pound,
Milk, 1 cup.

Mix together, and when it begins to boil, stir continually until it grows thick. Then it is ready to spread on the cake.

MOCHA CAKE

Flour, 1 cup,
Sugar, 1 cup,
Eggs, 2,
Milk, ½ cup,
Butter, 2 tablespoons,
Baking-powder, 1 teaspoon,
Vanilla, 1 teaspoon.

In making the layers, stir the sugar and eggs together, then add the flour. The milk and butter should be heated and put in last. Bake in 2 layers. This makes a small cake.

Filling for Mocha Cake
>Confectioner's sugar, 1 cup,
>Cocoa, 2 teaspoons,
>Butter, ¼ cup,
>Strong-made coffee, 2 tablespoons.

Put the filling between the layers, and on top.

MARSHMALLOW CAKE

>Butter, 1 cup,
>Sugar, 2 cups,
>Milk, 1 cup,
>Eggs, 4,
>Flour, 4 cups,
>Baking-powder, 3 large teaspoons,
>Vanilla, 1 teaspoon,
>Salt, ¼ teaspoon.

Bake the layers in 3 thick, or 4 thinner layers.

Filling for Marshmallow Cake
>Marshmallow candies, ½ pound,
>Granulated sugar, 1 cup,
>Egg, 1 (white only).

Put the marshmallows on an agate dish, and place in an open oven until they have melted and run together. In the meantime make a boiled icing with 1 cup of sugar and ⅓ cup of hot water, and boil until the syrup hairs; then pour over it the stiffly beaten white of 1 egg.

Add the melted marshmallows to this, beat slowly for 5 minutes, spread on the cake, between the layers, and on top. For the top layer put a number of marshmallows on a skewer, hold before the open fire, till they puff, and brown; then place them round the edge of the cake.

FUDGE CAKE

Butter, 1 cup,
Sugar, 1 cup,
Milk, 1 cup,
Flour, 3 cups,
Pecan nuts, ½ cup,
Grated chocolate, ¼ cup,
Eggs, 2,
Baking-powder, 1 teaspoon.

Cream the butter with the sugar, add the milk, and chocolate, eggs, sifted flour, and baking-powder, and last of all the nuts, broken and dredged with flour. Bake in layers, and put together with the fudge filling here given. Cover all with boiled icing.

Filling for Fudge Cake

Sugar, 2 cups,
Chocolate, ¼ cup,
Milk, ¾ cup,
Butter, 1 tablespoon,
Vanilla, 1 teaspoon.

Put into a porcelain-lined saucepan the sugar, chocolate, milk, and butter. The chocolate should be broken small. Boil over a hot fire for 6 minutes; then take from the range, add the vanilla, and beat until the mixture begins to thicken, then pour quickly over the cake layers.

LADY BALTIMORE CAKE

Butter, 1 cup,
Sugar, 2 cups,
Flour, 3½ cups,

Sweet milk, 1 cup,
Eggs, 6 (whites only),
Baking-powder, 2 level teaspoons,
Rosewater, 1 teaspoon.

Mix it as you would a white cake, and bake in 3 layers.

Filling for Lady Baltimore Cake

Granulated sugar, 3 cups,
Eggs, 3 (whites only),
Chopped raisins, 1 cup,
Figs, 5,
Nut-meats.

Cut the figs in very fine strips, and mix with them enough chopped nut-meats to make 1 cupful. Dissolve the sugar in a cup of boiling water. Beat the whites to a stiff froth.

Cook the sugar until it threads, then pour it slowly over the beaten whites of the eggs. Stir constantly while pouring it in.

Add to this icing the chopped raisins, nut-meats, and figs. Ice, and emboss the sides and top of the cake with this mixture.

SAND TARTS

Butter, ½ pound,
Granulated sugar, 1 pound,
Eggs, 3,
Vanilla extract, 1 teaspoon,
Flour,
Nutmeg.

Beat the butter to a cream and then add the sugar. Then add the yolks of the eggs and the whites of 2 of the eggs, which have all been beaten together. Add the vanilla, and just a little grated nutmeg.

Mix in barely sufficient flour to make a dough. Dust the baking-board thickly with granulated sugar. Take out a piece of the dough and roll it into a moderately thin sheet. Cut it out with round cutters and bake in a moderately hot oven until a light brown.

Dust the top of the sheet with sugar instead of flour, to prevent the roller from sticking.

FRUIT DROPS

Flour, 2 cups,
Sugar, 1½ cups,
Butter, 1 cup,
Eggs, 3,
Dates, ¾ pound,
Figs, ¼ pound,
English walnuts, 1½ pounds,
Soda, 2 teaspoons,
Cinnamon, 1 teaspoon,
Allspice, ½ teaspoon,
Salt, a pinch.

Cream the butter and sugar. Add the eggs, salt, flour, soda (which must be dissolved in 1 tablespoon of hot water).

Also add the dates and figs cut fine, the walnuts, cinnamon, and allspice. Mix all together. Knead with the hands, roll into little balls, and drop on buttered tins, and bake in a hot oven.

SURPRISE MACAROONS

Shredded cocoanut, 1 cup,
Brown sugar, 1 cup,
Butter, 1 cup,
Eggs, 2, well beaten,
Oatmeal, 1½ cups,

Chopped raisins, 1 cup,
Chopped pecans, 1 cup,
Soda, 1 level teaspoon,
Cinnamon, ½ teaspoon.

Dissolve the soda in a little hot water; mix all the ingredients well together, and drop, by small teaspoonsful, on paper into a greased baking-pan.

Bake in a moderate oven until brown. After taking from the fire, let it stand for a moment.

OATMEAL ROCK CAKES

Oatmeal, 3 cups,
Butter, 4 tablespoons,
Sugar, 10 tablespoons,
Eggs, 2.

Mix together, and drop from a teaspoon upon paper placed in a buttered pan. Bake in a moderate oven until quite brown.

OATMEAL SPICED COOKIES

Butter, ½ cup,
Lard, ½ cup,
Granulated sugar, 2 cups,
Sweet milk, 10 tablespoons,
Rolled oats, 3½ cups,
Chopped nut-meats, ¾ cup,
Flour, 3 cups,
Salt, ½ teaspoon,
Cinnamon, 1 level teaspoon,
Cloves, 1 level teaspoon,
Allspice, 1 level teaspoon,
Soda, 1 level teaspoon.

Mix together, beat vigorously. Drop from a spoon onto a greased pan, leave room for spreading. Bake in a medium oven. These cookies will keep for weeks if put into an airtight box.

GERMAN RINGS

>Flour, ½ pound,
>Sugar, 1 pound,
>Butter, 1 pound,
>Eggs, 2 (yolks and whites beaten separately),
>Ground cinnamon, 1 tablespoon.

Beat the yolks and whites separately. Make a dough of the flour, butter, and ¾ pound of the sugar, and add both yolks of the eggs, and half of the beaten whites.

Roll the dough in small pieces and form into rings. Dip these first into the remaining white of egg, and then into a mixture made of ¼ pound of the sugar, and 1 tablespoon of ground cinnamon. Bake until light brown.

RUSSIAN ROCK CAKE

>Butter, 1 cup,
>Sugar, ½ cup,
>Eggs, 3,
>Flour, 3½ cups,
>Ground cinnamon, 1 teaspoon,
>Nut-meats, 1 cup,
>Dates, 1 pound.

Mix the butter, sugar, and eggs, and beat all to a cream; add the spices, flour, nut-meats, and dates cut fine, and bake on buttered tins.

MARZIPAN
GERMAN

Almonds, 1 pound,
Powdered sugar, 1 pound,
Rosewater.

Blanch the almonds, and when perfectly dry, pound them, or grind them fine in a meat chopper, and add to this gradually, the sugar and rosewater. Cover a board thickly with powdered sugar, and on this, with the fingers, knead thoroughly the mixture.

Allow the mixture to remain on the board for an hour after kneading, and then roll it out to the thickness of about $\frac{1}{4}$ inch, and cut into small fancy shapes and allow these to harden.

If so desired the mixture may be pressed into a figured mold, and there allowed to harden, and then be turned out.

This does not require cooking, but may be placed in the oven for a few moments to dry.

SCOTCH SHORT-CAKE

Butter, $\frac{3}{4}$ pound,
Flour, 1 pound,
Powdered sugar, 1 pound,
Cinnamon, 1 tablespoon,
Eggs, 3.

Rub the butter and flour together; mix in the powdered sugar and the cinnamon. Mix into a dough with the 3 eggs well beaten, and roll it out into a sheet. Cut into round cakes, and bake in a quick oven. They will require but a few minutes.

SUPERIOR COOKIES

Butter, 1 cup,
Sugar, 2 cups,
Eggs, 2,
Cream, 4 tablespoons,
Baking-powder, 2 teaspoons,
Flour.

Use only as much flour as may be required to roll them out. Roll thin, and bake quick.

SUGAR COOKIES

Sugar, 2 cups,
Butter, 1 cup,
Eggs, 2,
Baking-soda, 1 teaspoon,
Carraway seed, 1 teaspoon,
Flour.

Use just enough flour to roll out. Bake in a moderate oven.

GINGER SNAPS

Butter, ½ pound,
Flour, 2 pounds,
Ground ginger, 1 tablespoon,
Brown sugar, ½ pound,
Molasses, 1 pint.

Rub the butter into the flour, and add the ginger and the sugar. Mix thoroughly, then add gradually the molasses, as the dough must be quite stiff—possibly you may not need the entire pint of molasses, it depends on the grade of flour used. Knead it thoroughly, and roll out into a thin sheet.

Cut with a small round cutter and bake in a moderate oven until the cakes are brown and crisp.

JACKSON SNAPS

Butter, ½ pound,
Sugar, 1 pound,
Egg, 1,
Lemon, 1,
Flour (sifted), 1 quart.

Beat the butter to a cream, adding the sugar and egg well beaten, also 1 cupful of water and the juice of 1 lemon, also the grated rind of the lemon.

Knead in the flour which has been sifted—possibly you may require a little more than a quart. The dough must be hard and elastic. Roll it out into a thin sheet, and cut out, and bake in a moderate oven until they are brown and crisp.

HERMITS

Sugar, 1½ cups,
Butter, ¾ cup,
Eggs, 2,
Soda, 1 teaspoon,
Cinnamon, 1 teaspoon,
Cloves, 1 teaspoon,
Nutmeg, 1 teaspoon,
Chopped raisins, 1 large cupful,
Flour.

Use only enough flour to roll out. Dissolve the soda in a little water before mixing. Put sugar or grated cocoanut, or nuts, on top before baking.

CRULLERS

Sugar, 1 cup,
Eggs, 2,
Sour milk, 1 cup,
Melted shortening, 3 tablespoons,
Salt, 1 level teaspoon,
Cream of tartar, 1 level teaspoon,
Baking-soda, 1½ teaspoons,
Flour, nutmeg, cinnamon.

Use flour enough to roll as soft as can be handled; spice to taste with the nutmeg and cinnamon; roll out, cut into shapes, and fry in deep hot fat till a delicate brown.

GRANDMOTHER HOLT'S CRULLERS

Sugar, 10 tablespoons,
Melted butter, 5 tablespoons,
Lard, 6 tablespoons,
Sweet milk, ½ cup,
Eggs, 3,
Soda, ¼ teaspoon,
Flour, nutmeg, salt.

Mix together, using only enough flour to make rolling out possible. Season to taste, with the nutmeg and salt. Shape, and fry in very hot lard.

CANDY

MOLASSES CANDY

Molasses, 1 quart,
Vinegar, ½ cup,
Sugar, 1 cup,
Butter, 1 heaping tablespoon,
Vanilla, 1 teaspoon,
Soda, 1 teaspoon.

Dissolve the sugar in the vinegar. Mix it with the molasses, and boil, stirring frequently, until it hardens by being dropped from the spoon into cold water.

Then stir in the butter and soda, the latter dissolved in hot water. Flavor to taste, with vanilla, give one final stir, and pour into buttered dishes.

While still hot, pull it white, into sticks, using butter or flour on the fingers.

ENGLISH MOLASSES CANDY

Molasses, 1 pound,
Brown sugar, 1 pound,
Butter, ½ pound,
Vanilla, or peppermint, 1 teaspoon.

Boil the sugar and molasses slowly together, until the mixture becomes stringy, then stir in the butter and a teaspoon of vanilla or peppermint. The longer it is cooked the more brittle it will be, and when brittle it will keep better, and be less apt to become sticky.

When sufficiently cooked pour into a buttered tin. Nuts may be added if desired, and if so, should be added when about to pour into the tin,—care being taken to stir them well into the candy.

WHITE SUGAR CANDY

> Granulated sugar, 3 cups,
> Cream of tartar, 1 salt-spoon,
> Vinegar, 2 tablespoons,
> Butter, 1 teaspoon,
> Cold water, ⅔ cup.

Place over a slow fire the vinegar, sugar, and water, and beat slowly until the sugar is dissolved, then add the butter and cream of tartar. Do not stir after the sugar commences to boil. Cook until a sample dropped in cold water will harden.

Flavor with vanilla. Half of it may be colored pink with fruit-coloring, or chocolate may be used.

When pulled, this makes a fine cream candy.

SEA FOAM

> Loaf sugar, 1 pound,
> Thick cream, 1 cup,
> Nut-meats, finely chopped, 1 cup.

Bring the sugar and cream to a soft boil, then take off the fire, and whip with an egg-beater, until soft and fluffy, like down. Stir in the nuts, and cut in irregular shapes.

Place them on **paraffin paper**, and allow them to cool before handling.

It is more difficult to make candy in warm weather than in

cold. It should be cooked a little longer in summer than in winter.

BUTTER SCOTCH

Brown sugar, 1 pound,
Butter, ¼ pound,
Ground ginger, ½ ounce.

Dissolve the sugar, add the butter, and keep stirring over the fire until it sets lightly, then add the ginger, stir it well in, and pour the whole into a buttered dish, and set in a cool place.

PEPPERMINT DROPS

Granulated sugar, 1 large cup,
Hot water, 4 tablespoons,
Confectioner's sugar, 4 tablespoons,
Oil of peppermint, a few drops.

Put the cup of sugar in a granite saucepan, together with the hot water, and when the mixture commences to boil continue to cook for 3 minutes only. Then add the confectioner's sugar, and a few drops of peppermint oil, which have been mixed together, and turning it quickly into the boiling syrup, stir it well.

Take from the fire, and set it in a larger pan of cold water; and, with a spoon, drop the hot liquid in spots, about the size of a nickel, on oiled paper, or on marble.

Do not place the lozenges so close together that they will be liable to run together.

CREAM PEPPERMINTS

White sugar, 1 pound,
Cream of tartar, ¼ teaspoon,
Oil of peppermint, 3 drops.

Dissolve the cream of tartar in a teacup of cold water, add to it the sugar, and place over the fire, and boil until a sample cooled in water can be rolled into a ball with the fingers. Then remove from the fire, allow it to cool a little, and then beat with a spoon until it turns white.

Add 3 drops of oil of peppermint, and mix it well into the candy. If the candy hardens too quickly while beating, set the bowl in a tin of boiling water. Make into balls with the hands.

MINT DROPS

Sugar, 1 pound,
Oil of peppermint, 3 drops,
Cream of tartar, ½ salt-spoon.

Dissolve the cream of tartar in half a cup of water, and put this, together with the sugar, over the fire, and stir until the sugar is dissolved and the mixture commences to boil.

Continue to boil until a sample, tested in water, becomes stringy; then add 3 drops of peppermint oil, stir it well in, then take from the fire, and when somewhat cooled, beat quickly until it begins to look opaque. Then pour into tiny fluted molds, or drop on oiled paper or marble. They will harden at once.

SAUERKRAUT CANDY

Take 2 cups of brown sugar, half a cup of boiling water, boil until it will harden in cold water; add cocoanut, grated, and pour, after beating well, upon a buttered dish.

COCOANUT DROPS

Grated cocoanut,
Granulated sugar,
White of egg.

To 1 grated cocoanut add the half of its weight of granulated sugar, and the white of 1 egg, beaten to a stiff froth.

Stir and mix well together, drop on buttered paper, or on waxed paper, and place in the oven and bake for 15 minutes.

PEANUT BRITTLE

Peanuts, 1 cup,
Granulated sugar, 1 pint.

Roast, shell, and blanch the peanuts. Put the sugar in a frying-pan, place on a moderate fire. Add no water, or any kind of liquid. Stir often with a metal spoon, or one of agate-ware. As the sugar heats it will at first lump, then as it grows hotter will gradually melt.

Do not let the syrup turn darker than weak coffee; and in stirring be careful not to allow it to splash on the skin, as it makes a painful burn.

When melted, and pale brown, stir in the nuts, then turn out quickly into a flat well-greased pan, resting in cold water.

Pound out the mixture as thin as possible, and put aside in a cold place to harden before breaking the candy into pieces.

PEANUT CANDY

Molasses, 2 cups,
Sugar, 1 cup,
Vinegar, ½ (small) cup,
Butter, 1 tablespoon,
Water, 1 cup,
Peanuts (roasted).

Place all except the peanuts in a kettle, and boil until brittle, then stir in the peanuts which have been shelled and skinned.

Pour out on a greased plate. English walnuts or hickory-nut meats may be used in the same manner.

NUT CANDY

Nut-meats, 1 cup,
Sugar, 1 cup,
Molasses, 1 cup.

Boil together until the mixture is brittle when dropped into cold water. Add the meats of either peanuts, hickory-nuts, walnuts, almonds, etc. Then take from the fire.

Pour into buttered pans, and mark into squares before it cools.

PENOTCHIE

Light-brown sugar, 3 cups,
Milk, 1 cup,
Butter, 1 teaspoon,
Vanilla extract, 1 teaspoon,
Nut-meats, 1 cup.

Any of the various nut-meats may be used. Put the sugar and milk over the fire, and boil till a sample dropped into cold water makes a soft, but firm ball in the fingers.

Then add the butter. Take from the fire, flavor with the vanilla, stir in the nut-meats which have been broken in little bits, turn out onto a shallow pan, well buttered, and mark into squares with a buttered knife.

NOUGAT

Sweet almonds, 1 pound,
Loaf sugar, 1 pound,
Lemons (juice only), 3.

Blanch the almonds, and with a sharp knife split each into several parts. Spread them over a large dish and place in a slow oven.

Powder the loaf sugar, and put it in a preserving-pan without any water at all, and set it on the back of the stove, or over a gentle fire and stir with a wooden spoon till the sugar is nearly dissolved.

The almonds should not be allowed to brown in the oven. Take them out and mix them with the juice of 3 lemons, and put the almonds, a few at a time, into the melted sugar, and allow them to simmer until a thick paste is formed, taking care to stir hard all the time.

Prepare a mold or square tin, well greased inside with olive-oil, and into it pour the mixture; smooth it evenly, and set it in a cool place to harden; then cut it into oblong blocks with a buttered knife.

FRENCH FONDANT

As fondant forms the base for many candies, it is of importance that in the making of such candies care in making the fondant be always exercised.

Fondant can be used at any time for the foundation of candies; when any of this mixture is left over in candy-making, it can be used after the lapse of time.

The regular formula for making fondant is as follows:

> Granulated sugar, 1 pound,
> Water, ½ pint,
> Flavoring.

Place a graniteware or enameled stewpan over the fire—not next to the blaze—and stir in the sugar and water, constantly stirring until all the sugar is dissolved. Then let the syrup boil for from 5 to 6 minutes, trying it by dropping a few drops into a glass of cold water. When it will form soft balls in the fingers take it from the fire and pour the syrup into a large platter that has been cooled in cold water.

When the syrup begins to thicken and cool, beat it rapidly with a wooden spoon. Add any desired flavoring before this beating.

After having beaten until white, knead it with the fingers, as kneading dough. This will cause the fondant to become smooth and of good consistency, which will enable it to be easily shaped to suit one's fancy.

CHOCOLATE COATING

Chocolate coating for almonds and creams is made by melting sweetened chocolate in a double-boiler.

Run a thick skewer into each nut, and dip into the melted chocolate until thoroughly coated.

Spread on buttered tins to dry, or on waxed paper.

CHOCOLATE BONBONS

Sweetened chocolate, ½ pound,
Gum arabic, 1 ounce,
Confectioner's sugar, 2 ounces.

The gum arabic should be dissolved in 1½ tablespoons of hot water. Put the chocolate into a boiler and cook until soft, then add the gum arabic, dissolved in water and stir till smooth. Add the sugar, mix all together, and then drop the chocolate, gradually, from the spout of the sugar-boiler, cutting off with a wire, to desirable size. When the candy is dry it is ready to eat.

CHOCOLATE CREAMS, NO. 1

Vanilla chocolate, 1 cake,
Vanilla extract, 2 tablespoons,

Powdered sugar, 3 cups,
Cornstarch, or arrowroot, 2 tablespoons,
Butter, 1 tablespoon.

Wash the salt from the butter. Stir the sugar and 1 cup of water together, and mix in the cornstarch, or arrowroot, and bring to a boil, stirring constantly to induce granulation. Boil about 10 minutes, and then add the butter.

Take from the fire, and beat as you would eggs, until it begins to look like granulated cheese. Then put in the vanilla extract. Butter your hands well. Make the cream into balls about the size of large marbles, and lay them on a greased dish.

During this time the chocolate should have been melted, by putting it, grated fine, into a tin pail, or a saucepan, and plunging it into another pail, containing boiling water.

When the chocolate is a black syrup add about two tablespoons of the powdered sugar to it, beat it smooth, turn it out on a hot dish, and roll the cream balls in it until sufficiently coated.

Lay them on a cold dry dish to dry, taking care that they do not touch each other.

CHOCOLATE CREAMS, NO. 2

Unsweetened chocolate, 2½ ounces,
Cooked fondant, 1 pound,
Flavoring.

Roll the fondant into small balls, and place on oiled paper to harden. Use only half of the fondant for this purpose, and put the other half of the fondant into the stewpan with 2½ ounces of chocolate and add a few drops of vanilla or other flavoring extract.

Put the stewpan into another vessel of boiling water, allowing the fondant and chocolate to melt together and form a thick cream.

Then remove from the fire, take the hardened-fondant balls, one at a time, either on a fork or on a sharpened stick, and dip into the chocolate-fondant, placing them immediately on a smooth oiled paper, in a cold place to harden.

BURNT ALMONDS

>Brown sugar, 1½ cups,
>Shelled and blanched almonds, 1 cup,
>Water, 3 tablespoons.

Put the sugar and water into a saucepan, place on the fire, and stir until the sugar is dissolved. When the sugar comes to a good boil, put in the almonds, and stir till the nuts are well covered and a little browned.

Turn on a buttered dish, and separate each nut. If not coated with candy, thoroughly, then repeat the process.

CHOCOLATE ALMONDS, NO. 1

>Sweet chocolate,
>Almonds,
>Vanilla extract.

Blanch the almonds. Grate or shave the chocolate into a bowl, set in a pan of boiling water. When the chocolate is melted put an almond on the point of a darning needle, and dip it into the melted chocolate. Then lay it on greased paper to dry. After all the nuts have been dipped and dry, dip a second time and a third time if so desired.

CHOCOLATE ALMONDS, NO. 2

>Vanilla chocolate, ½ pound,
>Butter, 2 tablespoons,
>Almonds.

Put the chocolate into a pan over boiling water, and when melted, stir in the butter, and add 2 tablespoons of boiling water.

The almonds, which have already been blanched, should have been dried between towels, and roasted in the oven till a light brown.

Dip the almonds into the coated mixture, and drop on paraffin paper to harden.

CHOCOLATE TAFFY

>Granulated sugar, 2 cups,
>Grated chocolate, 3 cups,
>Boiling water, ½ cup,
>Butter, 1 tablespoon,
>Vanilla extract, 2 teaspoons.

Cook until it will nearly crack when dropped into cold water, then add the butter, and continue to boil, until the candy snaps when tested in cold water. Take from the fire, flavor with the vanilla, cool and pull it, and cut it into any desired shapes.

CHOCOLATE CHIPS

>Chocolate,
>Molasses, 1 cup,
>Sugar, ⅔ cup,
>Butter, 1 heaping tablespoon,
>Vanilla extract.

First mix a candy of molasses for the filling. This should be made as follows: Boil together molasses, sugar, and butter until a little of it dropped into cold water is crisp, then add a flavoring of vanilla, and pour it out on buttered tins and when cool enough to handle, pull thin, and cut into small pieces.

When these pieces have become perfectly cold, dip them into melted sweetened chocolate, also flavored with vanilla, and lay the pieces on waxed paper to dry.

CHOCOLATE CARAMELS, NO. 1

Light brown sugar, 3 pounds,
Chocolate, ½ pound,
Butter, ¼ pound,
Cream, ½ cup,
Vanilla extract, 3 tablespoons.

Put into a porcelain kettle all except the vanilla and set it on the back of the stove and let it melt slowly—2 hours is not too long, if you wish the candy to be rich and smooth.

When melted let it heat stronger, and boil for about 10 minutes, then try it in cold water, and if it forms a ball of the consistency of putty, take from the fire, and beat, adding the vanilla, then turn into a buttered dish, and when set, mark off in squares.

CHOCOLATE CARAMELS, NO. 2

Brown sugar, 1 pound,
Grated, unsweetened chocolate, 4 ounces,
Thick molassses, 1 teaspoon,
Butter, 2 ounces,
Sweet milk, ⅓ cup,
Vanilla extract, 20 drops.

The butter should be unsalted if possible. Put all the ingredients into the saucepan except the vanilla, and boil, stirring constantly, for 20 minutes. Try, by dropping a little in a cup of cold water, and as soon as it will form a ball, and does not discolor the water, remove the pan from the fire.

Add the vanilla, and beat with a wooden spoon till cool; then pour into a shallow tin pan that has been greased with butter, and allow it to harden. Before it is quite hard, cut into blocks with a sharp knife.

CHOCOLATE NUT CANDY

Cocoa, or chocolate, 1 pound,
Pulverized sugar, 2 cups,
Cream, ½ cup,
Butter, 1 tablespoon,
Vanilla, 1 teaspoon,
Nut-meats, 1 cup.

Any nut-meats may be used except peanuts. Put the sugar, cream, cocoa, and butter in a saucepan, place over a quick fire, stir constantly to prevent burning, and at the end of 3 minutes test it by dropping a little in cold water. If it forms a soft ball, remove from the fire, and flavor with the vanilla, then heat the candy in the kettle till begins to thicken. Have ready the nuts, stir them into the candy then pour on buttered tins.

When nearly cold cut in squares. Instead of vanilla a teaspoon of cinnamon may be used for flavoring.

CHOCOLATE FUDGE, NO. 1

Unsweetened chocolate, 1 cake,
Brown sugar, 3 pounds,
Milk, 1 cup,
Butter, ½ pound,
Vanilla, 1 teaspoon.

Let the sugar, milk, and butter come to a boil, then add the cake of chocolate, and boil further till it thickens. Try it in water. Take from the fire, and season with vanilla.

Beat it till creamy—for about 5 minutes. Cool in a shallow pan, and mark it in squares before it hardens.

CHOCOLATE FUDGE, NO. 2

>Chocolate, 1 pound,
>Sugar, 2 pounds,
>Milk, or cream, 1 cup,
>Butter, $\frac{1}{8}$ pound,
>Vanilla, 1 teaspoon,
>Salt, a large pinch.

Dissolve the chocolate over the tea-kettle, then mix with it the sugar and cream, or milk, and return to the stove. After it comes to a boil stir in the butter and a large pinch of salt.

Boil till the mixture forms a very soft ball when dropped into cold water. It should have just consistency enough not to go to pieces when handled.

Beat it vigorously, stirring in the vanilla, and when the candy has slightly cooled, pour it into buttered pans, and when almost set, mark it in squares with a knife.

This also makes good icing for a chocolate cake.

NUT FUDGE

>Sugar, 3 cups,
>Milk, $1\frac{1}{2}$ cups,
>Butter, 1 large tablespoon,
>Vanilla, 1 teaspoon,
>Nut-meats, 1 cup.

Break the nut-meats in bits. Boil the sugar and milk together, slowly until perfect drops will form when dropped in cold water.

Then remove from the fire, add the butter and vanilla. Heat again till thick, then add the nut-meats, mix well, and turn into buttered plates and mark in squares with a knife, while still warm.

MAPLE CARAMELS

Maple sugar, 2 pounds,
Cream or milk, 1 quart.

Break the sugar into the milk,—half cream if so preferred, —and boil steadily till a little dropped in cold water will harden.

Then pour it into greased pans, and as it cools mark off into squares.

COFFEE CARAMELS

Brown sugar, 1 pound,
Strong coffee, 1 cup,
Cream, ½ cup,
Butter, 1 tablespoon.

Cook until brittle when dropped into cold water, then pour into buttered tins, and when nearly cold, mark off in squares.

MEXICAN KISSES

Brown sugar, 2 cups,
Sweet milk, ½ cup,
Butter, 1 heaping tablespoon,
English walnuts (broken in bits), 1 pound.

Put the sugar, and milk in a stewpan, and cook gently till a little dropped in cold water will ball when rubbed in the fingers. It will take about 10 minutes to reach this stage. Stir constantly while boiling as it scorches easily.

Add the butter, and as soon as melted, remove the pan from the fire and beat steadily till the mixture is creamy, and a bit granulated. Then stir in the walnuts or other nut-meats, beat hard, and turn into buttered pans, and set away to harden in a cool place.

GUM-DROPS

>Gum arabic, 1 pound,
>White sugar, 1 pound,
>Cornstarch and flavoring,
>Granulated sugar,
>Coloring if desired.

Dissolve the gum arabic in a pint and a half of water, strain, and add the pound of white sugar, and heat till all the sugar is dissolved. Flavor to taste, and color all, or a part of it if so desired. The flavoring and coloring should be added to the mixture while it is warm.

When about the consistency of honey, fill a shallow pan with cornstarch, then take a rounded stick, the size the gum-drop is desired to be, and make little indentations in the cornstarch.

Fill a thin-lipped pitcher with the mixture, and pour it gently into these starch-molds, cutting the stream with a wire.

When all the molds are filled, set the pan in a warm place for several days, till the drops are hardened enough to handle; then take them out of the molds and dampen them a little, and shape in granulated sugar.

LEMON-DROPS

>Lemon-juice,
>Loaf sugar.

Squeeze some lemon-juice into a pan and with it mix some of the best loaf sugar, pounded and passed through a sieve. Make a paste so thick that it can scarcely be stirred, and place it in a porcelain saucepan over a hot fire, and stir for about 5 minutes with a wooden spoon.

Then remove it from the fire, and drop from the point of a knife, upon waxed paper—ordinary writing paper will do.

When cool, the drops may easily be removed from the paper. Peppermint drops may also be made in the same manner, by substituting the essence of peppermint, also orange-drops made by substituting the juice of oranges.

CANDIED MINT LEAVES

Prepare fondant, and when the syrup is boiled, so that it "hairs," remove it from the fire, stir a little, and dip each small spray of mint into it, laying them afterwards on buttered paper to harden.

CANDIED VIOLETS

Candied violets may be prepared in the same way as candied mint leaves.

The syrup may be colored by using grape juice, and the stems made green with spinach leaves crushed, and the juice added to fondant.

DECORATING CAKES

Crystallized mint leaves, and violets, and candied fruits may be formed into most attractive decorations for cakes.

TO FASTEN CANDLES ON CAKES

Push a hot hat-pin, or a knitting needle into the bottom of the candle; remove, and put in a wooden toothpick while the wax is still soft. After the wax is hardened around the toothpick the candle may be easily placed in position on the cake.

MARRONS GLACÉS

Fresh chestnuts, 1 quart,
Butter, 2 teaspoons,
Lemon-juice, 2 tablespoons.
Syrup
Sugar, 2 quarts,
Vanilla bean, 1-inch length.

Use freshly gathered chestnuts if possible. Score each nut on one side with a sharp knife, then cover them with boiling water, cook for 5 minutes, and then drain and dry them. Add a teaspoon of butter to each pint of chestnuts, and placing them in a pan, shake them over the fire for 5 minutes, which will loosen both inner and outer skin and these must now be removed together, while the nuts are hot.

Cover the bared nuts with cold water, adding the 2 tablespoons of lemon-juice, and let them stand overnight, when the nuts will be firm, and will not break in cooking.

In the morning drain and let them dry, and then cover them with a syrup made of 2 pints of sugar and a cup of water, for each pint of nuts used—or in this case, 2 quarts of sugar, and 2 cups of water. Cook without boiling for 2 hours, or until the nuts look clear.

Drain off the syrup, taking care not to break the nuts, and reduce the syrup by rapid boiling. If the nuts are to be put away in syrup, then 5 to 8 minutes' boiling will be enough and in this case, when the syrup is cooked down, put back the nuts, and add the desired flavoring: This should be, either; an inch-length of vanilla bean for each quart of nuts, or, the juice and thin rind of one lemon, or, 2 tablespoons of maraschino.

After the flavoring is gently stirred in, pour the nuts and the syrup into small glasses, and seal when cold.

This makes an ideal flavoring for ices; or, the nuts and a little of the syrup may be served in frappé glasses with whipped cream.

Sweet potatoes may be prepared in the same manner instead of chestnuts.

CHESTNUTS GLACES

Chestnuts, 1 quart,
Granulated sugar, 1 pound,
Water, 2 cups.

Put a quart of fine large chestnuts into a frying-pan and roast, then skin them, and stick a wooden tooth-pick into each one. The chestnuts should not be allowed to brown.

Boil the sugar with 2 cups of water, to the candying stage, and then dip each nut into it. Stick the ends of the little skewers in a dish of brown sugar, to drain and harden.

CANDIED ORANGE-PEEL

Oranges, 6,
Granulated sugar, ½ pound,
Water, 1 cup,
Brandy.

Slice the oranges in pieces about a quarter of an inch thick. Remove all the pulp, and soak the rinds overnight in water sufficient to cover them. The water should be cold, and add to it salt in proportion of a flat tablespoon of salt to a quart of water.

In the morning put the rind on to boil, in fresh water, and cook until tender but not broken; then put the pieces on a sieve to dry.

Prepare a syrup of the granulated sugar and a cup of water, and boil until it begins to thicken, but is not at the crackling stage.

Dip the pieces of peel into the brandy, and then dip them into the syrup, which must be kept hot until the pieces have all been dipped and dried two or three times.

The next day reheat the syrup, and dip the pieces again, several times, and repeat this for 3 days, then dry off the pieces, and pack in tin boxes, with waxed paper between each layer of peel.

ORANGE BALLS
CALIFORNIA

Orange peel,
Sugar.

Soak the orange peel for 3 days in cold water, changing the water each day. Then put the peel in hot water, and boil until soft. Squeeze as dry as possible; chop fine and weigh it.

Take the same weight of sugar, and boil it with a little water until it hairs. Then add the chopped peel, boil a few minutes longer, take from the fire, cool, put on a baking-board sprinkled with granulated sugar, and mold into small balls. Roll these in sugar, and spread on a plate to dry

BEVERAGES

PUNCHES

PUNCH

>Plain soda-water, 4 bottles,
>Claret, 4 quarts,
>Brandy, ½ pint,
>Rum, Medford or Jamaica, 1 pint,
>Moselle, or Rhine wine, 1 pint,
>Vermouth, 1 gill,
>Pineapple, sliced, 1,
>Oranges, sliced, 4,

Mix, and sweeten with loaf-sugar, to taste.

FISH-HOUSE PUNCH

>Brandy, 1 pint,
>Jamaica, or Medford rum, 2 pints,
>Lemon-juice, 1 pint,
>Strong green tea, ½ pint,
>Water, 3 pints,
>Loaf-sugar, 1½ pounds.

Mix, strain, and before serving, add ice.

PHILADELPHIA FISH-HOUSE PUNCH

>Peach brandy, ¼ pint,
>Cognac, ½ pint,
>Jamaica, or Medford rum, ¼ pint,

Lemon-juice, ⅓ pint,
Apollinaris, 1 quart,
White sugar, ¾ pound.

Dissolve the sugar in one-half its volume of water before mixing. Mix all together, stir well, and serve with a large lump of ice in the bowl.

NAVY PUNCH

Jamaica rum, 2 quarts,
Brandy, 2 quarts,
White wine, 2 quarts,
Tea, 1 quart,
Lemons, the juice of 24,
Oranges, the juice of 6,
Water, 1 pint,
Soda-water, 6 bottles,
Light brown sugar.

Squeeze the juice of the lemons and oranges into a punch-bowl. Twelve of the lemons and all of the 6 oranges should be pared, before squeezing, and the peel placed in 1 pint of boiling water and allowed to stand until cold. Strain this water and pour it into the punch-bowl.

Next add the spirits and the tea, and mix well by stirring, and add a large block of ice.

Just before serving add the soda-water and sweeten to taste with the brown sugar, placing in the bowl some of the slices of orange and lemon for effect.

U. S. S. RICHMOND PUNCH

This celebrated punch is made from a stock, which can be kept in bottles, and at any time will produce an excellent punch by the addition of soda-water or champagne and ice, and is very useful in that it can be prepared on the spur of the moment. In making the stock, care should be used that the tea should not be drawn long enough before using to become bitter. When the stock has been made it should be tightly bottled, and placed in a comparatively cool place. The following is the composition of the stock:

> Jamaica rum, 1 quart,
> Brandy, 1 quart,
> Strong black tea, 1 quart,
> Port wine, 1 quart,
> Lemons, 12,
> White sugar, 3 cups,
> Curaçao, ½ pint.

Just before serving add 10 bottles of soda-water to 3 quarts of stock. Use plenty of ice.

CHAMPAGNE PUNCH

> Champagne, 2 quarts,
> Brandy, 1 pint,
> Rich lemonade, 1 pint,
> Curaçao, 1 gill,
> Syphon soda, 1 quart.

First make the lemonade, and to this add the curaçao and the brandy, a few minutes before the punch is to be served. Place a large block of ice in the bowl with the liqueur mixtures. Then add the soda and the champagne. The bowl may be further dressed with sliced oranges or with small fruits in season, such as strawberries, or cherries.

CHAMPAGNE PUNCH FOR TWELVE
CHAMBERLIN

>Champagne, 2 bottles,
>Brandy, ¼ bottle,
>Rum, ¾ tumbler,
>Strong black tea, 1 tumbler,
>Lemons, 3, strained,
>Powdered sugar, to taste.

CONGRESSIONAL PUNCH
CHAMBERLIN

Lemon-juice, 1 quart (very sweet),
Whisky, 1 quart,
Brandy, 1 pint,
Claret, 1 quart,
Champagne, 1 quart and 1 pint,
Oranges, bananas, etc., sliced,
Sweeten to taste.

REGENT PUNCH

>Strong green tea, 1½ pints,
>Jamaica rum, 1 pint,
>Brandy, 1 pint,
>Batavia arrack, 1 pint,
>Curaçao, 1 pint,
>Champagne, 1 quart,
>Lemon-juice, 1½ pints,
>Capillaire, 1½ pints,
>Pineapple, 1, sliced,
>Oranges, 2, sliced.

Mix all in a punch-bowl, and add ice and the champagne, just before serving. Sweeten further with sugar, if so desired.

Capillaire is a simple syrup made of sugar, or honey, and flavored with orange-flowers, or with orange-flower water.

CLARET PUNCH

Claret, 1 quart,
Sherry, ½ pint,
Maraschino, 1 liqueur-glass,
Pulverized sugar, ¼ pound,
Seltzer (siphon), 1 quart,
Ice, and the peel of 1 lemon.

Mix well, strain the punch, and add the ice and seltzer just before serving.

MADE DRINKS

APPLE TODDY

VIRGINIA

Old apple-brandy, 1 gallon,
Water, 1 gallon,
Loaf-sugar, 2 pounds,
Apples, large and sour, 8.

Bake the apples thoroughly without burning, and pour the gallon of scalding hot water over them. Let them stand in the water until cold, then put them through a colander, to remove the skins, seeds, and cores.

Add the sugar, and when dissolved pour in the brandy, and cover the crock or bowl tightly. When this is cold it may be served at once, or it may be placed in tightly corked bottles for future use.

APPLE TODDY
MARYLAND
Sour apples, well roasted, 18,
Boiling water, 1 gallon,
Sugar, 2 quarts,
Brandy, 1 quart,
Rum, Medford or Jamaica, 1 quart,
Sherry, 1 quart,
Madeira, 1 pint,
Arrack, ½ pint,
Peach brandy, ½ pint,
Orange bitters, ½ pint,
Grated nutmeg, 1,
Pineapple preserves, 2 tablespoons.

Pour the hot water over the apples, let it stand till it is cold, then put the apples through a colander, to take out the seeds, skins, and cores. Then add the other ingredients, and mix well together by stirring.

EGG-NOG
CHAMBERLIN
Pulverized sugar, 1¼ pounds,
Eggs, strictly fresh-laid, 12,
Best cognac, 1 quart,
Champagne, ½ pint,
Powdered nutmeg, 1 even tablespoon,
Fresh sweet milk, 2 quarts,
Sweet cream, 1 quart.

Thoroughly beat up the yolks of the eggs and incorporate them with the other ingredients by repeated stirring. Make the whites of the eggs into light snowy foamy whiteness, and place on top.

This receipt makes about 1 gallon of egg-nog.

CHERRY BOUNCE

Wild cherries, 6 quarts,
Medford rum, 1½ gallons,
Loaf-sugar, 1 pound,
Water, 2 quarts.

Put all into a 3-gallon demijohn. Shake well together, let stand for at least 3 months, sampling once in awhile, for it may need more sugar.

The longer it stands the better it becomes.

MIXED SINGLE DRINKS

MILK PUNCH

Brandy, 1 liqueur-glass,
Jamaica rum, 1 liqueur-glass,
Powdered sugar, 1 teaspoon,
Milk, 2 gills (1 tumblerful),
Nutmeg and lemon-peel.

Pour the liquors into the mixer first, then pour in the milk and sugar. Shake well, and strain into a large glass.

Sprinkle the nutmeg over the top, and squeeze in the lemon-peel.

GIN FIZZ

Powdered sugar, 1 teaspoon,
Lemon-juice, 4 dashes,
Gin, 1 liqueur-glass,
Carbonated water, and fine ice.

Mix the gin, lemon-juice and sugar in a glass, stir, shake thoroughly, in the mixer, strain into a glass, and fill up with carbonated water and fine ice.

RICKEY

Put a small piece of ice in a thin glass, and squeeze over it 1 lime. Put half the lime in the glass, and add a liqueur-glass of either whisky or gin, and fill the glass with carbonated water.

WHISKY SOUR

Squeeze the half of a lemon into the bottom of a glass, add a dash of carbonated water, and a little sugar. Mix this well, then fill the glass two-thirds full with shaved ice. Add a liqueur-glass of whisky, mix well, and strain. Then put in a slice of the lemon.

MINT JULEP, NO. 1

Whisky, ½ gill,
Sugar, 1 teaspoon,
French brandy, a dash,
Cracked ice,
Mint.

Fill a tall thin glass with finely cracked ice, and leave it for a few moments to become frosted on the outside. In another glass put the whisky, crush slightly the mint sprigs, so that its flavor will be imparted to the drink, add the sugar, and stir the mixture. No water must be used, as the melting ice will give all desired.

Pour this mixture into the tall glass, add a dash of French brandy, if at hand, trim the glass with a little sheaf of mint on one side, and put in a strawberry or a cherry to give it color.

MINT JULEP, NO. 2

Sugar, 1 cup,
Mint, 6 sprigs,

Strawberry juice, 1 gill,
Lemons, the juice of 4,
Cold water, 2 cups,
Boiling water, 1 cup,
Raspberry juice, 1 gill,
Cracked ice.

Boil the cold water and the sugar for 20 minutes, crush the mint, and pour the boiling water upon it, and allow it to stand 10 minutes, and then pour it into the syrup. To this add the strawberry, raspberry- and lemon-juices, and serve cold with the cracked ice.

MINT JULEP, NO. 3

Mint, 4 sprigs,
Whisky or brandy, 1 liqueur-glass,
Powdered sugar, ½ teaspoon,
Mint, 4 sprigs,
Seltzer, a dash,
Cracked ice.

Bruise 2 sprigs of the mint, place them in a mixing-glass, add the sugar and a dash of seltzer. Fill the tumbler with cracked ice, add the brandy or whisky, stir, shake well, and serve with a sprig or two on top.

PORT-WINE SANGAREE

Port-wine, one claret-glass,
Pulverized sugar, 1 teaspoon,
Cracked ice,
Grated nutmeg.

Mix, shake well, and serve with the grated nutmeg on top of the mixture, which should be put in a tall glass.

Sherry sangaree may be prepared in the same manner.

ORANGE COCKTAIL

Large oranges, 3,
Lemon, 1,
Sherry, 1 wine-glass.

Mix the juice of the oranges with that of the lemon, add the sherry, strain through cheese-cloth and chill. Add a cherry to each glass.

SHANDY GAFF

Put 2 or 3 pieces of ice in a large pitcher, and pour together, Bass and Ginger-ale at the same time.

BAMBOO

This is made from equal proportions of sherry and Italian Vermouth.

REMSEN COOLER

Remove the peel from a lemon, cutting it around, so that it will be in 1 piece and curl. Put this rind in a tall glass, around a piece of ice. Add a liqueur-glass of gin, and a bottle of soda.

CORDIALS.

MINT CORDIAL

Mint leaves (bruised), 1 small cup,
Oranges, large, 3,
Lemons, 6,
Sherry, ½ pint,
Sugar, 5 cups,
Water, 1 quart,

Red raspberries, 1 pint,
Siphon seltzer.

Soak the leaves in the juice of the oranges and lemons for half an hour, then add the sherry, a pint of raspberries, and a quart of thick, sugar-syrup made from boiling a quart of water and 5 cups of sugar for 10 minutes.

Mix thoroughly, place in the ice-chest, and just before serving add a siphon of seltzer.

Pour into a high glass tankard, and garnish with a bouquet of fresh mint.

ORANGE CORDIAL

Apple brandy, 2 quarts,
Oranges (skins only), 15,
Loaf sugar, 2 pounds.

Put the orange peel in the brandy, and let it stand for 3 weeks. Then take out the skins, and add 2 pounds of loaf sugar to the brandy, and let it stand for 6 weeks longer, then strain and bottle.

WINES

ELDER-BLOW WINE

Blossoms (pressed down), 1 quart,
Cold water, 1 gallon,
Sugar, 4 pounds,
Lemons, sliced, 3,
Yeast, 1 cake.

Pick from the stems enough blossoms to fill a quart measure when pressed down. Add a gallon of cold water, and steep for 24 hours.

Strain, and add the sugar, sliced lemons and yeast-cake.

Set away for 2 weeks, then strain carefully again, pour it into a jug, and after several months bottle.

CURRANT WINE

>Currants, 4 pounds,
>Sugar, 3 pounds,
>Water, 1 gallon.

Wash the currants, stems and all, in a large vessel; add the water and place in a cool cellar, stirring occasionally during 3 days. Press the currants through cloth, and strain the liquor, then add to it the sugar, and stir well.

Pour this into a cask, and when it ceases to ferment, bottle.

FRUIT PUNCHES.

CALIFORNIA FRUIT-PUNCH

Take equal quantities of unfermented white grape-juice, and apollinaris water.

Serve in a punch-bowl with a large lump of ice on which is laid grape leaves and a bunch of malaga grapes;—or a small quantity may be served in a glass pitcher.

STRAWBERRY PUNCH

>Strawberries, 1 quart,
>Raspberries, ½ pint,
>Sugar, 2 cups,
>Port-wine, 1 tumbler,
>Water, 1½ cups.

Pick the stems off of the berries and crush, and pass the juice through a fine sieve or cloth. Make a syrup with the sugar and water, and mix it with the juice. Add the port-wine, and place the whole on ice for several hours before serving.

Serve in small glasses.

ORANGE PUNCH

Oranges, 4,
White sugar, 1 pound,
Lemon, 1,
Water, 1 pint.

Take the rind from two of the oranges, grate it, and add to it the sugar and water. Stir together until the sugar is entirely dissolved, bring it to a boil, and continue to boil longer for 5 minutes.

When it has boiled 5 minutes take it from the fire, and when cold add the lemon and orange juices, and also about 1 quart of cold water, which is poured over it over cracked ice.

FRUIT PUNCH

Lemons, 12,
Oranges, 6,
Pineapple, ⅓,
Sugar,
Strawberries, or raspberries.

Squeeze the lemons and oranges, grate the pineapple, using only ⅓ of it, sugar to taste, strain the whole through a sieve, and add to this water enough to make a gallon.

Garnish it with a few strawberries and raspberries, or with maraschino cherries.

Serve cold, iced.

TUTTI FRUTTI CUP

Stoned cherries (cut in halves), 1 cup,
Pineapple (shredded), 1,
Crushed strawberries, 1 pint,
Bar-le-duc jelly, 1 small glass,
Powdered sugar,
Grated nutmeg,
Orange rind,
Granulated sugar, 3 cups,
Lemon-juice, ½ pint,
Cucumber (peeled), 1,
Ice, cherries, rosemary.

Place the stoned cherries, pineapples, strawberries, and bar-le-duc jelly in a large mixing-bowl. Sprinkle all with powdered sugar liberally, and also add a dusting of grated nutmeg and the grated rind of 1 orange.

Put this on the ice for 2 or 3 hours to chill and ripen.

Boil together in a saucepan, granite, the 3 cups of sugar and a quart of water, boiling for 10 minutes; then remove it from the fire and when cold stir into it the lemon, or lime-juice, and the cucumber, cut in dice.

When ready to serve, dress a block of crystal ice with large clusters of cherries and sprigs of rosemary.

Blend the two mixtures, quickly but thoroughly together, and pour slowly over the ice.

CLARET CUP, NO. 1

Claret, 1 quart,
Brandy, 2 liqueur-glasses,
Benedictine, or curaçao, 2 liqueur-glasses,
Lemons, 2,
Siphon soda, 1 quart,

Cucumber rind, 1, sliced,
Mint, 4 stalks,
Sugar, ice.

Mix well and serve in a high pitcher, with the cucumber rind and the mint at the top.

Champagne cup and Rhine-wine cup are made in the same manner by substituting those wines for the claret.

CLARET CUP, NO. 2

Sugar, ½ pound,
Lemons, 3,
Brandy, ½ tumbler,
Mint, 2 sprigs,
Green cucumber, 1,
Claret, 2 quarts,
Vichy, or seltzer, 2 bottles,
Pineapple, strawberry,
Ice, orange.

Dissolve the sugar in enough water to melt it and then allow it to cool. Place it in a large punch-bowl, and add to it the brandy and the lemon-juice. Whip this to a foam, then add the thin-cut rind of the lemon, the sprigs of mint, and the rind of the cucumber cut in strips, a quart of chipped ice, and the 2 quarts of claret and lastly the carbonated-water—either vichy or seltzer.

Stand the bowl in a larger one of chipped ice, cover the surface with slices of lemon, orange, pineapple, cut in little pieces, and a few strawberries.

The punch may be put into a large pitcher if more convenient; in either case, serve in glass cups.

SAUTERNE CUP

Sugar, 3 heaping tablespoons,
Boiling water, ½ pint.
Sugar, again, 1 cup,
Lemon, 1,
Oranges, 2,
Sauterne, 2 quarts,
Seltzer, 1 bottle,
Ice, mint,
Pineapple and strawberries.

Put the sugar (3 tablespoons) in a bowl with the boiling water, and stir it briskly till the sugar dissolves, then let it cool. When cool add to it the other cup of sugar, and a half pint of finely chipped ice. Whip these all up well, and then squeeze in the juice of 1 lemon and 2 oranges.

Just before serving add the sauterne and the seltzer, a few pieces of ice, slices of orange, pineapple and a few strawberries, and serve cold.

TEA PUNCH

Strong tea, 12 quarts,
Apollinaris, 12 pints,
Granulated sugar, 12 cups,
Lemon-juice, 3 pints,
Chipped, and lump ice.

In making the tea, allow at least 4 teaspoonfuls of good tea to each quart of boiling water. Let it stand for 10 minutes after it is made, then strain off the liquor from the leaves.

When it is cold, put a large lump of ice in a punch-bowl, and pour in the tea. Mix all the other ingredients, stir in, mixing well together, and keep it in a cold place, replenishing the serving bowl with this, and with ice, as required. This should make about 5 gallons.

A handful of mint leaves, floating on the surface of the serving-bowl is a pleasant addition to the flavor, and looks attractive.

Other fruits may be cut up and added.

FRUIT SYRUPS

PINEAPPLE SYRUP

Loaf sugar, 3 pounds,
Eggs (whites only), 2,
Pineapple juice, 1 quart.

Put the sugar into a granite pan or kettle, over the fire. Beat the whites of the eggs, and add them to 2 cups of clear water. Pour this over the sugar and set it over the fire to boil till clear. Remove it and let it get cold.

Pare and grate enough pineapple to make a quart of juice and strain it into the syrup. Boil for 10 minutes, and then bottle. Cover the corks with melted wax. This makes a delicious water-ice, and is better for flavoring than fresh pineapples.

LEMON SYRUP
FOR BOTTLING

Lemons, 18,
Water, 2 quarts,
Sugar, 6 pounds,
Eggs (shells and whites only), 2.

Scrub well 6 of the lemons, and chip off the thin yellow rind. Pour over this 1 pint of water and steep for an hour and then drain. Add 3 pints more of water, and the sugar, and put over the fire. When the sugar is dissolved, add the shells of the eggs, and also the whites, beaten to a froth, and stir until the scum rises and the syrup is clear.

Remove all the scum, add the strained juice of all the 18 lemons. Bring to the boiling point, skim, and bottle securely.

FRUIT SYRUP

> Red raspberries, 1 pint,
> Ripe currants, 1 quart,
> Granulated sugar, 2 cups,
> Cold water, 2 quarts.

Bruise the fruit in a preserving kettle, with a potato-masher, add to it the water and sugar, and let it cook until the sugar is dissolved. Let it heat gradually, and after it begins to boil remove it from the fire, drain in a jelly-bag, into a large bowl.

When it is clear and cool ice it, and sweeten it more, if it requires, and serve in small glasses.

SUMMER DRINKS

RASPBERRY SHRUB

> Red raspberries, 4 quarts,
> Vinegar,
> White sugar.

Cover the raspberries with vinegar in a closed stone jar. Keep them in a cool place for 24 hours, then strain through a sieve or cloth, not pressing too closely. To each pint of juice allow a pound of lump sugar broken in small bits. Put this over the fire to simmer quietly, gently stirring. Skim, as long as any scum arises. When cold bottle in dry bottles, and cork well.

CURRANT WATER

Raspberries, 1 cup,
Currants, 2 cups,
Sugar syrup, 1 cup.

Mash the raspberries and currants together, add a cup of water and bring to a simmer over the fire.

Make a sugar syrup of sugar and water boiled to the thread stage. Strain the currant and raspberry juices, and add to it the cup of sugar syrup, also a quart and a half of water, and stand the drink on ice until it is chilled.

FRENCH CREOLE DRINK

Pineapple, 1,
Lemon, 1,
Milk, 1 quart,
Sugar,
Ice.

Crush the pineapple, press the lemon, and strain the juices of both through a fine sieve, or through a piece of linen.

Add the milk, a piece of ice, and sweeten to taste.

GINGER-ALE JULEP

Granulated sugar, 1 scant cup,
Lemons, 6,
Mint, 6 stalks,
Pounded ice, 1 cup,
Ginger-ale, 2 bottles.

Put the sugar in a glass pitcher and squeeze upon it the juice of the lemons. When the sugar has dissolved stick half a dozen stalks of mint into the pitcher, bruising with the fingers some of the lower leaves.

Add a cup of pounded ice, then pour in the ginger-ale, and serve at once.

OLD COLONIAL GINGER CUP

Sultana raisins, ½ pound,
Currants, 1 cup,
Almond extract, 1 teaspoon,
Preserved ginger, ½ cup,
Oranges, 4,
Lemons, 2,
Powdered sugar, 2 cups,
Grated cocoanut, 3 tablespoons,
Ground cinnamon, ½ teaspoon,
Ginger-ale,
Shaved ice.

Steep the raisins and currants in 1 quart of boiling water for half an hour, then strain; and when cold add the almond extract, the preserved ginger, juices of the lemons and oranges, and also the sugar, cocoanut and cinnamon.

Mix well and place in the ice-box until thoroughly chilled, and when ready to serve, pour over all a quart of iced ginger-ale, serving in tall crystal glasses half filled with shaved ice.

GRAPE-JUICE

Grapes, 10 pounds,
Sugar, 3 pounds,
Water, 1 cup.

Put the grapes and water in a granite stewpan, heat until the pulps and stones separate, then strain through a jelly bag. Add the sugar to the juice, heat to the boiling point, and pour into bottles and seal.

For serving, dilute with crushed ice, or with ice-water.

BOTTLING LEMON-JUICE

>Lemons,
>White sugar.

Use 1 pound of sugar to each pint of lemon-juice. Squeeze the juice of the lemons, strain free from pulp and pits, add powdered white sugar and stir till the sugar is dissolved, then put away in small bottles, putting a teaspoon of olive-oil on the top of each bottle, before corking, then cork close.

When wanted for use uncork carefully, and remove the oil with a bit of cotton-wool. To use for lemonade, add one large tablespoon of juice to a gill of water.

PINEAPPLE LEMONADE

>Pineapple, 1,
>Lemons, 5,
>Sugar, 1 pound.

Peel and grate the pineapple and pour over it the juice of the lemons. Make a syrup of the sugar with a pint of water, boiling them together for 10 minutes.

Add the sugar syrup to the juices, put in a quart of cold water, and strain through a muslin cloth.

Serve in a glass filled with cracked ice, adding a cherry to each glass.

EGG LEMONADE

>Lemon, 1,
>Eggs, 2,
>Sugar and ice,
>Water.

Make a good plain lemonade, with half a lemon in each of 2 tumblers, add enough sugar to make it sweet as desired, beat an egg for each tumbler, and when well beaten, pour it into the tumbler with some cracked ice.

Fill the glass with filtered water, shake well, till the egg is fully mixed with the other liqud. Serve at once. This makes two drinks.

CHOCOLATE PARFAIT AMOUR

Rich milk, 1 pint,
Grated chocolate, 1 small cup,
Granulated sugar, 5 tablespoons,
Eggs, 3,
Vanilla extract, 1 teaspoon,
Whipped cream, 1 pint,
Finely chopped ice, 2 cups,
Apollinaris water,
Vanilla meringue.

Put the milk in a double boiler, and when almost boiling, stir in the chocolate, mixed with a little of the milk when cold. Also add the granulated sugar, and allow to boil till quite thick.

Remove from the fire, and while still warm, beat in the eggs and vanilla extract.

Place on ice until very cold, then stir in, lightly, the whipped cream and the chopped ice, diluting to the proper consistency with apollinaris water. Serve from tall cups that have been frosted with a vanilla meringue.

HAVANA AMANDE

Sweet almonds, 3 dozen,
Milk, 2 quarts,

Vanilla extract, 1 teaspoon,
Sugar, ½ pound.

Peel the almonds, and pound them to a pulp, and boil in the milk. Add the vanilla, and sweeten with the sugar. Let it cool, strain through a fine sieve, and place on the ice.

ROOT-BEER

Root-beer extract (Williams'), 1 bottle,
Compressed yeast cake, 1,
Sugar, 3 cups,
Warm water, 8 quarts,
Salt.

Dissolve the yeast cake in 1 cup of the warm water, mix with the sugar, and extract, and a little salt. Then add the warm water, and bottle it.

Set the bottles in a warm place for 12 hours, and then put them in a cool place.

To make orange-soda, or lemon-soda, substitute for the root-beer extract the juice of either a dozen lemons, or a dozen oranges. The fruits must be ripe. Orange-soda will require less sugar than lemon-soda.

For strawberry or raspberry flavor, take the desired quantity of fruit, crush, strain the juice, boil for 10 minutes, let it cool, and use this for the beverage in same manner as was used the root extract for root-beer.

Sarsaparilla, and vanilla extracts may be employed in the same manner as was the root extract.

GINGER BEER

Green ginger, sliced thin, 1½ ounces,
Yeast cake, ½,
Cream of tartar, 1 ounce,

Light-brown sugar, 1 pound,
Lemons, 2,
Boiling water, 1 gallon.

Scrub and slice the lemons very thin without paring. Mix the sugar, lemons, cream of tartar, and ginger together, add the boiling water, and stir over the fire till the sugar is dissolved, and then boil for about one minute longer.

Pour it into a large crock, and when cooled, add the half of a compressed yeast cake, which has previously been dissolved in a little warm water. Let it ferment for 24 hours, then strain and bottle.

Tie the corks down, and lay the bottles on their sides in the cellar. This is better at the end of a week than when newly made.

PART II
USEFUL INFORMATION

CLEANING AND REMOVING STAINS

JAVELLE WATER

Javelle water is excellent for removing stains from table linen, or other linen, and if carefully used is quite harmless, but the bleach is a strong one, and if permitted to stand for an instant after the discoloration has disappeared, the material is likely to be weakened, and in a short time a hole will appear.

The water is made as follows:

>Sal-soda, ½ pound,
>Boiling water, 1 pint,
>Chlorid of lime, ¼ pound,
>Boiling water, 1 quart.

Dissolve the sal-soda in a pint of boiling water, and in a separate vessel dissolve the chlorid of lime in a quart of boiling water.

When these two mixtures have dissolved then mingle them, and give the compound mixture a thorough stirring and leave the liquid to cool; when a clear portion will arise, which should be poured off and bottled and tightly corked. The bottles containing it should be kept in a dark place.

To use it, put a little of the bottled liquid into a basin, and wet the discolored linen with clear water, then put it into the basin containing the bleach. The stain should disappear in a moment—not a minute—and the material then at once plunged into clear cold water, and then into another supply of cold water, continuing this long enough to check any further action of the acid.

Only that portion of the linen that is stained should be wet with the javelle water as near as possible.

JAVELLE WATER
SECOND METHOD

Cold water, 1 gallon,
Chlorid of lime, 1 pound (1 can),
Sal-soda (common washing-soda), 4 pounds.

Place all on the fire and allow it to boil for 10 minutes. Take off and cool, and when cool put into bottles, fruit-jars, or stone jugs. Keep tightly corked.

A cup of this liquid in a tub of water will loosen the dirt in most soiled clothes, bleaching perfectly. It is also good for cleaning greasy cooking-utensils, drain-pipes, etc., and for removing all bad odors.

JAVELLE WATER
THIRD METHOD

Chlorid of lime, ½ pound,
Sal-soda, 1 pound.

Put the lime and soda into a wooden pail, pour on boiling water till the pail is full, to dissolve the soda. Let it remain for some hours, and next day stir it well, strain through a cloth and put it into bottles and cork, and keep in the dark.

For taking out stains, wet the linen with water, and rub some of the javelle water on the stain, then rub with washing-soap, and roll up tightly, and put it in, to boil.

OXALIC ACID

Oxalic acid may be used in the same manner as javelle water to remove stains, unless they are very deep-seated. It is prepared as follows:

Crystals of oxalic acid, 2 ounces,
Water, 1 gill.

Place the oxalic acid crystals in a bottle, add the water, and shake frequently until many of the crystals have dissolved, which may not, possibly, be before 12 hours. If the crystals are small it may be less. Then strain off the solution, 1 gill of which put into a gallon of water if the acid is to be used for a general bleach for clothes that have been made yellow by being long put away. But even in this case the clothes must be well wet before being put into the acid bath.

To use for taking out stains, add a gill of the solution to a pint of water, and the spot to be removed is touched with it, the same as with javelle water.

Both javelle water and oxalic acid are poison, and the bottles should be so labeled. They should not be used if there are abrasions on the hands.

REMOVING STAINS WITH SULPHUR MATCHES

Very small spots on white linen may be removed by wetting the heads of sulphur matches, one after the other, and rubbing them over the discoloration.

It is the sulphur in the composition which acts as a bleach.

TO CLEAN DECANTERS OR WATER-BOTTLES

Mix half a gill of vinegar with a handful of salt, and put a little of the liquid in each decanter, and shake well then rinse in clear water. Milk bottles should be washed first with cold water.

SOFT SOAP

Potash, ¾ pound,
Grease, 1 pound.

Soak the potash in cold water overnight, and next day boil it until the potash dissolves, then while still boiling hot, pour it over the grease which has been placed in the receptacle in which you intend to keep the soap.

Every day pour on more boiling water, according to the quantity of soap being made, and stir well.

Twenty-five pounds of grease will make about 1 barrel of soap. Pour on a kettle of hot water each day until it comes to the right consistency.

TO REMOVE SPOTS FROM CLOTHING

Sometimes the application of soap, ammonia, or gasoline to fabrics that have been soiled seems only to make the stains more prominent. This is partly because the cleaning agent was not suitable to the material.

No matter whether it is silk, wool, or cotton, there should always be a fresh piece of cloth placed underneath, to absorb the soiled fluid that soaks through, otherwise the cleaning-fluid, laden with dirt, has no place to go, and simply spreads over the original place. Several layers of some absorbent material should be used; layers of cheese-cloth are very good for this purpose.

It is also important that the fabric to be cleaned be spread out smoothly, so that it may be seen that no dirty ring is formed outside the stained portion. To prevent the formation of such a ring, the stained portion should be surrounded with cornstarch, which will prevent the cleaning-fluid from spreading. If there should be a ring formed outside the cleaned portion, it may in some cases be removed by holding it over the spout of a boiling tea-kettle.

The absorbent cloth should also be large enough to admit of moving the stained spot to a different place, so as not to rub in again, the old washed-out dirt.

Use a piece of old, but clean flannel for wetting and for

rubbing; and also have another clean piece for use in drying the spot as nearly as possible.

GREASE SPOTS ON LINEN OR COTTON

To remove grease spots from linen or cotton, use soap or weak lyes, and rub well with glycerin, and wash them out in warm water.

TO REMOVE GREASE SPOTS FROM WOOLENS

To remove grease spots from woolen goods use soapsuds, or ammonia.

TO REMOVE GREASE SPOTS FROM SILKS

To remove grease spots from silks, use benzine, ether, magnesia, chalk, or ammonia.

TWEED AND SERGE GARMENTS

For cleaning tweed and serge garments, a mixture of pure alcohol and salt is very useful. As much coarse common salt should be used as the alcohol will absorb, and the liquid should be applied as evenly as possible over the whole spot to be cleaned, using a brush to apply it.

TO REMOVE MILDEW FROM LINEN

To remove mildew from linen rub the linen well with soap, and then add a scraping of fine chalk. Cover well with the soap and chalk, and rub it well into the fabric. Put it in the air, and as it dries keep moistening it again. After two or three applications of the chalk and soap, the mildew will disappear.

Another method of removing mildew is by using chlorid of lime. For strong fabrics dissolve 4 tablespoons of dry chlorid of lime in half a pint of water, and let the mildewed article lie in this for 15 minutes; then wring it out gently, and put it into weak muriatic acid solution made of 1 part of muriatic acid and 4 parts of water.

For delicate fabrics the above solution of chlorid would be too strong, therefore the solution should be made of only 1 part of chlorid of lime to 12 parts of water, and furthermore the fabric should not be allowed to remain in the solution longer than 5 minutes.

IRON-RUST STAINS

Iron-rust stains are removed by using cream of tartar. If this be sprinkled on the stain and the damaged fabric be allowed to remain in the sun for a little while, the spot will disappear. If the first application is not entirely successful, a second will almost surely remove the stain.

TO REMOVE INK-SPOTS

To remove ink-spots from fabrics make a thick paste of milk and starch, and spread this on the spots and leave it for 2 days; and at the end of that time the spots will be hardly visible when the paste has been brushed off. It is, however, of use only if the spots are treated soon after they have been made.

TO REMOVE GRASS-STAINS

Grass-stains may be removed from clothing with common cooking-molasses, or with glycerin, by allowing the stained cloth to remain for 2 or 3 hours with either of these spread over the stained spot, then afterward washing out in lukewarm water. If the first application does not entirely remove the stain, then apply again.

TO TAKE A SCORCH-MARK OUT OF LINEN

A scorch-mark on linen, if not too brown, may sometimes be removed by moistening the linen with water, and laying in the sun. Repeat the moistening two or three times, and the mark will disappear.

TO REMOVE PAINT-STAINS

Turpentine is generally a very good liquid to use for removing paint-stains, and in this case it is always well to use if possible, the surrounding cornstarch, to prevent the turpentine from spreading.

STAINS MADE BY TAR

Stains made by tar are always best removed by the use of turpentine; and the spot should be surrounded with cornstarch, to prevent the spreading of the cleanser.

TO REMOVE COFFEE AND TEA STAINS

To remove stains of coffee and tea, rub the spots with a little borax, and soak for half an hour in cold water; then hold the fabric over the mouth of a deep bowl, and pour boiling water through the spot.

Another method of removing coffee stains, is to rub the stained portion with pure glycerin. This will remove stains of coffee and even of cream, from woolen and other materials. The stained place should be afterward well washed with lukewarm water, and ironed on the under, or wrong side, until dry.

TO REMOVE BLOOD-SPOTS

Blood-spots may be removed from the most delicate fabrics by dropping cold water quickly over the stains (that is, immediately after the blood-spots are made), and then covering the place with a thick layer of common laundry starch, finely powdered. When dry, brush off the starch, and it will be found that the stains are gone. This remedy, however, is of no use unless applied at once.

KEROSENE FOR WASHING CLOTHES

The washing of clothes can be made much easier by soaking them overnight, especially clothes that are particularly soiled, in water to which has been added a tablespoon of kerosene. In the morning wring out the clothes, and put them in a boiler, to which has been added another tablespoon of kerosene, then rinse through cold water, and hang them out.

TO REMOVE STAINS OF PEACHES

To remove peach-stains, place a tablespoon of sulphur on a plate, add a few drops of pure alcohol and ignite. Over this place a tin funnel, mouth downward, and wet the stain and hold over the smaller opening of the funnel, allowing the fumes of the sulphur to come in contact with every part of the stain. The action is a quick, chemical bleaching, which is effective for stains on white goods. Be careful to rinse the material immediately, and thoroughly in weak ammonia, and then launder as usual.

TO REMOVE BERRY- OR FRUIT-STAINS FROM THE HANDS

To remove fruit-stains from the hands, use the fumes from a few sulphur matches, lighting them one by one, and holding the fingers over the fumes. If the stains are large, light a bunch at a time.

TO REMOVE FRESH FRUIT-STAINS FROM FABRICS

To remove fresh fruit-stains from fabrics, first try by pouring boiling water over them; if this fails, then rub them with a half-lemon, dipped into salt, and then wash the garment.

Javelle water will surely take out the stains, but the utmost care must be used in using javelle water—or rather in washing away every trace of the cleaning-fluid after the stain has been removed—else the result will be a hole.

REMOVING SPOTS ON WOOLEN CLOTH

Spots on woolen cloth may be removed by using sulphuric ether, which should always be applied with a piece of the same material as that of the goods being cleaned if possible. This method is recommended by a prominent woolen-cloth manufacturer

TO CLEAN IVORY HANDLES OF KNIVES

Knives which have ivory handles that may have become darkened, may be cleaned by rubbing the handles with half a lemon, which has been dipped in salt. After treating them thus, then wash in warm water, and wipe dry.

TO CLEAN CHAMOIS GLOVES

Make a strong lather, put the gloves on the hands, and go over all parts of the gloves with this lather, squeezing and rubbing as if washing the hands. Rinse them in the same manner, always in cold water. Wipe them with a soft linen cloth, getting as much of the water out of them as possible, while the gloves are still on the hands.

Dry them, and push them in shape with a glove-stretcher, and do not under any circumstances, rub the soap into them.

TO CLEAN WHITE PLUMES

Cut some soap (white) into small pieces, and put it into boiling water, adding a little pearl-ash. When the mixture has dissolved put the plumes into it, and draw them through the hand till they look clean, then put them into a clean lather, and rinse in cold water to which is added a little bit of blue.

TO WASH FINE LACE

Sew the lace to a piece of white cotton cloth and wet thoroughly, and rub copiously with naphtha soap. Let it stand for several hours—overnight if possible. Gently wash until the lace is clean. When dry take carefully from the cloth, and pull the lace into shape and pick out the edge; then press down on the wrong side laying it on a felt cloth.

"Brown spots" may be removed from lace or from fine embroidery, by repeated soaping and putting in the sun.

TO RESTORE BLACK LACE

Water, ½ cup,
Borax, 1 teaspoon,
Alcohol, 1 teaspoon.

Squeeze the lace through this mixture, then rinse in a cup of hot water in which an old kid glove has been boiled. Pull out the edges till almost dry, then press for 2 days between the leaves of a heavy book.

Another method is, to lay the lace on a clean smooth board, and moisten it all over with a piece of black silk dipped in a solution of 1 teaspoon of borax to a pint of warm water. Iron it while still damp, covering the lace with a piece of cloth, or between sheets of thick brown paper.

A method for cleaning black lace is to make a solution of 2 parts of alcohol and 1 part water, and after soaking the lace in this, dry it in the air, and stiffen with a very thin solution of gum arabic.

TO CLEAN JET PASSEMENTERIE

To clean jet passementerie, rub it with a cloth or a soft brush, dipped in equal parts of alcohol and water, and then dry it with a clean cloth.

TO CLEAN SOILED SILK EMBROIDERY

To clean soiled silk embroidery use spirits of wine, and dip a camel's-hair brush in it and brush the trimming until all the dirt is removed.

HOW TO USE MAGNESIA

When using magnesia as a cleanser, first dampen the stained place, then moisten the magnesia, and rub it vigorously on the stain, and allow it to dry thoroughly, when the magnesia powder may be easily shaken out.

TO DRY-CLEAN A RUG

Beat the rug till no more dust flies from it, then lay it flat on the floor, and spread over it, powdered fuller's earth. Rub the powder in with a brush as if you were scouring, and then roll the rug up, and leave it for a week before brushing and beating. When well beaten and swept, take a dishpan half full of water, to which add a cup of ammonia, and dipping a broom into the pan, sweep with the broom, the wrong way of the nap. This will leave the rug looking fresh and clean.

TO CLEAN AN OIL-PAINTING

Take the picture from the frame, and lay it on the table face upward. Prepare a bowl of tepid water and go carefully over the entire surface of the picture using a soft sponge.

Then take a large white potato, peel it, and cut in half, and after wiping it off, go over the picture with the smoothly cut part of the potato, while it is still moist from the cutting.

Do not rub hard, and the dirt will soon begin to soften and make a suds, quite black, continue to rub it until all the stains and spots disappear, and then carefully wash with the tepid water and the sponge.

Never use soap on an oil-painting. It may clean it, but the chemicals in soap do damage. Later, wipe the fly-specks and soot off, with tepid water and pearline, using a sponge. After it is cleaned and dried, varnish with picture varnish applied with a bristle-brush. Spread quickly, and don't go over the same place twice.

TO CLEAN GILT FRAMES

Beat up the white of an egg, add to it a pinch of soda, and brush this mixture over the frames. Then wash with soft water and dry with a white flannel cloth.

TO CLEAN A MIRROR

First rub the surface with a rag dipped in a little methylated spirit, then sprinkle with a little finely powdered blue. Wipe quite clean, and polish with a silk duster.

TO CLEAN BRASS AND SILVERWARE

Take half a cup of whiting and fill the cup with cold water; pour this into a bottle, and add 1 ounce of ammonia; shake well, before using. Wet a flannel cloth with this, and rub the silver or brass.

CARE OF FURNITURE

FURNITURE POLISH, NO. 1

A good furniture polish is easily made as follows:

> Turpentine, 1 tablespoon,
> Vinegar, 1 tablespoon,
> Olive-oil, 2 tablespoons.

This should always be well shaken just before using.

FURNITURE POLISH, NO. 2

> Beeswax, 1 ounce,
> Castile soap, ½ ounce,
> Turpentine, 1 pint.

Pare the soap and wax, and put them in a quart bottle and add the turpentine. Let it remain for 24 hours, and shake the bottle well to mix the ingredients. Next day shake it well again, and fill the bottle with water. On the following day it should be of the consistency of thick cream, and is then ready for use. Always just before using shake it well.

CEMENT

A good cement can be made by mixing powdered rice with a little cold water, slowly adding to it boiling water, till the right consistency is obtained, then pour into a saucepan, and boil it for a minute.

This paste is almost transparent, and is well adapted for

fancy paper-work, for which a strong and colorless cement is required.

CEMENT FOR BROKEN GLASS

Plaster of Paris, mixed into a paste with white of egg, makes a strong cement for mending broken glass or china.

Another excellent cement is made as follows: Into a small bottle press as much isinglass as will fit in; then pour in, by degrees, unsweetened gin, which will gradually dissolve the isinglass, if the bottle is kept in a warm place.

CHINESE CEMENT

Orange shellac (broken small), 4 ounces,
Rectified spirits, 3 ounces.

Digest together in a warm place till dissolved, then apply to the broken parts and these will adhere so that should the article break again it will break in another place. The mixture should be about the consistency of molasses. It is good for mending porcelain, glass, fancy-works, jewelry, etc.

WATERPROOF GLUE

Waterproof glue may be made from 3 parts gum shellac, and 1 part india rubber; these being dissolved separately, in ether, under the influence of heat, and the two solutions afterward mixed and kept for a time in a sealed bottle.

Water, either hot or cold, and most acids and alkalies will have no effect on this glue.

LACQUER FOR TOILET SILVER

Methylated spirits, 1 pint,
Shellac, 1 ounce.

Put the shellac in a bottle and dissolve with the methylated spirits, cork the bottle tightly, and let it stand for 24 hours, then pour off the clear liquid.

Heat the metal slightly, and paint the solution over it with a camel's-hair brush. Any metal ornament may be lacquered in the same way.

A little of this solution may be added with good results to the powder ordinarily used to clean silverware.

PAINTING BRASS-WORK WITH SHELLAC

If brass chandeliers, stair rails, and so forth, are painted with a coating of shellac, they will long keep their polish.

While the fixtures are still bright and fresh they should be given a coating of white shellac, such as is used by painters. The best quality of shellac should be used, and applied with a camel's-hair brush.

In the case of brasswork that is not fresh, it should first be thoroughly scoured and polished, and dried with a soft cloth, then carefully painted, avoiding too wet a brush, as that will make streaks, or look smeary. When properly painted with shellac, the beds, chandeliers, etc., will not need attention for a long time.

TO CLEAN TARNISHED SILVER

Water, 1 gallon,
Cyanid of potassium (fused), 1 pound.

This preparation is used by a noted firm of silverware manufacturers. The same proportions made in smaller quantities will be of great use, as the cleaning fluid may be kept and used any number of times.

Dip the silver and leave it entirely covered for 4 or 5 minutes, then wash off with cold water, then with hot water, soap and sponge, then with cold water again, wipe dry, with a soft cloth, and polish with chamois and jeweler's rouge.

TO CLEAN ALUMINUM

Dissolve 20 grammes of borax in water, and a third as much ammonia as you have of water. Shake well together, apply, and polish until the white glittering effect is seen that is always on new aluminum articles.

GILDING MIXTURE

Take equal parts of copal varnish and turpentine, and enough Japan drier to give a glisten. Add bronze powder enough to bring to the consistency of mucilage and apply with a sizing brush.

TO WRITE ON METALS

Muriatic acid, 1 ounce,
Nitric acid, ½ ounce,
Beeswax.

To write on iron, steel, silver or gold, mix the above acids and use as follows: Cover the place in which you wish to write with melted beeswax, and when the wax is cold, write the name, or words plainly with a file-point, or with an etching needle, carrying the writing through the wax, and cleaning all the wax out of the letter.

Then apply the mixed acids with a feather, carefully filling all parts of each letter. Let the acid remain for from 1 to 10 minutes, according to the appearance desired, and then put on some water, which will dilute the acid and stop the process.

Either of the acids separately would cut iron or steel, but it requires the mixture of the two to take hold of either gold or silver. After the acids are washed off it is well to apply a little oil.

IMITATION OF GROUND GLASS

In many rooms, especially in apartments, where windows or door should have been furnished with ground glass, a good imitation of ground glass may be made as follows:

Take a soft piece of putty and tie it closely in a piece of cheese-cloth, and pat the plain glass with it until every part is covered with a thin white coating. When this covering has dried so that it will not rub off, brush the putty over with one coat of white varnish. The window may then be cleaned like a pane of plain glass.

TO CLEAN SPOTS FROM MAHOGANY

Mahogany tables and desks are frequently disfigured by white marks caused by the standing of hot dishes upon them without a mat between. To remove the stains, rub on a few drops of sweet oil, and afterward polish with a little spirits of wine, using a soft cloth.

PUTTING RODS IN CURTAINS

When running brass rods through window, or sash curtains, put an old glove-finger over the end of the rod that is being pushed through the hem. It will prevent the rod from tearing the material.

TO DESTROY SILVER-BUGS

Oil of pennyroyal, 2 ounces,
Oil of sassafras, 2 ounces,
Alcohol, 4 ounces.

Let it mix well and then sprinkle where the bugs have been congregating.

TO RID A CLOSET OF MOTHS

Place some bricks in the closet, and take a tin or iron pan and after having heated the pan red hot, pour into it hot vinegar, and placing the pan on the bricks, close the door as soon as the vinegar commences to hiss on the heated surface of the pan, and keep the closet-door closed for the remainder of the day.

CARE OF THE HAIR

FALLING HAIR

> Glycerin, 1½ ounce,
> Eau de Cologne, ¼ pint,
> Liquid ammonia, 1 dram,
> Oil of rosemary, ½ dram,
> Oil of organum, ½ dram,
> Tincture of cantharides, 1 ounce.

Mix and agitate well for 10 minutes. A few drops of essence of musk, or other perfume, may be added if so desired.

HAIR TONIC, NO. 1

> Cologne, 8 ounces,
> Tincture of cantharides, 1 ounce,
> Oil of lavender, ½ dram,
> Oil of rosemary, ½ dram.

Apply to the roots of the hair daily. It is necessary that the scalp be absolutely clean; shampooing at least once a week, while using the tonic.

BRILLIANTINE FOR THE HAIR

Brilliantine is used to give the hair a gloss, and to keep it smooth.

> Sweet almond oil, 8 fluid ounces,
> Alcohol, 4 fluid ounces,

Glycerin, 1 fluid ounce,
Oil of geranium, 12 drops.

HAIR TONIC, NO. 2

Phenic acid, 2 grammes,
Tincture nux vomica, 7 grammes,
Tincture cinchona rub, 30 grammes,
Eau de Cologne, 120 grammes.

This is a good tonic for the hair, and also for removing dandruff from the scalp.

POWDER FOR OILY HAIR

A powder to clean oily hair is made as follows:

Powdered orris, ¼ pound,
Bergamot rind, 1⅓ drams,
Cassia flowers, 1½ drams,
Coarsely ground cloves, ¼ drams.

Mix all, and put through a sieve. The best way of using is to rub into the hair at night, and let it remain until morning, then brush it out. This will perfume the hair.

TO KEEP THE HAIR CURLED

The following mixture will keep the hair curled:

Gum arabic, 1 ounce,
Moist sugar, ½ ounce,
Hot water, ¾ pint,
Alcohol, 2 fluid ounces,
Bichlorid of mercury, 6 grains,
Sal-ammoniac, 6 grains.

The mercury and sal-ammoniac should be dissolved in the alcohol before mixing with the other ingredients. At the last add enough water to make the whole mixture measure 1 pint.

Perfume with cologne or lavender water. Moisten the hair with the fluid before putting it in papers or curlers.

This is too strong a solution to be applied repeatedly, as it would surely have a destructive effect on the hair follicles, and for that reason it should not be applied too frequently, nor at too short intervals. An occasional use, however, is practically harmless.

EGG SHAMPOO

A good egg shampoo can be easily made as follows:

> Egg, 1,
> Hot rain-water, 1 pint,
> Spirits of rosemary, 1 ounce.

Beat the mixture thoroughly and use it warm. Rub it well into the scalp, and rinse several times in clear water.

HENNA AS A STAIN FOR THE HAIR

Henna is a vegetable stain, quite harmless, and producing an attractive reddish tint to the hair. For home use it will be found much safer than anything else.

Shampoo the hair and dry, and then apply the stain of henna.

CARE OF THE EYEBROWS

Before brushing the eyebrows rub them with vaseline. This will help them to run in the one direction.

TO GROW HEAVY EYEBROWS

The following recipe for promoting the growth of the eyebrows is very good, and is perfectly harmless:

Vaseline, 2 ounces,
Cantharides, ⅛ ounce,
Oil of rosemary, 15 drops,
Lavender extract, 15 drops.

Mix thoroughly, and apply to the eyebrows with a tiny toothbrush once a day until the growth is sufficiently stimulated, and then less often.

This ointment may be used for the eyelashes also, but in this case apply carefully, for it will inflame the eyes if it gets into them.

TO DARKEN THE EYEBROWS

Make a strong brew of sage tea, strain it through a muslin, and to a pint of the liquid add a tablespoon of alcohol. Apply this to the eyebrows with a brush. It is perfectly harmless, and will, in fact, stimulate the growth of the eyebrows.

CHINESE EYELASH STAIN

Gum arabic, 1 dram,
India ink, ½ dram,
Rose-water, 4 ounces.

Powder the ink and gum, and triturate small quantities of the powder until there is obtained a uniform black liquid in a powder, and then add the rose-water. Be careful not to get this stain in the eyes.

CARE OF THE SKIN

ALMOND MEAL

> Orris-root, powdered, 4 ounces,
> Wheat flour, 4 ounces,
> White Castile soap, powdered, 1 ounce,
> Borax, 1 ounce,
> Oil of bitter almonds, 10 drops,
> Oil of bergamot, 2 drams,
> Tincture of musk, 1 dram.

Mix well, and pass through a sieve. This should be used instead of soap.

ALMOND MILK

> Jordan almonds, 30,
> Distilled water, ½ pint,
> Sugar.

Blanch the almonds, and bruise them to a fine powder, by pounding in a mortar, in which has been placed also the distilled water. Add also a lump of sugar, so that the oil will not separate from the mixture.

The almonds should be pounded as finely as possible, and it will take some time. When pounded to an impalpable powder, then strain through cheese-cloth.

To make the milk richer, increase the number of almonds used with the same quantity of water. The preparation is both soothing and bleaching.

THE LEMON BATH

The lemon bath is a great invigorator, an excellent cleanser, and has a most soothing, refreshing, and softening influence on the skin. It is prepared as follows:

Cut five lemons in slices, and leave them to soak in a basin of water for half an hour. After the bath-water has been drawn from the faucet, the lemon-water should be added and the whole vigorously stirred.

BATH BAGS

> Oatmeal, 4 pounds,
> Bran, 2 quarts,
> Almond meal, 1½ pounds,
> White Castile soap, 1 pound,
> Violet sachet, 3 ounces.

Have the soap dried and powdered. Mix all together, and keep in glass jars, from which to fill small cheese-cloth bags, to use as sponges. The bags should be about 4 inches square, and filled as needed.

ROUGE

A simple preparation of rouge is made as follows:

> Carmine, ½ dram,
> Oil of almonds, 1 dram,
> French chalk, 2 ounces.

Mix thoroughly, and it will be found that the chalk absorbs the oil, making an adhesive powder. One advantage in using this rouge is that it does not contain any mercury.

FACE POWDER

Rice flour, 3 ounces,
Rice starch, 3 ounces,
Carbonate of magnesia, 1½ ounces,
Pulverized boric acid, ¾ ounce,
Powdered orris, ¾ dram,
Essence of citron, 7 drops,
Essence of bergamot, 7 drops.

Mix the essences with the magnesia, and then combine with the powder. Strain before using.

LIP SALVE

Spermaceti ointment, ½ ounce,
Balsam of Peru, 7½ grains,
Alkanet, 7½ grains,
Oil of cloves, 2 drops.

Mix the alkanet with the spermaceti ointment, in a bottle or in a dish, and let it stand over a gentle heat till the liquid is rose-colored, then put it through a strainer. When cool, stir in the balsam and let it settle.

When it is clear pour off the liquid, leaving the sediment, then add the cloves to the liquid. When it becomes cold, it should be hard, but it will not get hard if in the course of making it has been subjected to too much heat; therefore, it should simply be allowed to get warm.

COLD CREAM

Sweet oil of almonds, 75 grains,
Virgin wax, 20 grains,
Spermaceti, 8 grammes,
Perfume.

Melt all together, and stir for 20 minutes, and when cooling add any desired perfume.

ORANGE-FLOWER CREAM

Oil of sweet almonds, 4 ounces,
White wax, 6 drams,
Spermaceti, 6 drams,
Borax, 2 drams,
Glycerin, 1½ ounces,
Oil of neroli, 15 drops,
Oil of orange-skin (bigarde), 15 drops.

Melt the sweet almond, wax, and spermaceti, and add to it the orange-flower water. Dissolve the borax in the mixture, and then pour it slowly into the blended fats, stirring continuously. This is a good "food for the skin."

FOR MOIST HANDS

Tincture of belladonna, ½ ounce,
Eau de Cologne, 3 ounces.

Mix the two well, and use when desired during the day, always washing the hands in hot water and drying them quickly just before applying the lotion. Rub it well into the skin.

(Keep this out of the way of children and ignorant persons.) After having applied the lotion, the hands should be rubbed with a little talcum powder.

ORRIS POWDER FOR PERSPIRATION

Phenic acid, 3 fluid drams,
Alcohol, 5½ fluid drams,
Starch, 6¼ ounces,

Florentine orris, 5½ ounces,
Essence of violet, 32 minims.

Dissolve the acid in the alcohol, add the violet essence, then the starch, and then the orris.

TO REMOVE TAN

Bathe in pure lemon-juice. First wash the skin thoroughly with warm water and a pure soap; then after drying thoroughly with a soft towel, apply the lemon-juice with a wad of absorbent cotton.

Peroxid of hydrogen, diluted with water and applied in the same manner, will also remove tan.

PEROXID AS A FACE BLEACH

When using peroxid as a face bleach it should be left on the face for an hour or two after it dries. Instead of washing it off with water, rub the skin with a good cold cream, and the skin will be much smoother and softer.

TO REMOVE A MOTH-PATCH

Cocoa-butter, 2½ drams,
Castor oil, 2½ drams,
White precipitate of mercury, 1½ grains,
Essence of rose, 10 drops.

Apply the mixture to the moth-patch night and morning.

PERFUMES

COLOGNE

The following is a very good recipe for making cologne:

> Essence of lemon, 10 grammes,
> Essence of cedrat (citron), 10 grammes,
> Essence of bergamot, 10 grammes,
> Essence of fine lavender, 10 grammes,
> Essence of rosemary, 4 grammes,
> Essence of thyme, 2 grammes,
> Alcohol, 2 quarts.

Mix the essences with the alcohol, and filter through paper.

BLENDING OF PERFUMES

In making sachet-bags, the blending of the perfumes is of much importance. The two odors that mix most perfectly are violet and heliotrope; and the addition of a little sandal-wood to these will produce an exquisite odor.

Rose and heliotrope blend very sweetly; and lilac and violet make a dainty combination.

A little sandal-wood or orris-root added to almost any combination of odors will increase the pungency, and make the result more lasting.

SCENT-BAGS

An old-fashioned filling for scent-bags is made as follows:

> Coriander seed, ¼ pound,
> Powdered orris-root, ¼ pound,

Aromatic calamus, ¼ pound,
Damask-rose leaves, ¼ pound,
Lavender blossoms, 2 ounces,
Mace, ½ ounce,
Cinnamon, ¼ ounce,
Cloves, ¼ ounce,
Powdered musk, 2 drams.

Beat each separately, then mix well together.

VIOLET SACHET-POWDER

The following is a very good recipe for making a pleasant sachet-powder.

Powdered orris, 1 ounce,
Powdered bergamot-peel, ¼ ounce,
Powdered acacia, ¼ ounce,
Musk, 20 grains.

Bottle for 10 days, at the end of which time it is ready for use.

ROSE SACHET-POWDER

Lavender leaves, ⅛ pound,
Dried rose-leaves, ½ pound,
Powdered orris-root, ¾ pound,
Civet, 8 grains,
Powdered musk, 10 grains.

Mix thoroughly and keep air-tight until ready to make up into sachets. If the odor of musk is not agreeable it may be omitted.

ROSE SACHET

Dried rose-leaves, ½ pound,
Ground sandal-wood, ¼ pound,
Attar of rose, ⅛ ounce.

Keep in a tightly corked bottle when not needed for use to fill the bags.

HELIOTROPE SACHET

Dried rose-leaves, ¼ pound,
Powdered orris-root, ½ pound,
Powdered tonka bean, 2 ounces,
Vanilla bean, 1 ounce,
Attar of almonds, 2 drops.

Powder all and mix by sifting them together.

LAVENDER SMELLING-SALTS

Carbonate of ammonia, 8 ounces,
Oil of cloves, 1 fluid ounce,
Oil of lavender, ½ fluid ounce,
Oil of bergamot, ½ fluid ounce,
Oil of cassia, ½ fluid ounce.

Crush the ammonia into very small pieces, and put it into a smelling-bottle; mix the oils thoroughly, and pour just enough into the bottle to barely cover the ammonia, keeping the remainder to replenish the smelling-bottle when required.

TO MAKE POTPOURRI JARS

Whole allspice (crushed), 2 ounces,
Stick cinnamon (broken coarsely), 2 ounces,
Orris-root (bruised and shredded), 1 ounce,
Lavender flowers, 2 ounces,
Oil of rose, 5 drops,
Good cologne, ¼ pint,
Rose petals,
Salt.

Gather the rose leaves in the morning and let them stand in a cool place to dry. Toss them lightly, then put them in a large covered dish in layers. Sprinkle each layer freely with salt.

Add to this several mornings, till enough stock of leaves has been gathered. Shake up, or stir every morning, and let the whole stand 10 days after the last petals are added.

Transfer to a glass fruit-jar, in the bottom of which have been placed the allspice and cinnamon. Let it stand 6 weeks closely covered, when it is then ready for the permanent jar.

Add to it now the orris, lavender, and a small quantity of any other sweet-scented dried leaves that may be desired, and mix all together, and put it into the permanent rose-jar, in alternate layers; with the rose stock and the few drops of rose-oil, and pour over the whole, the fourth of a pint of good strong cologne.

This will last for years; though from time to time one may add a little lavender, or orange-flower water, or any nice perfume, and at some seasons, may even add a few more fresh rose-petals.

TO MAKE POTPOURRI JARS
ANOTHER METHOD

Violet powder, ½ ounce,
Orris-root, ½ ounce,
Mace, ½ teaspoon,
Rose powder, ½ ounce,
Heliotrope powder, ½ ounce,
Cinnamon, ¼ teaspoon,
Cloves, ½ teaspoon,
Oil of roses, 4 drops,
Oil chiris, 10 drops,
Oil melissa, 20 drops,
Oil eucalyptus, 20 drops,

> Bergamot, 10 drops,
> Alcohol, 2 drams.

Use fresh rose-leaves for the vehicle to hold the powders. It is best to gather the leaves when the roses are in their richest bloom. Pack them in a jar in layers, about 2 inches deep, and sprinkle about 2 tablespoons of fine, dry salt on each layer.

Continue this until the jar is full, adding fresh leaves and salt daily, and keep it in a dark, dry, cool place.

A week after the last layer is gathered, turn out the salted petals on a broad platter, mix, and toss together until the mass is loosened; then incorporate them thoroughly with the formula given above, pack them in a clean permanent jar, cover lightly, and set it away to ripen.

If not in its permanent jar it will be ready for permanent jars in a fortnight, and if well-covered will be good and fragrant for 25 years, if not longer.

PERFUMED BEADS

Old-fashioned perfumed beads are made in the following manner:

> Powdered red-rose petals, 4 ounces,
> Carmine, 20 grains,
> Tincture of musk, 1 dram,
> Gum tragacanth.

Mix all the ingredients together, and add enough of the gum tragacanth to mold into spheres; pierce them before they are perfectly dry. They can be highly polished, or can be incised in various fashions.

ATTAR OF ROSE

Rose leaves,
Salt,
Olive oil.

Pick enough rose leaves to make a quart when closely pressed down. Put a layer of these in a 2-quart glass fruit-jar, and sprinkle lightly with salt, then cover with a thin layer of absorbent cotton wet with olive oil.

Fill the jar with alternate layers in the same manner, and put on the rubber cover and set the jar in the sun daily for 2 weeks or longer, if the weather be cloudy.

Uncover, and press the oil from the leaves and cotton, and place it in very closely corked vials.

SIMPLE REMEDIES, AND FIRST AIDS

USES FOR HOT WATER

In case of colic—Apply to the abdomen a large square of house flannel which has been dipped into boiling water and wrung out by twisting it in a towel. After twisting or wringing, the flannel should be given one shake, folded into a light soft pad, and applied, and covered with waterproof, or thick flannel.

Headache, or neuralgia—The same kind of application to the nape of the neck, and to the forehead, gives great relief, no matter to what specific cause the headache may be due.

Lumbago—Thick flannel wrung out of boiling water will also assuage lumbago. When applied for this purpose the flannel should be changed every 10 or 15 minutes, having the fresh one wrung out and ready to go on, before the other one comes off.

Constipation—This may in many cases be cured without the use of drugs, by drinking a hot tumbler of water every night before going to bed, and another tumbler, next morning, half an hour or so, before breakfast.

Indigestion—A small tumbler of hot water, drank half an hour before dinner, is frequently of great service to sufferers from indigestion. The same, taken shortly after meals, is often found beneficial.

Sprains and strains—The very best thing to relieve the pain of a sprain is to immediately envelope the injured part in a piece of thick flannel which has been wrung out of boiling water.

Fomentations of this kind should be kept up until the pain lessens.

Sleeplessness—Give hot spinal douches—that is, pouring hot water down the spine from a jug, or a big sponge. These douches are of more value for the cure of sleeplessness than sleeping draughts, for they cannot do harm, and in most cases soothe the nerves, draw blood from the brain, and induce sleep.

Convulsions—The immediate treatment of convulsions in young children is a hot bath—not too hot, remember. You should be able to bear your own elbow quite comfortably in the water. The elbow is much more sensitive than the hand, and can therefore, better test the heat, if a bath thermometer be not at hand. If a bath thermometer is obtainable let the temperature of water be not over 100 degrees Fahrenheit.

Overstoutness—The drinking of hot water, combined with a diet from which farinaceous foods, sugar, potatoes, and beer are eliminated, does much toward reducing a too superabundant amount of fat. The water should be taken in this manner:

Take from ½ pint to 1 pint in the morning, either in bed, or while dressing; and take the same quantity an hour and a half before each meal, and half an hour before bedtime.

The water should not be gulped down, but slowly sipped; taking from 5 to 15 minutes to drink—it can be rewarmed during the drinking, if necessary. By taking it in this manner uncomfortable distention is avoided. It is best to begin with a smaller quantity, and increase as it is found to agree.

VEGETABLES AS MEDICINE

Asparagus benefits the kidneys.
Potatoes contain salts and potash.
French beans and lentils give iron.

Celery is good for rheumatism and neuralgia.

Tomatoes stimulate the healthy action of the liver.

Lettuce is good for tired nerves, and induces sleep.

Cabbage, cauliflower, and spinach are beneficial to anemic people.

Food specialists vote spinach as the most precious of vegetables. It contains salts of potassium and much iron.

It is claimed that carrots form blood, beautify the skin, and improve the appetite.

For that tired feeling that comes in the spring, the best vegetables are, parsley, horseradish, mustard, dock, dandelion and beet-tops, as they clear the blood, and regulate the system.

MUSTARD PLASTERS

To make a mustard plaster take equal parts of mustard and flour; stir together with a little warm water, just sufficient to make it into a thick paste. Spread it on a piece of linen that is large enough to fold over and prevent the paste from touching the skin. Apply the plaster to that part of the skin that it is desired to irritate.

Ginger plasters may be made in the same manner, as mustard plasters, and produce the same results and do not blister.

CURE FOR SEASICKNESS

A glass of hot milk with a generous dash of cayenne will often cure seasickness.

SICK HEADACHE

The juice of half a lemon, in a cup of black coffee, without any sugar, has been found to cure a sick headache.

TO CURE A BILIOUS ATTACK

A strong, unsweetened lemon, taken before breakfast, will prevent and will cure a bilious attack.

GRAPE- AND PINEAPPLE-JUICE

These are great blessings in the sickroom. Only the juice of either should be swallowed. It allays thirst, and is nourishing, acting beneficially upon the liver and kidneys.

FOR SPRAINS

If the ankle is sprained, rest is all important. Bandage the part and keep this bandage soaked with water as hot as the patient can bear, or with witch-hazel.

For a sprained wrist, use the same treatment and put the arm in a sling.

FOR NOSE BLEED

Lay the sufferer on his back, with arms elevated above the head, and apply the coldest water obtainable to the nose, forehead, and back of the neck.

FAINTING

Lay the patient on his back, and do not raise the head, but allow it to remain at the same level as the rest of the body. Loosen the collar, and anything tight about the neck and body, and apply smelling-salts to the nose, and bathe the face and head with cold water, dashing it on.

When the patient is able to swallow, administer brandy. The all-important point is to keep the patient's head low.

HYSTERICS

Hysterics may be treated in the same manner as fainting.

HICCOUGHS

Severe cases demand drastic treatment, such as hot mustard plasters laid directly on the pit of the stomach. For milder cases cloths dipped in either hot vinegar, brandy, or whisky, will sometimes give immediate relief.

TO STOP THE FLOW OF BLOOD

In case of an accident when the flow of blood from a wound is excessive, an application of equal parts of flour and sugar, mixed well, will effectually check the flow until the arrival of a physician.

RELIEF FOR BURNS

Slight burns and scalds may be relieved by wrapping the parts in a soft cloth saturated with a strong solution of borax.

A dressing of carbolized vaseline, olive-oil, or the white of egg, are all excellent to exclude the air from a burn.

If blisters have formed, they should be opened by pricking, and dressed at once, to protect from the air.

TO REMOVE A SPLINTER

To extract a splinter from the flesh with but little pain, nearly fill a wide-mouthed bottle with hot water, place the injured part over the mouth of the bottle, and press tightly down. The suction will draw the flesh down, and in a minute or two the splinter will come out.

STINGS OF INSECTS

To relieve the stings of insects apply ammonia, or peroxide to the affected part. An old-time cure was as follows:

Take the sting out with a needle and then with the place

tightly squeezed, suck, and afterwards apply a liniment of powdered chalk and olive-oil to the part.

FOR BURNING FEET

Arnica diluted with warm water is soothing for tired and burning feet. After the lotion has dried in, rub the feet gently, using a good toilet-cream of sweet-almonds.

Always draw the blood from the ankle or the instep, toward the toes. Support the instep or the ball of the foot with the left hand, while rubbing with the right; using the downward motion on the outside of the foot, or ankle. A rotary motion on the instep is very restful.

LIME-WATER

Put a heaping teaspoon of pure slaked lime into 1 quart of boiled or distilled water. Cork, and shake several times during the first hour. Then let the lime settle, and after 24 hours pour off the clear liquid. Keep in a dark bottle, and well stoppered.

TOOTH-POWDER

The following recipe gives an excellent tooth-powder, easily made, and pleasant to use:

>Peruvian bark, ½ ounce,
>Myrrh, ½ ounce,
>Powdered Orris-root, ½ ounce,
>Chalk, 1 ounce.

Flavor very strongly with wintergreen.

INDEXES

ALPHABETICAL INDEX

A

Alligator pear cocktail, 19.
  Salad, 171.
Almond blancmange, 229.
  Meal, 325.
  Milk (Soup), 26.
  Milk (Lotion), 325.
  Velvet cream, 229.
Almonds, Burnt, 265.
  Chocolate, 265.
  Salted, 196.
Aluminum, to clean, 318.
Amande, Havana, 297.
American Macaroni, 106.
  Woodcock, 205.
Anchovy paste, 21.
Angel cake, 244.
Apple and banana salad, 179.
  Cake, 233.
  Cress and celery salad, 177.
  Custard pie, 219.
  Florentine, 234.
  Soufflé, 224.
  Toddy, 280, 281.
Apples, baked, 131.
  Steamed, 132.
Artichokes, fonds of, 23.
Asparagus, Cream of, 26.
Aspic jelly, 177.
  Queen's, 177.
  Salmon, 169.
  Tomato, 176.
  Tongue in, 61.
Attar of rose, 335.

B

Bacon with kidneys, 81.
Bahia salad, 172.
Baked apples, 131.
  Calf's liver, 79.
  Cheese omelette, 136.
  Fillet of flounder, 46.
  Liver, 79.
  Onions, 113.
  Pears, 196.
  Quinces, 195.
Baked sole, 46.
Bamboo, 285.

Banana and apple salad, 179.
Barbecued ham, 207.
Bar-le-duc, Currant, 193.
Bath bags, 326.
  Buns, 6.
Batter pudding, 214.
Bean salad, 172.
Béchamel sauce, 152.
Beef-heart, braised, 78.
Beer, Ginger, 298.
  Root, 298.
Beets, cream of, 25.
Berry stains, to remove, 310.
Beverages, 276.
  Apple toddy, 280, 281.
  Bamboo, 285.
  California fruit punch, 287.
  Champagne punch, 278.
    Chamberlin's, 279.
  Cherry bounce, 282.
  Chocolate parfait amour, 297.
  Claret cup, 289, 290.
    Punch, 280.
  Currant water, 294.
    Wine, 287.
  Egg lemonade, 296.
  Egg nog, 281.
  Elderblow wine, 286.
  Fish house punch, 276.
  Fruit punch, 288.
  Gin fizz, 282.
  Ginger ale julep, 294.
    Beer, 298.
  Grape juice, 295.
  Lemon syrup, 292.
  Milk punch, 282.
  Mint julep, 283, 284.
  Navy punch, 277.
  Old Colonial ginger cup, 295.
  Orange cocktail, 285.
    Cordial, 286.
    Punch, 288.
  Philadelphia fish-house punch, 276.
  Pineapple lemonade, 296.
    Syrup, 292.
  Port wine sangaree, 284.
  Raspberry Shrub, 293.

Beverages—Cont'd
  Regent punch, 279.
  Remsen cooler, 285.
  Rickey, 283.
  Root beer, 298.
  Sauterne cup, 291.
  Shandy gaff, 285.
  Strawberry punch, 287.
  Tutti frutti cup, 289.
  U. S. S. Richmond punch, 277.
  Whisky sour, 283.
Bilious attack, 339.
Bisque, tomato, 31.
Black bean soup, 31.
Blackberry pudding, 217.
  Soup, 37.
Black fruit cake, 235.
Blancmange, almond, 229.
Blending of perfumes, 330.
Bloodspots, to remove, 309.
Blood, to stop the flow of, 340.
Blueberry pudding, 216.
Bonbons, chocolate, 263.
Bordelaise sauce, 153.
Bottling lemon juice, 296.
Boudins of veal, 83.
Braised beef-heart, 78.
Brass, how to clean, 314.
Brasswork, shellac for, 317.
Brazilian shrimps, 47.
Breads, 3.
  Times for cooking bread, 3.
  Bath buns, 6.
  Berlin pancakes, 11.
  Boiled connifeia, 14.
  Cheese straws, 15.
  Cinnamon coffee bread, 17.
  Egg puffs, 14.
  English crumpets, 14.
  Fried connifeia, 17.
  German pancakes, 10.
  Graham gems, 7.
    Loaf, 5.
  Minute biscuit, 8.

INDEX

Breads—Contd.
Nut bread, 4.
Oatmeal wafers, 12.
Parker house rolls, 5.
Pop-overs, 13.
Pulled bread, 5
Rice griddle cakes, 9.
Pancakes, 10.
Waffles, 9
Richmond thin biscuits, 8.
Sally Lunn, 12.
Virginia, 13.
Scotch scones, 14.
Soda biscuits, 7.
Sour milk cakes, 10.
Waffles, 8.
Washington rolls, 6.
Whole-wheat cakes, 11.
Yorkshire breakfast cake, 15.
Pudding, 16.
Bread pudding, 213.
Sauce, 154.
Bridget cake, 242.
Brilliantine for the hair, 321.
Broiled eggplant, 116.
Broth, Scotch, 35.
Brown Betty, 218.
Butter sauce, 147.
Carrots, 126.
Sauce, 147.
Brunswick stew, 87.
Burning feet, how to relieve, 341.
Burns, relief for, 340.
Burnt almonds, 265.
Butter, lemon, 156.
Scotch, 258.
Tomato, 155.

C

Cabbage, red, 114.
Red, pickled, 190.
Cadillac chicken, 90.
Cake, 235.
Angel, 244.
Apple, 233.
Black fruit, 236.
Bridget, 242.
Caramel, 245.
Coffee, 240.
Composition, 237.
Crullers, 255.
Grandmother Holt's, 255.
Dark fruit, 236.
Dried apple, 242.
Fruit, 238.
Fruit drops, 249.
Fudge, 247.
German loaf, 243.
Rings, 251.
Gingerbread, 243.
Ginger snaps, 253.

Cake—Contd.
Hermits, 254.
Jackson snaps, 254.
Lady Baltimore, 247.
Marshmallow, 246.
Marzipan, 252.
Minnehaha, 244.
Mocha, 245.
Oatmeal rock cakes, 250.
Spiced cookies, 250.
Pound cake, 240, 241.
Russian rock, 251
Sand tarts, 248.
Scotch short-cake, 252.
Spice cake, 239
Sugar cookies, 253.
Superior cookies, 253.
Surprise macaroons, 249.
White cake, 241.
White fruit cake, 239.
Yellow frosting, 235.
Cakes, decorating, 272.
Placing candles upon, 272.
With fillings, 244.
California fruit punch, 287.
Orange marmalade, 195.
Calf's head cheese, 53.
Liver, baked, 79.
Canape Lorenzo, 21.
of Chicken livers, 21.
Candied mint leaves, 272.
Orange peel, 274.
Violets, 272.
Candles, to fasten on cakes, 272.
Candy, 256.
Burnt almonds, 265.
Butter Scotch, 258
Chestnuts, glacés, 274.
Chocolate almonds, 265.
Bonbons, 263.
Caramels, 267.
Chips, 266
Coating, 263.
Creams, 263, 264.
Fudge, 268, 269.
Nut candy, 268.
Taffy, 266.
Cocoanut drops, 259.
Coffee caramels, 270.
Cream peppermints, 258.
English molasses, 256.
French fondant, 262.
Fudge, 268, 269.
Gum drops, 271.
Lemon drops, 271.
Maple caramels, 270.
Marrons, glacés, 273.
Mexican kisses, 270.
Mint drops, 259.

Candy—Contd
Molasses, 256.
Nougat, 261.
Nut candy, 261.
Nut fudge, 269
Orange balls, 275.
Peanut brittle, 260.
Candy, 260.
Penotchie, 261.
Peppermint drops, 258.
Sauerkraut, 259.
Sea foam, 257.
White sugar, 257.
Caramel cake, 245.
Custard, 220.
Caramels, chocolate, 267.
Coffee, 270.
Maple, 270.
Care of the eyebrows, 323.
Furniture, 315.
Hair, 321.
Skin, 325.
Carrot balls, 126.
Carrots, browned, 126.
Cream of, 28.
Mashed, 125.
Casserole of liver and rice, 60.
Cauliflower, cream of, 29.
Scalloped, 114.
Caviar, 20.
Celery, apple and cress salad, 179
With chestnuts, soup, 27.
Cream of, 24.
Cutlets, 127.
Fritters, 127.
Hors d'œuvre, 23.
Pineapple salad, 180.
Tomato salad, 176.
Cement, 315.
For broken glass, 316.
Chinese, 315.
Chafing-dish receipts, 198.
American woodcock, 205.
Barbecued ham, 207.
Cheese fondue, 206.
Creamed oysters, 199.
Shrimps, 201.
Curried oysters, 198.
Eggs and tomato scramble, 202.
English monkey, 206.
Hard-shell clams, 200.
Lobster, à la Newburg, 201.
Mock terrapin, 207.
Oysters à la Parisienne, 199.
Panned oysters, 198.
Scotch woodcock, 205.

INDEX

Chafing-dish receipts— Contd.
 Scrambled eggs with sausage, 202
 Shrimps with French peas, 208
 Soft-shell clams, 200
 Spanish rarebit, 204
 Welsh rarebit, 203
Chamberlin's boiled ham, 76.
 Champagne punch, 279.
 Terrapin, 49
Chamois gloves, to clean, 311
Champagne punch, 278, 279.
Cheese balls, 159.
 Calf's head, 53.
 Custard, 52.
 Fondue, 205
Cheese omelette, baked, 136.
 Pork, 54.
 With Scrambled eggs, 137
 Straws, 15, 159.
 Veal, 54
Cherries, jellied, 231.
Cherry Bounce, 282.
 Pudding, 216.
 Salad, 181.
Chestnut and celery soup, 27
 Cream (dessert), 231
 Cream (soup), 28.
 Croquettes, 131.
 Compote, 231.
 Grape-fruit salad, 179
 Patties, 70
 Purée, 29, 30
 Salad, 171, 172
 Sauce for fowls, 155.
 Stuffing for turkey, 75
Chestnuts in brown sauce, 130.
 French, 129.
 Glacés, 274.
 Stewed, 130.
 White sauce, 129.
Chicken cadillac, 90.
 Casserole, 84.
 Creole, 86.
 French, 91.
 Gumbo, 33
 Jellied, 88, 89.
 Luau-ed, 87.
 Mousse, 62.
 Riced in shells, 62.
 Salad, 164.
 Stewed à l'espagnole, 86.
 Sour, 91.
 Terrapin, 92.
Chi Lo, Chinese, 94.
Chilli con carne, 61.
 Mexican, 60, 93.

Chilli con carne—Contd.
 Sauce, 187.
Chinese cement, 316
 Eyelash stain, 324.
 Pudding and rice, 102.
Chocolate almonds, 265.
 Bonbons, 263
 Caramels, 267
Chocolate chips, 266.
 Coating, 263
 Cream, 228
 Creams, 263, 264.
 Fudge, 268, 269.
 Nut candy, 268.
 Parfait amour, 297.
 Pie, 219.
 Pudding, 225
 With creamy sauce, 226
 Taffy, 266.
Chowder, clam, 32.
 Corn, 32
Chrysanthemum salad, 181
Chutney, 189.
Cinnamon coffee bread, 17.
Citron sauce, 156
Clam chowder, 32.
Clams, hard-shell, 200.
 Soft-shell, 200
Claret cup, 289, 290.
 Punch, 280
 Sauce, 156.
 Soup, 36.
Clothing, to remove spots from, 306.
Cocktail, Alligator pear, 19.
 Fruit, 20
 Orange, 285.
 Oyster, 19.
Cocoanut drops, 259.
Codfish balls, 42.
 Cakes, 43.
Coffee bread, cinnamon, 17
 Cake, 240.
 Stains, to remove, 309
Cold cream, 327.
 Rice Pudding, 211.
Collops in batter, 94
Composition cake, 237.
Compote, chestnut, 231.
Cookies, oatmeal, spiced, 250.
 Sugar, 253.
 Superior, 253.
Cordials, 285.
 Mint, 285.
 Orange, 286.
Corn chowder, 32.
 Fried, 124.
 Fritters, 124.
 Green, omelette, 123.
 Pudding, 124.
Correct sauces to serve with fish, 39.

Cotton, to remove grease spots from, 307
Crab and tomato salad, 169
Cream, Almond velvet, 229
 Asparagus, 26.
 Beets, 25.
 Carrots, 28.
 Cauliflower, 29.
 Celery, 24
 Chestnuts, 28, 231.
 Chocolate, 228.
 Dressing, 163
 Mushrooms, 25.
 Onions, 112
 Orange flower, 328.
 Peppermints, 258.
 Tunis fruit, 230.
Creamed eggs, 139.
 Oysters, 199.
 Salmon, 41.
 Scallops, 46.
 Shrimps, 201.
Creams, chocolate, 263, 264.
Cress, celery and apple, salad, 179
Croquettes, Chestnut, 131.
 Hominy, 128
 Lobster, 64.
 Nut, 66.
 Nut and crumb, 67
 Somerset Club, 67.
 Sweetbread, 57
 Sweet potato, 110
Croutes of herring, 22
Crullers, 255
Cucumber catsup, 184, 185.
 Fritters, 115.
 Pickles, Grandmother Holt's, 184
 Sauce, 148, 149.
 With raw tomatoes, 175
 With tomato jelly, 174.
 Stuffed, 115
Cup, Claret, 289, 290.
 Old colonial ginger, 295.
 Sauterne, 291.
 Tutti frutti, 289.
Currant bar-le-duc, 193
 Soup (see lemon), 37.
 Water, 294
 Wine, 287
Curried oysters, 198.
Curry, 69.
Curtain rods, putting into curtains, 319.
Custard, caramel, 220.
 Cheese, 52.
 Soufflé, 222
Cutlets, celery, 127.
 Fish, 47.
 Vegetarian, 98.

347

INDEX

D

Dark fruit cake, 236.
Decanters, how to clean, 305.
Decorating cakes, 272.
Desserts, 211.
  Almond blancmange, 229.
  Almond velvet cream, 229.
  Apple cake, 233.
  Custard pie, 219.
  Florentine, 234.
  Soufflé, 224.
  Batter pudding, 214.
  Bread pudding, 213.
  Brown Betty, 218.
  Caramel custard, 220.
  Cherry pudding, 216.
  Chestnut compote, 231.
  Cream, 231.
  Snow, 230.
  Chocolate pie, 219.
  Pudding, 225.
  Pudding with creamy sauce, 226.
  Cold rice pudding, 211.
  Cream chocolate, 228.
  Egyptian pudding, 215.
  Fig pudding, 217.
  Florentine cream, 227.
  Frappéd figs, 224.
  German balloons, 214.
  Farina pudding, 228.
  Fruit tarts, 232.
  Graham pudding, 213.
  Guava sherbet, 224.
  Ingredients for mincemeat, 220.
  Jellied cherries, 231.
  Lemon cream, 226.
  Pudding, 221.
  Molded farina, 227.
  Pineapple sponge, 223.
  Porcupine, 232.
  Prune soufflé, 223.
  Pumpkin pie, 219.
  Rice pudding, 211.
  Rothe gruetze, 225.
  Russian rice, 212.
  St. Denis Indian pudding, 213.
  Steamed blackberry pudding, 217.
  Blueberry pudding, 216.
  Soufflé custard, 222.
  Strawberry sponge, 222.
  Trautmansdorf rice pudding, 212.
  Tunis fruit cream, 230.
  Washington pudding, 218.

Deviled salmon, 41.
  Tomatoes, 119.
Dressings for salads, 160.
  Turkey, 74, 75.
Dried apple cake, 242.
Duck and orange salad, 165.
Dundee Scotch marmalade, 194.

E

Egg lemonade, 296.
Egg nog, 281.
Eggplant, broiled, 116.
  à la Creole, 117.
  Turkish, 116.
Egg puffs, 14.
  Shampoo, 323.
  Timbales, 142.
  Toast, Swiss, 138.
Egg and tomato scramble, 202.
  Tomato toast, 138.
Eggs, 133.
  Baked cheese omelette, 136.
  Baked, and with stuffed tomatoes, 66.
  Creamed, 139.
  Fried savory, 141.
  Japanese, 140.
  Mexican, 140.
  In molds, 139.
  Omelette, celestine, 136.
  Aux haricots, 135.
  Oyster omelette, 134.
  Scrambled with cheese, 137.
  With sausage, 202.
  With tomatoes, 137.
  With spaghetti, 141.
  Spanish eggs (Huevos), 141.
  Stuffed, 139.
  Swiss egg toast, 138.
  Tomato and egg toast, 138.
  Tomato omelette, 135.
  Venetian, 140.
Egyptian pudding, 215.
English brawn, 53.
  Crumpets, 14.
  Molasses candy, 256.
  Monkey, 206.
Elderblow wine, 286.
Entrées, 51.
  Calf's head cheese, 53.
  Casserole liver and rice, 60.
  Cheese custard, 52.
  Chestnut patties, 70.
  Chicken mousse, 62.
  Chilli con carne, 61.
  Mexican, 60.

Entrées—Contd.
  Curry, 69.
  English brawn, 53.
  Genoa ramekins, 51.
  German globes, 68.
  Gnocchi, 52.
  Haddock ramekins, 51.
  Hawaiian curry, 69.
  Hassenpfeffer, 63.
  Italian veal cheese, 54.
  Lobster, à la Creole, 64.
  Lobster croquettes, 64.
  Lobster Patties, 63.
  Marrow bones, 55.
  Nut croquettes, 66.
  Nut and crumb croquettes, 67.
  Pâté de foie gras, 59.
  Pork cheese, 54.
  Riced chicken in shells, 62.
  Somerset Club croquettes, 67.
  Spinach loaf with sardines, 65.
  Stuffed tomatoes with baked eggs, 66.
  Sweetbread croquettes, 57.
  Patties, 58.
  Tomato soufflé, 65.
  Tongue in aspic, 61.
  Veal soufflé with mushroom sauce, 56.
  Terrapin, 56.
Eyebrows, the care of, 323.
  to darken, 324.
  to grow heavy, 323.
Eyelash stain, Chinese, 324.

F

Face powder, 327.
Fainting, 339.
Farina, molded, 227.
  Pudding, German, 228.
Fig pudding, 217.
Figs, frappéd, 224.
Fish, 38.
  Codfish balls, 42.
  Cakes, 43.
  Correct sauces to serve with, 39.
  Cutlets, 47.
  Flounders, baked fillet of, 46.
  Mackerel, 47.
  Oysters, à la creole, 44.
  à la poulette, 45.
  Paste, 48.
  Salmon, creamed, 41.

348

INDEX

Fish—Contd.
  Deviled, 41.
  Loaf, 49.
  Scallops, creamed, 46.
  Shad, baked, stuffing for, 44.
    Planked, 43.
  Shrimps, Brazilian, 47.
  Sole, baked 46.
  Terrapin, stewed, 49.
  Timbales, 50.
    Cases for, 49.
  Times for cooking, 38.
Fish-house punch, 276.
  Philadelphia, 276.
Fish salads, 165.
Fish scalloped with peppers, 123.
Flounders, baked fillet of, 46.
Florentine cream, 227.
Flower salads, 181.
Fonds of artichoke, 23.
Fowls, chestnut stuffing for, 155.
Frapped Figs, 224.
French chestnuts, 129.
  Chicken, 91.
  Creole drink, 294.
  Dressing, 160.
  Fondant, 262.
  Macaroni, 105.
  Peas, with shrimps, 208.
Fried connifela, 17.
  Corn, 124.
  Eggs, savory, 141.
  Peppers, green, 120.
  Potato balls, 110.
  Tomatoes, green, 117.
    Ripe, 118.
Fricandeau of veal, 82.
Fricase de pollos, 85.
Fritters, celery, 124.
  Corn, 124.
  Cucumber, 115.
Fruit cake, 238.
  Black, 236.
  Dark, 236.
  White, 239.
Fruit cocktail, 20.
Fruit cream, Tunis, 230.
  Drops, 249.
  Punch, 287, 288.
  Salads, 178.
  Soups, 37.
  Stains, to remove, 310, 311.
  Syrups, 292, 293.
Fudge cake, 247.
  Chocolate, 268, 269.
  Nut, 269.

G

Genoa ramekins, 51.

German balloons, 214.
  Farina pudding, 228.
  Fruit tarts, 232.
  Globes, 68.
  Loaf cake, 243.
  Pancakes, 10.
  Potato salad, 171.
  Rings, 253.
  Turnips, 125.
Gilding mixture, 318.
Gilt frames, to clean, 314.
Gin fizz, 287.
Ginger ale julep, 294.
  Beer, 298.
  Pear, 193.
  Snaps, 253.
Glass, cement for, 318.
  Ground, imitation of, 319.
Glue, waterproof, 318.
Gnocchi, 52.
Goulashe, 92.
Graham gems, 7.
  Loaf, 5.
  Pudding, 213.
Grandmother Holt's crullers, 255.
  Cucumber pickles, 184.
Grape-fruit and chestnut salad, 179.
Grape juice, 295.
  In the sick room, 339.
Grapes, spiced, 192.
Grass stains, to remove, 308.
Grease spots, to remove, 307.
Green corn omelette, 123.
  Mayonnaise, 162.
  Tomato and onion pickle, 186.
Griesmehl soup, 36.
Guava sherbet, 224.
Gum drops, 271.
Gumbo, 33.

H

Haddock ramekins, 51.
Hair, the care of, 321.
  to keep curled, 322.
  Tonics, 321, 322.
Ham, barbecued, 207.
  Boiled, 76.
  Boiled with rice, 102.
Hard-shell clams, 200.
Hassenpfeffer (Sour rabbit), 63.
Hawaiian curry, 69.
  Taro, 30.
Havana amande, 297.
Headache, 338.
Heliotrope sachet, 332.
Henna, 323.
Hermits, 254.
Herring salad, 167, 168.
Hiccoughs, 340.

Hollandaise sauce, 150.
Hominy croquettes, 128.
Hors d'oeuvres, 19.
  Alligator pear cocktail, 19.
  Anchovy paste, 21.
  Canape of chicken livers, 21.
  Canape Lorenzo, 21.
  Caviar, 20.
  Celery, 23.
  Croutes of herring, 22.
  Fonds of artichoke, 23.
  Fruit cocktail, 20.
  Italian toast, 22.
  Oyster cocktail, 19.
  Rings of onions or eggs, 23.
  Tomato, 20.
Horseradish sauce, 154.
Huevos (Spanish eggs), 141.
Hungarian goulashe, 92.
Hysterics, 339.

I

Imitation of ground glass, 319.
Ingredients for mincemeat, 220.
Ink-spots, to remove, 308.
Iron-rust, to remove, 308.
Italian macaroni, 104.
  Toast, 22.
  Veal chrese, 54.
Ivory handles, to clean, 311.

J

Jackson snaps, 254.
Japanese eggs, 140.
  Salad dressing, 164.
Javelle water, 303, 304.
Jellied cherries, 231.
  Chicken, 88, 89.
Jelly, Tomato, 174.
  Venison, 192.
Jet passamenterie, 313.
Julep, Ginger ale, 294.
  Mint, 283, 284.

K

Kerosene for washing clothes, 310.
Kidneys and bacon, 81.
  Stewed à la Creole, 81.

L

Lace, to wash, 312.
  Black, to restore, 312.

INDEX

Lacquer for silver, 316.
Lady Baltimore cake, 247.
Lavender smelling salts, 332.
Lemonade, egg, 296.
　Pineapple, 296.
Lemon bath, 326.
　Butter, 156.
　Cream, 226.
Lemon drops, 271.
　Juice, for bottling, 296.
　Pudding, 221.
　Soup, 37.
　Syrup, 292.
Lentil soup, 35.
Lily salad, 182.
Lime water, 341.
Linen, to remove grease spots from, 307.
　To remove mildew from, 307.
　To remove scorch spots from, 309.
Lip-salve, 327.
Liver, baked, 79.
　With rice, in casserole, 60.
Lobster, à la Creole, 64.
　Croquettes, 64.
　à la Newburg, 201.
　Patties, 63.
　Salad, with cream dressing, 166.
　Soup, 32.
Louisiana gumbo, 33.
Luan-ed chicken, 87.
Lyonnaise potatoes, 109.

M

Macaroni, 103.
　American, 106.
　French, 106.
　Italian, 104.
　Mexican, 105.
　Spanish, 104.
Macedoine loaf, 95.
Mackerel, 47.
Made drinks, 280.
Magnesia, how to use as a cleanser, 313.
Mahogany, to clean spots from, 319.
Maitre d'hôtel sauce, 151.
Maple caramels, 270.
Marmalade, California orange, 195.
　Dundee Scotch, 194.
　Rhubarb, 194.
Marrons glacés, 273.
Marrow bones, 55.
Mashed carrots, 125.
Marshmallow cake, 246.
Mayonnaise dressing, 161.

Mayonnaise dressing— Contd.
　Green, 162.
　Without oil, 162.
Marzipan, 252
Measured angel cake, 244.
Meat salads, 164.
Meats, 71.
　Beef-heart, braised, 78.
　Chicken, Cadillac, 90.
　Casserole, 84.
　Creole, 86.
　French, 91.
　Fricase de pollos, 85.
　Jellied, 88, 89.
　Luan-ed, 87
　Stewed, à l'espagnole, 86.
　Sour, 91.
　Terrapin, 92
　Chilli con carne, 93.
　Chi lo, Chinese, 94.
　Collops in batter, 94.
　Goulashe, Hungarian, 92.
　Ham, boiled, 76.
　Spanish steak, 77.
　Kidneys and bacon, 81.
　Stewed, à la Creole, 81.
　Liver, baked, 79.
　Calf's baked, 79.
　Macedoine loaf, 95.
　Pigeon pie, 77.
　Rabbit, stewed, 82.
　Stew, Brunswick, 87.
　Spanish, 88.
　Substitutes for meat, 96.
　Times for cooking meats, 71.
　Tongue à la juive, 80.
　Ragout, 79.
　T u r k e y, chestnut stuffing for, 75.
　Dressings, 74, 75.
　Roast, with oysters, 73.
　Stuffing, 74.
　Veal, boudins of, 83.
　Fricandeau of, 82.
　Vegetarian cutlet, 98.
　Loaf, 96, 97.
　Roast, 99.
　What to serve with meats, 72.
Melting codfish cakes, 43.
Metals, to write on, 318.
Mexican eggs, 140.
　Kisses, 270.
　Macaroni, 105.
　Rice, 101.
　Stuffed peppers, 122.
Mildew, to remove, 307.

Milk punch, 282.
Mincemeat, ingredients for, 220.
Minnehaha cake, 244.
Mint cordial, 285.
　Drops, 259.
　Julep, 283, 284.
　Leaves, candied, 272.
　Sauce, 152.
Minute biscuit, 8.
Mirrors, to clean, 314.
Mixed single drinks, 282.
Mocha cake, 245.
Mock terrapin, 207
Moist hands, 328.
Molasses candy, 256.
Molded farina, 227.
Moth patch, to remove, 329.
Moths, to rid a closet of, 320.
Mushrooms, cream of, 25.
　Stewed, 128.
Mustard pickle, 188
　Plasters, 338.
　Sauce, 148.

N

Navy punch, 277.
Nose-bleed, 339.
Nougat, 261.
Nut bread, 4.
　Candy, 261.
　Candy chocolate, 268.
　Croquettes, 66.
Nut and crumb croquettes, 67.
Nut fudge, 269.

O

Oatmeal, rock cakes, 250.
　Spiced cookies, 250.
　Wafers, 12.
Oil painting, to clean, 313.
Oily hair, powder for, 322.
Okra, stewed with tomatoes, 118.
Old colonial ginger cup, 295.
Omelette, baked cheese, 136.
　Celestine, 136.
　Green corn, 123.
　Haricots, 135.
　Oyster, 134.
　Remarks, 133.
　Tomato, 135.
Onions, baked, 113.
　Bermudas, stuffed, 113.
　Creamed, 112.
　Scalloped, 112.

INDEX

Orange balls, 275.
  Cocktail, 285.
  Cordial, 286.
  Marmalade, 195.
  Peel, candied, 274.
  Punch, 288.
Orange-flower cream, 328.
Orris powder, for perspiration, 328
Oxalic acid, for removing stains, 304
Ox-tongue à la juive, 80.
Oyster cocktail, 19.
  Omelette, 134.
  Salad, 165.
Oysters, creamed, 199.
  Curried, 198.
  À la Parisienne, 199.
  Panned, 198.
  À la poulette, 45.
  With roast turkey, 73.

P

Paint stains, to remove, 309.
Pancakes, Berlin, 11
  German, 10.
  Rice, 10.
Panned oysters, 198.
Parfait amour, Chocolate, 297.
Parker house rolls, 5
Parsley sauce, 147.
Paté de foie gras, 59.
Patties, Chestnut, 70.
  Lobster, 63.
  Sweetbread, 58.
Peach purée, 37.
  Stains, to remove, 310.
Peaches, sweet pickled, 190.
Peanut brittle, 260.
  Candy, 260.
Pear, Ginger, 193.
Pears, baked, 196.
Penotchie, 261.
Pepper catsup, 185.
  Salad, 173.
  Sauce, 152
Peppers, à la Creole, 121
  Green, fried, 120.
  Green, stuffed, 120.
  Scalloped with fish, 123.
  Stuffed, 121.
Peppermints, Cream, 258.
  Drops, 258.
Perfumed beads, 334.
Perfumes, 330.
Peroxid as a face bleach, 329
Philadelphia fish-house punch, 276.

Piccalilli, Red, 188
Pickles, 184
  Almonds, salted, 196.
  Cabbage, Red 190.
  Chilli sauce, 187
  Chutney, 189.
  Currant bar-le-duc, 193.
  Cucumber catsup, 184-185.
  Cucumbers, Grandmother Holt's, 184
  Grapes, spiced, 192.
  Marmalade, California orange, 195
  Dundee Scotch 194
  Rhubarb, 194.
  Mustard pickle 188
  Peaches, sweet pickled, 190.
  Peanuts, salted, 196.
  Pear, Ginger, 193.
  Pears, baked, 196.
  Pepper catsup, 185.
  Piccalilli, Red, 188.
  Pineapple, sweet pickled, 191
  Quinces, baked, 195.
  Tomato pickle, 186
Pickles, Tomato, green and onion, 186
  Tomato preserves, 192
  Venison jelly, 192
  Watermelon rind sweet-pickled, 191.
Pigeon pie, 77.
Pie, Apple custard, 219.
  Chocolate, 219
  Pigeon, 77.
  Pumpkin, 219.
Pilau, Turkish, 103.
  West India, 102.
Pineapple and celery salad, 180.
  Juice in the sick room, 339.
  Lemonade, 296.
  Sponge, 223.
  Soup (see lemon), 37.
  Sweet-pickled, 191.
  Syrup, 292.
Planked shad, 43.
Plasters, mustard, 338.
Plumes, to clean, 312
Poi, 30.
Polish for furniture, 315.
Pompadour salad, 172.
Pop-overs, 13.
Poppy salad, 182.
Porcupine, 232
Pork cheese, 54.
Port wine sangaree, 284
Potato balls, fried, 110.
  Salad, German, 171.
  Soufflé, 109.
Potatoes, Lyonnaise, 109

Potpourri jars, 332-333.
Pound cake, 240-241
Prune soufflé, 223.
Puchero, 34
Pudding, Batter, 214.
  Blackberry, 217.
  Blueberry, 216.
  Bread, 213.
  Cherry, 216.
  Chinese, with rice, 102
  Chocolate, 225
  Chocolate, with creamy sauce, 226.
  Corn 124
  Egyptian, 215
  Farina German, 228
  Fig, 217
  Graham, 213.
  Lemon, 221.
  Rice, 211
  Squash, 127
  St Denis Indian, 213.
  Trautmansdorf, rice, 212
  Washington, 218
Pulled bread, 5
Punch, 276
  California fruit, 287
  Champagne, 278-279
  Claret, 280
  Fish house, 276
  Fruit, 288
  Milk, 282
  Navy, 277
  Orange, 288
  Philadelphia fish-house, 276
  Strawberry, 287.
  Tea, 281.
  U. S. S. Richmond, 277.
Purée, Chestnut, 29-30.
  Peach, 37.

Q

Queen's aspic, 177.
Quinces, baked, 195.

R

Rabbit, stewed, 82.
Ranickins, Genoa, 51.
  Haddock, 51.
Raspberry shrub, 293.
  Soup (see lemon), 37.
Red cabbage, 114.
  Pickled, 190.
  Piccalilli, 188.
Regent punch, 279.
Removing spots from clothing, 306-307.
Rhubarb marmalade, 194.
Rice, 100.
  With Chinese pudding, 102.

INDEX

Rice—Contd.
With ham, 102.
Griddle cakes, 9.
Liver in casserole, 60.
Mexican, 101.
Pancakes, 10.
Pilau, Turkish, 103.
West India, 102.
Pudding, 211.
Trautmansdorf, 212.
Rizotto, 100.
Spanish, 101.
Waffles, 9.
Riced chicken in shells, 62.
Richmond thin biscuits, 8.
Rickey, 283.
Rings of eggs, 23.
Onions, 23
Rizotto, 100.
Roast turkey with oysters, 73.
Rock cake, Russian, 251.
Rock cakes, oatmeal, 250.
Rods, to put into sash curtains, 319.
Root beer, 298.
Rose sachet powder, 331.
Salad, 183.
Rothe gruetze, 225.
Rouge, 326.
Rug, to dry-clean, 313.
Russian rock cake, 251.

S

Sachet powders, 331-332.
Salad dressings, 160.
Salads, 158.
Alligator pear, 171.
Apple and banana, 179.
Apple, cress and celery, 179.
Bahia, 172.
Bean, 172.
Celery and pineapple, 180.
Cheese balls, 159.
Straws, 159.
Cherry, 181.
Chestnut, 171-172.
Chicken, 164.
Chrysanthemum, 181.
Dressings, 160.
Boiled, 162-163.
Cream, 163.
French, 160.
Japanese, 164.
Mayonnaise, 161-162.
Duck and orange, 165.
Fish, 165.

Salads—Contd.
Grape-fruit and chestnut, 179.
Grapes, white, 178.
Herring, 167-168.
Lamb, 164.
Lily, 182.
Lobster, 166.
Oyster, 165.
Pepper, 173.
Pompadour, 172.
Poppy, 182.
Potato, German, 171.
Queen's aspic, 177.
Radish, 173.
Rose, 183.
Salmon aspic, 169.
Shad-roe, 166.
Spanish, 173.
Sweetbread, 164.
Tomato aspic, 176.
With Celery, 176.
With Crab, 169.
With Cucumber, 175.
Frappé, 175.
Jelly, 174.
Jelly and Cucumber, 174.
Tongue, 165.
Tulip, 183.
Salmon aspic, 169.
Creamed, 41.
Deviled, 41.
Loaf, 40.
Salted almonds, 196.
Peanuts, 196
Sally Lunn, 12-13.
Sand tarts, 248.
Sandwiches, 209.
Sangaree, Port-wine, 284.
Sardines with spinach loaf, 65.
Sauerkraut candy, 259.
Sauces, 143.
Bechamel, 152.
Bordelaise, 153.
Bread, 154.
Brown, 146-147.
Brown butter, 147.
Chestnut, for fowls, 155.
Citron, 156.
Claret, 156.
Cucumber, 148-149.
Espagnol, 153.
Hollandaise, 150.
Horseradish, 154.
Lemon butter, 156.
Maître d'hôtel, 151.
Mint sauce, 152.
Mustard sauce, 148.
Parsley sauce, 147.
Pepper sauce, 152.
Sauce tartare, 151.
Tomato butter, 155.
Tomato sauce, 154.
Vinaigrette, 149.
White sauce, 146.

Sauces—Contd.
What to serve with various meats, 145.
Sauces to serve with fish, 39.
Sausage and scrambled eggs, 202.
Sauterne cup, 291.
Scalloped cauliflower, 114.
Fish and peppers, 123.
Scotch broth, 35.
Scones, 14
Short-cake, 252.
Woodcock, 205.
Scorch-marks, to remove from linen, 309.
Scrambled eggs and cheese, 137.
Eggs and sausage, 202.
Tomato and egg, 137-202.
Sea foam candy, 257.
Seasickness, cure for, 338.
Serge garments, to clean, 307.
Shad, baked, stuffing for, 44.
Planked, 43.
Shad-roe salad, 166.
Shampoo, egg, 323.
Shandy gaff, 285.
Shellac for brasswork, 317.
Sherbet, Guava, 224.
Shrimps, Brazilian, 47.
Creamed, 201.
With French peas, 208.
Sick headache, relief for, 338.
Silk, to remove grease-spots from, 307.
Silver, to clean, 313, 317.
Silver bugs, to destroy, 319.
Silver, lacquer for, 316.
Simple remedies, 336.
Skin, the care of, 325.
Smelling salts, 332.
Soda biscuit, 7.
Soft gingerbread, 243.
Soft-shell clams, 200.
Soft soap, 305.
Sole, baked, 46.
Somerset Club croquettes, 67.
Soufflé, Apple, 224.
Custard, 222.
Potato, 109.
Prune, 223.
Spinach, 111.
Tomato, 65.
Veal, 56.

INDEX

Soups, 24.
  Almond milk, 26.
  Asparagus, Cream of, 26
  Beets, Cream of, 25
  Beef-tea, 36
  Black bean, 31
  Blackberry, 37
  Caldo (see puchero), 34
  Carrots, Cream of, 28
  Cauliflower, Cream of, 29
  Celery, Cream of, 24
  Chestnuts, Cream of, 28
    With celery, 27
    Puree, 29-30.
  Chicken gumbo, 33
  Clam chowder, 32
  Claret soup, 36
  Corn chowder, 32
  Currant soup, 37
  Griesmehl, 38.
  Lemon soup, 37
  Lentil soup, 35
  Lobster soup, 32
  Louisiana gumbo, 33
  Mushrooms, Cream of, 25.
  Peach purée, 37.
  Pineapple, 37.
  Pot, 30
  Puchero, 34.
  Raspberry, 37.
  Scotch broth, 35.
  Taro, 30
  Tomato bisque, 31
  What to serve with soups, 24.
Sour chicken, 91.
  Milk cakes, 10.
  Rabbit (Hassenpfeffer), 63.
Snaps, Ginger, 253.
  Jackson, 254
Spaghetti with eggs, 141.
Spanish eggs (Huevos), 141
  Macaroni, 104.
  Rarebit, 204
  Rice, 101.
  Salad, 173.
  Steak, 77.
  Stew, 88.
Spice cake, 239.
Spiced grapes, 192.
Spinach loaf with sardines, 65.
  Soufflé, 111.
Splinter, how to remove, 340.
Spots removed from fabrics, 307.
Sprains, 339.
Squash pudding, 127.

Steamed apples, 132.
Stew, Brunswick, 87
  Spanish, 88
Stewed chestnuts, 139
  Chicken, à l'espagnole, 86
  Kidneys à la Creole, 81
Stewed Mushrooms, 138
  Rabbit, 82
  Terrapin, 49.
  Tomato and okra, 118
Stings of insects, 340
St. Denis Indian pudding, 213
Strawberry punch, 287
  Sponge, 222
Stuffed Bermuda onions, 113.
  Cucumbers, 115
  Eggs, 139
  Peppers, 121.
    Green, 120.
    Mexican, 122.
    Spanish, 122.
  Tomatoes, 119
  Tomatoes with baked eggs, 66.
Substitutes for meats, 56
Sugar cookies, 253
Sulphur matches for removing stains, 305
Summer drinks, 293
Superior cookies, 253
Surprise macaroons, 249
Sweetbread croquettes, 57.
  Patties, 58.
  Salad, 164.
Sweet pickled peaches, 190.
  Pineapple, 191.
  Watermelon rind, 191.
Sweet potato croquettes, 110.
Swiss egg-toast, 138.
Syrups, fruit, 292-293.
  Lemon, 292
  Pineapple, 292.

T

Taffy, Chocolate, 266.
Tan, to remove, 329.
Tar stains, to remove, 309.
Taro, 30
Tarts, German fruit, 232.
  Sand, 248.
Tea punch, 291
Tea stains to remove, 309.
Terrapin, Chicken, 92.
  Stewed, 49.
  Veal, 56.

Timbale cases for creamed fish, 49
Timbales, Egg, 142
Tins for cooking bread, 3
  Cake, 3
  Fish, 38.
  Meats, 71
  Vegetables, 108
Tomato aspic, 176
  Bisque, 31
  Butter, 155
  and Celery salad, 176
  and Egg, scramble, 202
  and Egg, toast, 138
  Frappé, 175
  Hors d'oeuvre, 20
  Jelly, 174
  Omelette, 135
  Pickle, 186
  Preserves, 192
  Sauce, 154
  Soufflé, 65
Tomatoes, deviled, 119
  Raw, with cucumber, 175
  Scrambled with eggs, 137
  Stewed with okra, 118
  Stuffed, 119
Tooth powder, 341
Trautmansdorf rice pudding, 212
Tulip salad, 183.
Tunis fruit cream, 230.
Turkey, Chestnut stuffing for, 75
  Dressing, 74-75.
  Stuffing, 74
Turkish eggplant, 116.
  Pilau, 103.
Turnips, German, 125
Tutti frutti cup, 289
Tweed garments, to clean, 307.

U

Useful information, 301.
Uses for hot water, 336.
U. S. S. Richmond punch, 277.

V

Veal, boudins of, 83.
  Fricandeau of, 82.
  Soufflé, 56.
  Terrapin, 56
Vegetable roast, 99.
  Salads, 170
Vegetables, 107.
  Apples, baked, 131.
    Steamed, 132.
  Cabbage, Red, 114.
  Carrot balls, 126.
  Carrots, browned, 126.

353

INDEX

Vegetables—Contd.
  Mashed, 125.
  Cauliflower, scalloped, 114.
  Celery cutlets, 127.
  Fritters, 127.
  Chestnut croquettes, 131.
  Chestnuts, in brown sauce, 130.
  French, 129.
  Stewed, 130.
  In white sauce, 129.
  Corn, fried, 124.
  Fritters, 124.
  Omelette, 123.
  Pudding, 124.
  Cucumber fritters, 115.
  Stuffed, 115.
  Eggplant, broiled, 116.
  À la Creole, 117.
  Turkish, 116.
  Hominy croquettes, 128.
  Mushrooms, stewed, 128.
  Onions, baked, 113.
  Bermudas, stuffed, 113.
  Creamed, 112.
  Scalloped, 112.
  Peppers, à la Creole, 121.
  Green, fried, 120.
  Green, stuffed, 120.

Vegetables—Contd.
  Scalloped with fish, 123.
  Peppers, stuffed, 121.
  Mexican, 122.
  Spanish, 122.
  Potato balls, 110.
  Soufflé, 109.
  Potatoes, Lyonnaise, 109.
  Spinach loaf with sardines, 65.
  Pudding, 111.
  Soufflé, 111.
  Squash pudding, 127.
  Sweet potato croquettes, 110.
  Tomatoes, deviled, 119.
  Green, fried, 117.
  Ripe, fried, 118.
  Stewed, with okra, 118.
  Stuffed, 119.
  Times for cooking vegetables, 108.
  Turnips, German, 125.
Vegetables, as medicine, 337.
Vegetarian cutlet, 98.
  Loaf, 96-97.
Venetian eggs, 140.
Venison jelly, 192.
Vinaigrette sauce, 149.
Violet sachet powder, 331.
Violets, candied, 272.

W

Waffles, 8-9.
Washing clothes with kerosene, 310.
Washington pudding, 218.
  Rolls, 6.
Water bottles, to clean, 305.
Watermelon rind, sweet-pickled, 191.
Waterproof glue, 316.
Welsh rarebit, 203
West India pilau, 102.
Whisky sour, 283.
White cake, 241.
White fruit cake, 239.
  Grapes, salad, 178
  Plumes, to clean, 312.
  Sauce, 146.
  Sugar candy, 257
Whole-wheat cakes, 11
Wine, Currant, 287.
  Elderblow, 286.
Woolen cloth, to clean, 307, 311.
Writing on metals, 318.

Y

Yellow frosting, 235.
Yorkshire breakfast cake, 15.
  Pudding, 16.

GENERAL INDEX

CHAPTER I

Breads.

Times for cooking bread and cake, 3.
Nut bread, No. 1, 4.
Nut bread, No. 2, 4.
Pulled bread, 5.
Graham loaf, 5.
Parker house rolls, 5.
Washington rolls, 6.
Bath buns, 6.
Graham gems, 7.
Soda biscuit, 7.
Minute biscuits, 8.
Richmond thin biscuits, 8.
Waffles, 8.
Rice Waffles, 9.
Rice griddle cakes, 9.
Rice pancakes, 10.
Sour milk cakes, 10.
German pancakes, 10.
Berlin pancakes, 11.
Whole wheat cakes, 11.
Oatmeal wafers, 12.
Sally Lunn, 12.
Virginia Sally Lunn, 13.
Popovers, 13.
Egg puffs, 14.
Scotch scones, 14.
English crumpets, 14.
Cheese straws, 15.
Yorkshire breakfast cake, 15.
Yorkshire pudding, 16.
Boiled connifela, 16.
Fried connifela, 17.
Cinnamon coffee bread, 17.

CHAPTER II

Hors D'œuvres.

Oyster cocktail, 19.
Alligator pear cocktail, 19.
Fruit cocktail, 20.
Caviar, 20.
Tomato, 20.
Anchovy, 21
Canapés of chicken livers, 21.
Canapé Lorenzo, 21.
Croûtes of herring, 22.
Italian toast, 22.
Fonds of artichoke, 23.
Rings of onions and eggs, 23.
Celery, 23.

CHAPTER III

Soups.

What to serve with soup, 24.
Cream of celery, 24.

Cream of mushrooms, 25.
Cream of beets, 25.
Almond milk cream soup, 26.
Cream of asparagus, 26.
Chestnut and celery soup, 27.
Chestnut cream, 28.
Cream of carrots, 28.
Cream of cauliflower, 29.
Chestnut purée, No. 1, 29.
Chestnut purée, No 2., 30.
Taro, or Poi, 30.
Tomato bisque, 31.
Black bean soup, 31.
Lobster soup, 32.
Clam chowder, 32.
Corn chowder, 32.
Chicken gumbo, 33.
Louisiana gumbo, 33.
Puchero, 34.
Scotch broth, 35.
Lentil soup, 35.
Beef tea, 36.
Griesmehl soup, 36.
Claret soup, 36.
Lemon soup, 37
Blackberry soup, 37.
Peach purée, 37.

CHAPTER IV.

Fish

Times for cooking fish, 38
Correct sauces to serve with fish, 39.
Salmon loaf, No. 1., 40.
Salmon loaf, No 2., 40.
Creamed Salmon, 41.
Deviled Salmon, 41.
Codfish balls, 42.
Melting codfish cakes, 43.
Planked shad, 43.
Stuffing for baked shad, 44.
Oysters à la creole, 44.
Oysters à la poulette, 45.
Creamed scallops, 46.
Baked sole, or fillet of flounders, 46.
Brazilian shrimps, 47.
Mackerel (Chamberlin), 47.
Fish cutlets, 47.
Fish paste, 48.
Stewed terrapin (Chamberlin), 49.
Timbale cases for creamed fish, 49.
Fish timbales, 50.

CHAPTER V.

Entrées.

Genoa ramekins, 51.
Haddock ramekins, 51.

INDEX

Cheese custard, 52.
Gnocchi, 52.
Calf's head cheese, 53.
English brawn, 53.
Pork cheese, 54.
Italian veal cheese, 54.
Prepared marrow bones, 55.
Veal terrapin, 56.
Veal soufflé and mushrooms, 56.
Sweetbread croquettes, 57.
Sweetbread patties, 58.
Pâté de foie gras, No. 1., 59.
Pâté de foie gras, No. 2., 59.
Casserole liver and rice, 60.
Chilli con carne, No. 1., 60.
Chilli con carne, No. 2., 61.
Tongue in aspic, 61.
Chicken mousse, 62.
Riced chicken in shells, 62.
Hassenpfeffer (Sour rabbit), 63.
Lobster patties, 63.
Lobster à la creole, 64.
Lobster croquettes, 64.
Spinach and sardines, 65.
Tomato soufflé, 65.
Stuffed tomato and eggs, 66.
Nut croquettes, 66.
Nut and crumb croquettes, 67.
Somerset Club croquettes, 67.
German globes, 68.
Curry, 69.
Hawaiian curry, 69.
Chestnut patties, 70.

CHAPTER VI.
Meats.

Time-table for cooking meats, 71.
What to serve with meats, 72.
Roast turkey with oysters, 73.
Turkey stuffing, 74.
Turkey dressing No. 1., 74.
Turkey dressing, No. 2., 75.
Chestnut stuffing for turkey, 75.
Boiled ham, 76.
Boiled ham (Chamberlin), 76.
Spanish steak, 77.
Pigeon pie, 77.
Braised beef-heart, 78.
Baked liver, 79.
Baked calf's liver, 79.
Tongue ragoût, 79.
Ox-tongue, à la juive, 80.
Kidneys and bacon, 81.
Stewed kidney à la creole, 81.
Stewed rabbit, 82.
Fricandeau of veal, 82.
Boudins of veal, 83.
Chicken in casserole, No. 1., 84.
Chicken in casserole, No. 2., 84.
Fricase de pollos, 85.
Stewed chicken a l'espagnole, 86.
Creole chicken, 86.
Luau-ed chicken, 87.
Brunswick stew, 87.
Spanish stew, 88.
Jellied chicken, No. 1., 88.
Jellied chicken, No. 2., 89.
Cadillac chicken, 90.
Sour chicken, 91.

French chicken, 91.
Chicken terrapin, 92.
Hungarian goulashe, 92.
Chilli con carne, 93.
Chinese Chi Lo, 94.
Collops in batter, 94.
Macedoine loaf, 95.
Vegetarian loaf, No. 1., 96.
Vegetarian loaf, No. 2., 97.
Vegetarian cutlet, 98.
Vegetable roast, 99.

CHAPTER VII.
Rice and Macaroni.

Boiled rice, 100.
Rizotto, 100.
Mexican rice, 101.
Spanish rice, 101.
Rice and ham, 102.
Rice and Chinese pudding, 102.
West India pilau, 102.
Turkish pilau, 103.
Remarks on macaroni, 103.
Italian macaroni, No. 1., 104.
Italian macaroni, No. 2., 104.
Spanish macaroni, 104.
Mexican macaroni, 105.
French macaroni, 105.
American macaroni, 106.

CHAPTER VIII.
Vegetables.

Times of cooking vegetables, 108.
Lyonnaise potatoes, 109.
Potato soufflé, 109.
Fried potato balls, 110.
Sweet potato croquettes, 110.
Spinach soufflé, 111.
Spinach pudding, 111.
Creamed onions, 112.
Scalloped onions, 112.
Stuffed Bermuda onions, 113.
Baked onions, 113.
Red cabbage, 114.
Scalloped cauliflower, 114.
Stuffed cucumbers, 115.
Cucumber fritters, 115.
Broiled eggplant, 116.
Turkish eggplant, 116.
Eggplant à la creole, 117.
Fried green tomatoes, 117.
Fried ripe tomatoes, 118.
Stewed tomatoes and okra, 118.
Deviled tomatoes, 119.
Stuffed tomatoes, 119.
Fried green peppers, 120.
Stuffed green peppers, 120.
Stuffed peppers, 121.
Peppers à la creole, 121.
Mexican stuffed peppers, 122.
Spanish stuffed peppers, 122.
Peppers scalloped with fish, 123.
Green corn omelette, 123.
Fried corn, 124.
Corn fritters, 124.
Corn pudding, 124.
German turnips, 125.
Mashed carrots, 125.

INDEX

Browned carrots, 126.
Carrot balls, 126.
Squash pudding, 127.
Celery fritters, 127.
Celery cutlets, 127.
Hominy croquettes, 128.
Stewed mushrooms, 128.
French chestnuts, 129.
Chestnuts in white sauce, 129.
Chestnuts in brown sauce, 130.
Stewed chestnuts, 130.
Chestnut croquettes, 131.
Baked apples, 131.
Steamed apples, 132.

CHAPTER IX.
Eggs.

Omelettes, 133.
Oyster omelette, 134.
Omelette aux haricots, 135.
Tomato omelette, 135.
Baked cheese omelette, 136.
Omelette celestine, 136.
Scrambled eggs with tomatoes, 137.
Scrambled eggs with cheese, 137.
Tomato and egg toast, 138.
Swiss egg toast, 138.
Creamed eggs, 139.
Stuffed eggs, 139.
Eggs in molds, 139.
Mexican eggs, 140.
Venetian eggs, 140.
Japanese eggs, 140.
Huevos, 141.
Fried savory eggs, 141.
Eggs with spaghetti, 141.
Egg timbales, 142.

CHAPTER X.
Sauces.

Remarks on sauces, 143.
Sauces to serve with various meats, 145.
White sauce, 146.
Brown sauce No. 1., 146.
Brown sauce, No. 2., 147.
Brown butter sauce, 147.
Parsley sauce, 147.
Mustard sauce, 148.
Cucumber sauce, No. 1., 148.
Cucumber sauce, No. 2., 149.
Vinaigrette sauce, 149.
Hollandaise sauce, No. 1., 150.
Hollandaise sauce, No. 2., 150.
Sauce tartare, No. 1., 151.
Sauce tartare, No. 2., 151.
Maître d'hôtel sauce, No. 1., 151.
Maître d'hôtel sauce, No. 2., 151.
Mint sauce, 152.
Pepper sauce, 152.
Béchamel sauce, 152.
Espagnol sauce, 153.
Bordelaine sauce, 153.
Bread sauce, 154.
Horseradish sauce, 154.
Tomato sauce, 154.
Chestnut sauce for fowls, 155.
Tomato butter, 155.
Lemon butter, 156.
Citron sauce, 156.
Claret sauce, 156.

CHAPTER XI.
Salads.

Remarks on salads, 158.
Cheese balls, 159.
Cheese straws, 159.
Salad dressings, 160-164.
  French, No. 1., 160.
  French, No. 2., 160.
  Mayonnaise, No. 1., 161.
  Mayonnaise, No. 2., 161.
  Mayonnaise, without oil, 162.
  Green mayonnaise, 162.
  Boiled, No 1., 162.
  Boiled, No. 2., 163.
  Cream, 163.
  Japanese salad, 164.
Meat salads, 164.
  Chicken, 164.
  Lamb, 164.
  Sweetbread, 164.
  Duck and orange, 165.
  Tongue, 165.
Fish salads, 165.
  Fish, 165.
  Oyster, 165.
  Shad roe, 166.
  Lobster, with cream dressing, 166.
  Herring, No. 1., 167.
  Herring, No. 2., 168.
  Tomato and crab, 169.
Salmon aspic, 169.
Vegetable salads, 170.
  Remarks, 170.
  German potato, 171.
  Alligator pear, 171.
  Chestnut, No. 1., 171.
  Chestnut, No. 2., 172.
  Bean, 172.
  Bahia, 172.
  Pompadour, 172.
  Pepper, 173.
  Radish, 173.
  Spanish, 173.
Tomato jelly, 174.
Tomato jelly and cucumbers, 174.
Raw tomatoes and cucumbers, 175.
Tomato frappé, 175.
Tomato and celery salad, 176.
Tomato aspic, 176.
Aspic jelly, 177.
Queen's aspic, 177.
Fruit salads, 178.
  Remarks, 178.
  White grapes, 178.
  Grapefruit and chestnut, 179.
  Apple, cress and celery, 179.
  Apple and banana, 179.
  Celery and pineapple, No. 1., 180.
  Celery and pineapple, No. 2., 180.
  Cherry, 181.
Flower salads, 181.
  Remarks, 181.
  Chrysanthemum, 181.
  Lily, 182.
  Poppy, 182.
  Rose, 183.
  Tulip, 183.

INDEX

CHAPTER XII.
Pickles and Relishes.

Grandmother Holt's cucumber pickles, 184.
Cucumber catsup, No. 1., 184.
Cucumber catsup, No. 2., 185.
Pepper catsup, 185.
Green tomato and onion, pickle, 186.
Tomato pickle, 186.
Chilli sauce, No. 1., 187.
Chilli sauce, No. 2., 187.
Mustard pickle, 188.
Red piccalilli, 188.
Chutney, 189.
Pickled red cabbage, 190.
Sweet pickled peaches, 190.
Sweet pickled watermelon rind, 191.
Sweet pickled pineapple, 191.
Spiced grapes, 192.
Venison jelly, 192.
Tomato preserves, 192.
Currant bar-le-duc, 193.
Ginger pears, 193.
Rhubarb marmalade, 194.
Dundee Scotch marmalade, 194.
California orange marmalade, 195.
Baked quinces, 195.
Baked pears, 196.
Salted almonds, 196.
Salted peanuts, 196.

CHAPTER XIII.
Chafing-Dish Receipts.

Panned oysters, 198.
Curried oysters, 198.
Creamed oysters, 199.
Oysters à la Parisienne, 199.
Hard-shell clams, 200.
Soft-shell clams, 200.
Lobster à la Newburg (Chamberlin), 201.
Creamed shrimps, 201.
Scrambled eggs and sausage, 202.
Egg and tomato scramble, 202.
Welsh rarebit, No. 1., 203.
Welsh rarebit, No. 2., 203.
Spanish rarebit, No. 1., 204.
Spanish rarebit, No. 2., 204.
American woodcock, 205.
Scotch woodcock, 205.
English monkey, 206.
Cheese fondue, 206.
Mock terrapin, 207.
Barbecued ham, 207.
Shrimps with French peas, 208.

CHAPTER XIV.
Sandwiches.

Apple and celery, 209.
Baked beans, 209.
Caviar, 209.
Celery, 209.
Chicken and almond, 210.
Club sandwich, 210.
Cucumber, 210.
Egg, 210.
Green pepper, 210.
Ham and olive, 210.
Lettuce-mayonnaise, 210.
Mutton, 210.
Nut sandwich, 210.
Sardine, 210.
Watercress, 210.

CHAPTER XV.
Desserts.

Rice pudding, 211.
Cold rice pudding, 211.
Russian rice, 212.
Trautmansdorf rice pudding, 212.
Bread pudding, 213.
St. Denis Indian pudding, 213.
Graham pudding, 213.
German balloons, 214.
Batter pudding, 214.
Egyptian pudding, 215.
Steamed blueberry pudding, 216.
Cherry pudding, 216.
Steamed blackberry pudding, 217.
Fig pudding, 217.
Washington pudding, 218.
Brown Betty, 218.
Pumpkin pie, 219.
Apple custard pie, 219.
Chocolate pie, 219.
Ingredients for mincemeat, 220.
Caramel custard, 220.
Lemon pudding, 221.
Strawberry sponge, 222.
Soufflé custard, 222.
Pineapple sponge, 223.
Prune soufflé, 223.
Apple soufflé, 224.
Frappéed figs, 224.
Guava sherbet, 224.
Rothe gruetze, 225.
Chocolate pudding, 225.
Chocolate pudding, with cream sauce, 226
Lemon cream, 226.
Florentine cream, 227.
Molded farina, 227.
German farina pudding, 228.
Cream chocolate, 228.
Almond blancmange, 229.
Almond velvet cream, 229.
Tunis fruit cream, 230.
Chestnut snow, 230.
Chestnut cream, 231.
Chestnut compote, 231.
Jellied cherries, 231.
German fruit tarts, 232.
Porcupine, 232.
Apple cake, 233.
Apple Florentine, 234.

CHAPTER XVI.
Cake.

Remarks on cake, 235.
Yellow frosting, 235.
Black fruit cake, 236.
Dark fruit cake, 236.
Composition cake, 237.
Fruit cake, 238.
White fruit cake, 239.
Spice cake, 239.

INDEX

Coffee cake, 240.
Pound cake, No. 1., 240.
Pound cake, No. 2., 241.
White cake, 241.
Bridget cake, 242.
Dried apple cake, 242.
German loaf cake, 243.
Soft gingerbread, 243.
Measured angel cake, 244.
Minnehaha cake, 244.
Caramel cake, 245.
Mocha cake, 245.
Marshmallow cake, 246.
Fudge cake, 247.
Lady Baltimore cake, 247.
Sand tarts, 248.
Fruit drops, 249.
Surprise macaroons, 249.
Oatmeal rock cakes, 250.
Oatmeal spiced cookies, 250.
German rings, 251.
Russian rock cake, 251.
Marzipan, 252.
Scotch short cake, 252.
Superior cookies, 253.
Sugar cookies, 253.
Ginger snaps, 253.
Jackson snaps, 254.
Hermits, 254.
Crullers, 255.
Grandmother Holt's crullers, 255.

CHAPTER XVII.
Candy.

Molasses candy, 256.
English molasses candy, 256.
White sugar candy, 257.
Sea foam, 257.
Butter Scotch, 258.
Peppermint drops, 258.
Cream peppermints, 258.
Mint drops, 259.
Sauerkraut candy, 259.
Mint drops, 259.
Peanut candy, 260.
Nut candy, 261.
Penotchie, 261.
Nougat, 261.
French fondant, 262.
Chocolate coating, 263.
Chocolate bonbons, 263.
Chocolate creams, No. 1., 263.
Chocolate creams, No. 2., 264.
Burnt almonds, 265.
Chocolate almonds, No. 1., 265.
Chocolate almonds, No. 2., 265.
Chocolate taffy, 266.
Chocolate chips, 266.
Chocolate caramels, No. 1., 267.
Chocolate caramels No. 2., 267.
Chocolate nut candy, 268.
Chocolate fudge, No. 1., 268.
Chocolate fudge, No. 2., 269.
Nut fudge, 269.
Maple caramels, 270.
Coffee caramels, 270.
Mexican kisses, 270.
Gum drops, 271.

Lemon drops, 271.
Candied mint leaves, 272.
Candied violets, 272.
Decorating cakes, 272.
Candies on cakes, 272.
Marrons glacés, 273.
Chestnut glacés, 274.
Candied orange peel, 274.
Orange balls, 275.

CHAPTER XVIII.
Beverages

Punch, 276.
Fish house punch, 276.
Philadelphia fish house punch, 276.
Navy punch, 277.
U. S. S. Richmond punch, 277.
Champagne punch, 278.
Champagne punch (Chamberlin), 279.
Congressional punch (Chamberlin), 279.
Regent punch, 279.
Claret punch, 280.
Apple toddy, Virginia, 280.
Apple toddy, Maryland, 281.
Egg nog (Chamberlin), 281.
Cherry bounce, 282.
Milk punch, 282.
Gin fizz, 282.
Whisky sour, 283.
Rickey, 283.
Mint julep, No. 1., 283.
Mint julep, No. 2., 283.
Mint julep, No. 3., 284.
Port wine sangaree, 284.
Orange cocktail, 285.
Shandy gaff, 285.
Bamboo, 285.
Remsen cooler, 285.
Mint cordial, 285.
Orange cordial, 286.
Elderblow wine, 286.
Currant wine, 287.
California fruit punch, 287.
Strawberry punch, 287.
Orange punch, 288.
Fruit punch, 288.
Tutti frutti cup, 289.
Claret cup, No. 1., 289.
Claret cup, No. 2., 290.
Sauterne cup, 291.
Tea punch, 291.
Pineapple syrup, 292.
Lemon syrup, 292.
Fruit syrup, 293.
Raspberry shrub, 293.
Currant water, 294.
French creole drink, 294.
Ginger ale julep, 294.
Old colonial ginger cup, 295.
Grape juice, 295.
Lemon juice (bottled), 296.
Pineapple lemonade, 296.
Egg lemonade, 296.
Chocolate parfait amour, 297.
Havana amande, 297.
Root beer, 298.
Ginger beer, 298.

INDEX

PART II.

CHAPTER XIX.

Cleaning and Removing Stains.

Javelle Water, No. 1., 303.
Javelle water, No. 2, 304.
Javelle water, No. 3., 304.
Oxalic acid, 304.
Removing stains with sulphur matches, 305.
Decanters, and water-bottles, 305.
Soft soap, 305.
Spots on clothing, 306.
Grease on linen or cotton, 307.
Spots on woolen clothes, 307.
Spots on tweed, or serge, 307.
Spots on silk, 307.
Mildew, 307.
Iron-rust, 308.
Ink-spots, 308.
Grass stains, 308.
Scorch marks, 309.
Paint stains, 309.
Tar, 309.
Coffee and tea stains, 309.
Blood spots, 309.
Kerosene for washing clothes, 310.
Peach stains, 310.
Peach stains on the hands, 310.
Fresh fruit stains, 311.
Spots on woolen cloth, 311.
Ivory handled knives, 311.
Chamois gloves, 311.
White plumes, 312.
Fine lace, 312.
Black lace, 312.
Jet passementerie, 313.
Silk embroidery, 313.
Magnesia, how to use, 313.
Rug, to dry-clean, 313.
Oil paintings, 313.
Gilt frames, 314.
Mirrors, 314.
Brass and silverware, 314.

CHAPTER XX.

Care of Furniture.

Furniture polish, No. 1., 315.
Furniture polish, No. 2., 315.
Cement, 315.
Cement for broken glass, 316.
Chinese cement, 316.
Waterproof glue, 316.
Lacquer for toilet silver, 316.
Painting brass-work with shellac, 317.
Tarnished silver, 317.
Aluminum, 318.
Gilding mixture, 318.
Writing on metals, 318.
Imitation of ground glass, 319.
Spots on mahogany, 319.
Curtain rods, 319.
Silver bugs, 319.
Moths, 320.

CHAPTER XXI.

Care of the Hair.

Falling hair, 321.
Hair tonic, No. 1., 321.
Brilliantine for the hair, 321.
Hair tonic No. 2., 322.
Powder for oily hair, 322.
To keep the hair curled, 322.
Egg shampoo, 323.
Henna, 323.
The eyebrows, 323.
Heavy eyebrows, 323.
To darken the eyebrows, 324.
Chinese eyelash stain, 324.

CHAPTER XXII.

Care of the Skin.

Almond meal, 325.
Almond milk, 325.
Lemon bath, 326.
Bath bags, 326.
Rouge, 326.
Face powder, 327.
Lip salve, 327.
Cold cream, 327.
Orange-flower cream, 328.
Moist hands, 328.
Perspiration, 328.
Tan, 329.
Peroxid as a face-bleach, 329.
Moth patch, 329.

CHAPTER XXIII.

Perfumes.

Cologne, 330.
Blending of perfumes, 330.
Scent bags, 330.
Violet sachet powder, 331.
Rose sachet powder, 331.
Rose sachet, 331.
Heliotrope sachet, 332.
Lavender smelling salts, 332.
Potpourri jars, 332-333.
Perfumed beads, 334.
Attar of rose, 335.

CHAPTER XXIV.

Simple Remedies and First Aids.

Uses for hot water, 336.
Vegetables, as medicine, 337.
Mustard plasters, 338.
Cure for seasickness, 338.
Sick headache, 338.
Bilious attack, 339.
Grape and pineapple juice, 339.
Sprains, 339.
Nose-bleed, 339.
Fainting, 339.
Hysterics, 339.
Hiccoughs, 340.
Bleeding, 340.
Burns, 340.
Splinter, 340.
Stings of insects, 340.
Burning feet, 341.
Lime water, 341.
Tooth powder, 341.

WEIGHTS AND MEASURES USED IN COOKING

LIQUID MEASURES

15 drops make one salt-spoon,
4 salt-spoons make one teaspoon,
4 teaspoons make one table-spoon,
4 table-spoons make one gill,
2 gills make one cup (or 1 half-pint),
4 gills make one pint,
2 pints make one quart.

$1/2$ cup equals 1 gill,
1 cup equals 2 gills,
2 cups equal 1 pint,
4 cups equal 1 quart.

4 wine-glasses equal 1 cup,
8 wine-glasses equal 1 pint,
16 wine-glasses equal 1 quart.

PROPORTIONATE WEIGHTS AND MEASURES

In measuring for weights, those articles which are not liquid, such as flour, lard, sugar, etc., the "heaping" spoonful equals 2 "level" or liquid spoonfuls.

1 heaping table-spoon of butter weighs 1 ounce.
1 heaping table-spoon of lard, or solid fat, weighs one ounce.
1 heaping table-spoon of granulated sugar weighs 1 ounce.
2 heaping table-spoons of coffee weigh 1 ounce.
2 heaping table-spoons of flour weigh 1 ounce.
2 heaping table-spoons of powdered sugar weigh 1 ounce.
1 heaping table-spoon of butter weighs 1 ounce.

1 cup of butter, or sugar, weighs $1/2$ pound.
2 cups of solid butter weigh 1 pound.
4 cups of flour weigh 1 pound.
2 cups of granulated sugar weigh 1 pound.
3 cups of meal weigh 1 pound.
1 pint of milk, or water, weighs 1 pound.
1 pint of liquids, generally, weighs 1 pound.
9 large, or 10 medium, eggs weigh 1 pound.
8 heaping table-spoons of dry material, gener

PROPORTIONS IN WHICH TO MI

Mix 1 heaping teaspoon of baking-powder to 2 cups of flour.
Mix 1 teaspoon of cream of tartar and half a teaspoon of soda with 2 cups of flour.
Mix 1 level teaspoon of soda with 2 cups of molasses.
Mix 4 heaping teaspoons of corn-starch with 1 quart of milk.